T0330447

LEARNING THROUGH COLLECTIVE MEMORY WORK

Bristol Studies in Comparative and International Education

Series Editors: **Michael Crossley, Leon Tikly,
Angeline M. Barrett**, University of Bristol and
Julia Paulson, University of Saskatchewan

This series critically engages with education and international development
from a comparative and interdisciplinary perspective. It emphazises work
that bridges theory, policy and practice, supporting early career researchers
and the publication of studies led by researchers in and from the
Global South.

Find out more about the new and forthcoming titles in the series:

bristoluniversitypress.co.uk/
bristol-studies-in-comparative-and-international-education

LEARNING THROUGH COLLECTIVE MEMORY WORK

Troubling *Testimonio* in Post-war Peru

Goya Wilson Vásquez

BRISTOL
UNIVERSITY
PRESS

First published in Great Britain in 2025 by

Bristol University Press
University of Bristol
1–9 Old Park Hill
Bristol
BS2 8BB
UK
t: +44 (0)117 374 6645
e: bup-info@bristol.ac.uk

Details of international sales and distribution partners are available at bristoluniversitypress.co.uk

British Library Cataloguing in Publication Data
A catalogue record for this book is available from the British Library

ISBN 978-1-5292-3786-3 hardcover
ISBN 978-1-5292-3788-7 ePub
ISBN 978-1-5292-3789-4 ePdf

Cover design: Blu Inc
Front cover image: Goya Wilson Vásquez
Bristol University Press uses environmentally responsible print partners.
Printed and bound in Great Britain by CPI Group (UK) Ltd, Croydon, CR0 4YY

FSC
www.fsc.org
MIX
Paper | Supporting
responsible forestry
FSC® C013604

Contents

Series Editors' Preface

Angeline M. Barrett (University of Bristol, UK)
Julia Paulson (University of Saskatchewan, Canada)

This book tackles seriously the question of how research bears witness to and works in reparative ways with people whose lives are deeply affected by violent conflict. The word *testimonio* in the book's subtitle refers to a well-established research methodology that is also used pedagogically, to make visible the 'lived experiences of students and educators' (Rodriguez-Campo, 2021: 4). However, Goya Wilson Vásquez is mainly interested in it as a methodology, employed by a group of young Peruvians, whose parents were involved with an insurgency organization, during the civil war that ran through the last two decades of the 20th century.

The *testimonios* constructed by the participants are central to this book. Within the pages of this book, you will meet members of the collective known as HIJXS de Perú (sons and daughters of Peru), as they speak to you in their own words about their memories of childhoods that were, in every way, shaped by the dehumanizing punishment and imprisonment endured by adult members of their families, many of whom remain imprisoned. The *testimonios* however are not an end point or output of the research but, rather, the starting point for a critical examination of the 'poetics' and 'politics' of memory work. For, you will also in the pages of this book meet the researcher, herself a member of the HIJXS group, as she researches with, alongside and apart from the other participants. Drawing on literature on narrative inquiry, she tackles such issues as the slipperiness of memory and its refraction by the time and place where memory work is conducted. Wilson Vásquez never diminishes the uncompromising realism of *testimonios* while also recognizing their 'poetics' as 'constructed art'.

At first glance, *Learning through Collective Memory Work* may not appear to be a book about education. It is not concerned with education institutions, although the young people at its centre were all university students when they constructed their *testimonios*. It is however concerned with *testimonio* as pedagogy and the potential for learners to connect their experiences and knowledge to those offered through *testimonios*. Wilson Vásquez's rigorous reflections on methodology offers valuable insights for researchers concerned with the legacies of violence, the possibilities of memory and the limits of reconciliation. It makes an important contribution to studies of education, memory and transitional justice in conceptualizing *testimonio* not just as pedagogical tool and teachable moment, but as methodology and political praxis. The book also expands the literature exploring the potential of narrative methods and methodology for comparative and international education (Trahar, 2008).

Learning through Collective Memory Work adds to a growing number of the books in the Bristol Studies in Comparative and International Education series concerned with contexts of violence, transitional justice and educational possibilities. Together with David Oakeshott's *Schooling, Conflict and Peace in the Southwestern Pacific* it focuses on how young people experience and respond to intergenerational legacies of violent conflict. We recommend it unreservedly as a text that prompts us all to be more empathetic, reflexive and creative researchers.

References

Rodriguez-Campo, M. (2021) 'Testimonio in education', in *Oxford Research Encyclopedia of Education*.

Trahar, S. (2008) 'It starts with once upon a time...', *Compare: A Journal of Comparative and International Education*, 38(3), pp 259–266.

Acknowledgements

This book is the result of more than a decade-long collaborative process with the HIJXS de Perú collective, and I would like to thank them and our families, including our chosen families.

To the HIJXS group, for cultivating a sense of belonging that made possible the sharing of our lives with certain complicity ... to those whose lives are in this book and those who could not be named here but whose stories did spill into ours and made their way into my writings. For all those long hours and never-ending nights of endless conversations about everything and nothing, sharing stories, hopes, tears and laughs when we (un)fixed the world and the word.

To other hijxs, as H.I.J.O.S. groups and as individuals around the world, for the inspiration, it is your stories and the multiple ways of telling them that showed us other possibilities.

To my mother, who will not read this book but whose profound words along the way made it possible, for trusting me with her stories because it was from her that I learnt about change as a constant possibility in our lives. To all our parents and grandparents for their love, convictions and struggles ... for their legacies, the good and the bad, and the in-betweenness.

We are thankful to all the friends, *compañerxs* and colleagues from collectives, institutions and academic spaces in many countries who contributed by listening, reading, discussing and encouraging the efforts to turn our work into a published book. To all those people who stood by our side in supportive roles, listening to my ramblings and my complaints about academia, the British weather or the traffic in Lima. I had people who acted as listeners and readers of early drafts, political compasses, or providers of critical and creative ideas. Others shared their enthusiasm, recommended readings and films, sent care packages across the Atlantic, edited my writing, and pushed me with their precise questions. There were also long conversations, spilled with humour and sarcasm at the toughest times, and plenty of tears over the years with people who helped me regain my confidence at crucial moments and helped me navigate my own fears as well as academia.

To my partner for encouraging me to take the leap and being there, for her (mis)understanding, the conversations, the fights, the meals, the love and the laughter ...

Together, all who have been part of this journey demonstrate the importance of collective work in the face of violence. This book reaffirms the necessity of opening the conversation and listening differently, for a dialogue with other knowledge, from these silenced memories of the sons and daughters of ordinary people who joined the armed groups during the internal war in Peru. Perhaps it will help us understand ourselves and imagine other ways of living.

1

Introduction

You may observe as you read this book that I, the author, shift between using the pronouns 'I', 'we' and 'they'. This reflects the challenges of producing academic work out of activist research, and how much the relationships from which this book unfolded complicated its writing. I became involved in the group I was working with, the HIJXS de Perú, a community connected by their parents' participation in the Tupac Amaru Revolutionary Movement. Since then, I have been a member, the writer/ researcher … but I live abroad. I have felt both an accomplice and an intruder in crafting and editing *testimonio*, counter-memories of Peru's violent past and violent present.

Peru's internal war between 1980 and 2000 resulted in the death and disappearance of almost 70,000 people, an overwhelming majority of them rural, indigenous and poor (TRC, 2003b). In its simplest depiction, it was fought between state forces and two insurgent groups, the Partido Comunista del Peru – Sendero Luminoso (PCP-SL), a Maoist group, and the Tupac Amaru Revolutionary Movement (MRTA) inspired by the Cuban revolution. Beyond this, the war also involved *ronderos* (peasant militias) and self-defence committees, paramilitary groups and a large business community linked to the military.

Twenty years after the Truth and Reconciliation Commission (TRC) published its Final Report, in 2023 the struggles over memory continue. The state's official narrative celebrates a successful fight against 'terrorism'. Even in competing accounts, there is a marked effort to delineate 'victims' and 'perpetrators' (Coxshall, 2005; Drinot, 2009; Theidon, 2010).[1] This has meant that several stories, those that do not fit such

---

[1] See Coxshall's argument about how the TRC could not 'fully complicate the dichotomy between "victim" and "perpetrator"' (Coxshall, 2005: 218). See Drinot (2009) for how the

clear-cut roles for the characters, remain absent from all reports and most public conversations.

This book deals with a corner of those stories. It is an inquiry into the process of producing *testimonio* as collective memory work with a group of young adults who call themselves HIJXS de Perú[2] and are connected by their parents' involvement in the MRTA. They experienced state repression, which included the killing, disappearance, torture, exile or imprisonment (a few are still in prison) of their relatives who were deemed 'terrorists'. They grew up stigmatized as the 'children of the terrorists' in the post-war period, thus falling between the cracks of the victim–perpetrator dichotomy and thereby inhabiting a sort of 'borderlands' (Anzaldúa, 1987). Over the 20-year war and subsequent transition to democracy in the early 2000s, this stigma silenced their stories.

The book explores the politics of breaking their silence through the vehicle of *testimonio*. Literally translated as testimony in English, *testimonio* in Spanish has resonances missing in English. It refers to a genre of testimonial narratives and highlights its relationship with a Latin American tradition of personal accounts from marginalized voices that are connected with larger societal and historical issues. *Testimonios* are a form of counter-history that aims to raise awareness to transform past and present injustices.

In the field of education, working with *testimonio* aligns with Latin American thinkers such as Paulo Freire with his concept of 'situated praxis' and 'critical consciousness' and Orlando Fals-Borda with his methodology of 'thinking-feelingly'. This approach to education goes hand in hand with what is known as 'critical pedagogy' which makes explicit power structures and relations in everyday life. From here, and in this book, education is understood as a doing-thinking-feeling-reflecting together in a common effort to understand the realities which we seek to transform.

Since the 1990s, *testimonio* has been used in educational spaces (for example, schools, teachers' education, academia) for its potential as a pedagogical tool, research method and teaching practice within critical pedagogies and social justice education frameworks (Carey-Webb and Benz, 1996; Latina Feminist Group, 2001; Haig-Brown, 2003; Beverley, 2004; Rodriguez-Campo, 2021). This rich tradition can nevertheless become problematic for the protagonists of *testimonio*. This inquiry calls for problematizing traditional notions and readings of *testimonio* to promote a more critical and productive

---

    dichotomy is applied (and more or less problematized) according to opposite 'ontologies of the violence' that produce it.

[2]   Translated as 'Sons and Daughters for Identity and Justice, against Oblivion and Silence, from Peru'.

engagement with testimonial narratives, including their pedagogical potential as learning resources.

This book presents a critical engagement with *testimonio* as a process, drawing from a collective memory work developed over a period of ten years with the HIJXS de Perú group. I am author, researcher, and myself became a troubled and troubling part of the collective. This is achieved by a methodology that approaches *testimonio* through *cycles of inquiry*, which is then theorized as three movements for memory work. The first movement operates within a 'realist' mode. It involves producing the stories to be retold as *testimonio*. The second, 'politics of memory', inquires into the process of *testimonio*-making, particularly the conditions under which such stories are produced and the shifting silences enacted. The third, 'poetics of memory', explores the problematics of writing violence and how such explorations lead to a further 'troubling' (Lather, 2007) of both the realist *testimonio* and its politics that complicates memory, voice and representation for qualitative activist inquiry in post-war contexts (see Figure 1.1).

The first movement re-presents the narratives produced with the collective from a traditional testimonial stance. The six *testimonios* are crafted as 'realist tales', carefully edited rewritings based on recorded conversations with the protagonists of the HIJXS group. The testimonial narratives perform as

Figure 1.1: Cycles of inquiry in memory work

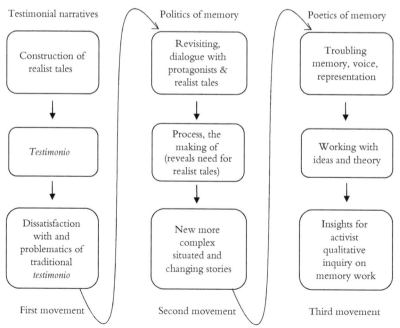

Testimonial narratives	Politics of memory	Poetics of memory
Construction of realist tales	Revisiting, dialogue with protagonists & realist tales	Troubling memory, voice, representation
Testimonio	Process, the making of (reveals need for realist tales)	Working with ideas and theory
Dissatisfaction with and problematics of traditional *testimonio*	New more complex situated and changing stories	Insights for activist qualitative inquiry on memory work
First movement	Second movement	Third movement

resistance texts and counter-narratives of Peru's internal war, arising from a collective desire to 'speak up'. The book starts with the narratives, instead of relegating them to an appendix, as traditional social research typically does. The intention is not to simply redress the violence (including epistemic violence) already exercised upon the protagonists' lives. It is also a deliberate attempt to situate their stories within the public narratives of the Peruvian war, a necessary condition for a deeper understanding of past and present political violence.

The second movement, 'politics of memory', troubles the realist *testimonio* by revisiting it and reflecting with its protagonists on how narratives are affected by the changes in their conditions of production: the relationship between participants as individuals and as a collective, the entanglements with places/spaces, and the shifting character of silences. It also acknowledges the need for *testimonio* as realist tales at methodological level to provide the object of troubling but also for political/activist reasons. Doing politics in a context of state and societal repression demands realist tales as a means for political action, a necessary step for breaking the silences and for claiming recognition.

The third movement, 'the poetics of memory', engages with ideas and theory from feminist poststructuralists and Latin American memory work to further trouble both the realist *testimonio* and its politics for a more creative understanding of the process of producing *testimonio* within memory work. This understanding complicates memory, voice and representation, particularly by inquiring into the problematics of the fact/fiction binary in light of activist research. It reflexively discusses the epistemological stances of and tensions within the inquiry and its implications for qualitative inquiry about memory work in repressive contexts.

While three neatly defined movements of memory work suggest a linear methodological journey from writing the story, revisiting and then theorizing the process, in practice this was and remains far messier. Movements overlap and feed into each other, all anchored in the relationships constructed with the protagonists. The journey was more one of travelling unmapped territories via an iterative process that goes 'through cycles of action and reflection' (Heron and Reason, 2001), which meant that the whole cycle repeated itself within each movement. However, framing the process requires imposing some 'order' on it to make possible both the writing and reading of our work, and to finally break the silences by sharing our *experiencia* (meaning both experience and experiment).[3]

---

[3]   I retain the Spanish word to express the double connotation of experience and experiment (or an experience of experimenting) used by popular education movements in Latin America (see Holdren and Touza, 2005).

A concern for and a critique of methodology runs through this book. The object of inquiry is the production of *testimonio* with the HIJXS de Perú group. The book is organized as a cycle of story-making over time and space, bearing witness to the testimonial process, and engaging the reader with three movements of memory work. The inquiry 'troubles' normative conceptions of *testimonio* by revisiting its practices over a six-year period (2007–2013) in two separate locations (Cuba and Peru), and 'troubles' its process of becoming by using creative writing while drawing on Lather's (2007) 'troubling' stance and Anzaldúa's (1987) 'borderlands' idea to explore *testimonio* as a place of in-between-ness: private–public, individual–collective, activism–research, telling–writing, and ultimately real–imagined.

The book starts with the construction and display of *testimonio* as 'realist tales' (a traditional use of testimonial writing), drawing on the collective memory work conducted in Cuba in 2007, where I met the HIJXS. It then explores the dialogues with the protagonists of the testimonial narratives when the work is 'taken back' to Peru when we return to the country in 2012–2013, where we embark on 'troubling' the *testimonio* by revisiting the recorded testimonials and intervening at the same time in the memory struggles over the internal war, which then results in new and more complex stories. The book ends with a further troubling of the process of writing *testimonio* within academia in the Global North as doctoral research (United Kingdom, 2010–2016), reflecting on qualitative inquiry, memory work and the uses of *testimonio* as pedagogical tool in the aftermath of war.

The contribution of this book lies in its expansion of the critical field of inquiry through three movements of memory work, and as such the book's structure is an illustration of, as well as the foundation for, its analysis. Traditional *testimonio* usually ends in the first movement with the representation of the realist tales. Scholarly research on *testimonio* tends to start with an existing testimonial narrative (already produced by a first movement) and continues with the third movement to critically engage with ideas and theories for a reading of testimonials. The innovative part rests not only in incorporating the second movement, where I re-enter into dialogue with the protagonists about the testimonial narratives, but in presenting the three movements together as a possibility for a different understanding of *testimonio* and, ultimately, memory, voice and representation, resulting from inquiring into the making of testimonial narratives through activist research.

This book explores testimonial narratives and collective memory as pedagogical tools and research methodology in the specific context of the Peruvian post-war. The situatedness of the inquiry contributes to revert the notion of war-torn countries as pure devastation, proposing instead to learn from them as sites of knowledge production and creativity with much to offer to transitional justice, curricula development, teacher training, educational resources, peace and conflict studies, and methodologies for research that pursues social justice.

Testimonio and terrorism: a Peruvian tale

For most, Peru's transition to democracy after the internal war had already happened with the end of Alberto Fujimori's authoritarian regime (1990–2000). After all, Peru had a transitional government (2000), an internationally renowned TRC (2003), a reparations plan with its national victim register (2005), a national memory museum (2015), and Fujimori was imprisoned for corruption and human rights violations following a landmark trial (2007). The milestones were all reached, however underneath the success story lay simmering the unaddressed root causes of the internal war. The structural violence and the strategic use of the 'terrorist' discourse continue to play out in the 'new' democracy while the Fujimori regime maintains its tight grip on public institutions, political processes and the legacies of the violence itself.

When Alberto Fujimori was elected in 1990, a 'self-coup'[4] was unimaginable. Only two years in his presidency, Fujimori allied with military forces to dissolve the National Congress, suspend the Constitution and purge the judiciary, assuming extraordinary powers and shifting power to the military. An example was the use of new anti-terrorist legislation and 'faceless judges' in military courts to prosecute terrorism.[5] The dismantling of democratic institutions came together with the imposition of neoliberal policies called 'the shock' for their impact, setting in motion a decade of authoritarian rule backed by the armed forces.

At the moment I finish this manuscript (2024), the country is facing the latest iteration of an endemic crisis of which the early release of Fujimori from prison is only a symptom. In the preceding seven years Peru has had six presidents, only two of them democratically elected, and almost all presidents since the 1980s have been charged with corruption or human rights violations, with a few imprisoned. On top of this, COVID-19 revealed a deeply broken system that proved deadly, positioning Peru as the most lethal country during the pandemic. Popular mobilizations have changed authorities more than once and called for new elections, and the latest

---

[4] Unlike other military coups in Latin America, in Peru, the democratically elected president was its protagonist, overthrowing his own government to impose authoritarian rule backed by the armed forces.

[5] Amnesty International's report on the effects of the anti-terrorist legislation states that 'between 1992 and 1997, all "terrorism-related" offences were tried before so-called "faceless judges" (jueces sin rostro), in trials that were not public. These judges sat behind tinted glass and talked to the defendants through microphones which distorted their voices' (Amnesty International, 2003: 10).

2021 election embodied a long unfulfilled promise to represent Andean communities, those most affected by the violence during and after the war.

The conservative elite in Lima, allied with right-wing political parties controlling the parliament and the military, did not accept the democratically elected president Pedro Castillo and after less than two years of constant harassment managed to oust him and seized power in 2022. The parliament brought Dina Boluarte, former vice-president, to fill the presidential seat. The response was quick and massive. Popular mobilization came mostly from the Andean territories against the removal of a government that they felt was theirs (Durand, 2023). Some protestors called for Castillo to be reinstated and others for new elections or even a new constitutional process. Mobilizations were met with a wave of lethal state violence, Andean provinces became heavily militarized under a state of emergency, and authorities and mass media accused protesters of being terrorists. More than 50 people were killed in the first two months and several were detained under suspicion of terrorism. The violence and its impunity were heavier and deadlier in the provinces, echoing the internal war. The terrorist discourse played a central role against the widespread mobilization, a political strategy developed during the internal war that has only amplified since to delegitimize and dehumanize people exercising their right to protest, while legitimizing their violent eradication. It is this ongoing legacy that the book unpacks through a cycles of memory work lens.

Indeed, testimonial memory work with the HIJXS group has been systematically, inevitably marked and shaped by the pervasive deployment of the terrorist discourse in post-war political life. Peru's insurgent groups, including the MRTA to which the parents of the HIJXS group belong, were and still are defined as terrorist. Anti-terrorist legislation not only perpetuates prosecution of former members of now-defeated armed groups but also criminalizes social protest and popular mobilization, as brutally seen in 2023. Moreover, 'apologia' for terrorism, a very loose term referring to advocating or supporting terrorism and terrorist groups or activities, is also criminalized within the legal framework. The definition is arguably loose enough to perpetuate the politics of fear that Burt (2008) examines in *Political Violence and the Authoritarian State in Peru*, and the impunity of past and present state violence as argued by Robin Azevedo and Romero Barrios (2023) in 'Socio-political crisis, massacre and dehumanization'.

In Peru, the word 'terrorista' morphed in colloquial conversation to 'terruco' in the early 1980s and was later shortened to 'tuco'. Aguirre (2012)'s history of 'terruco' shows how it was used during the Peruvian internal war both as an insult and to stigmatize particularly racialized sectors of society, initially those in the armed groups but also indigenous people from the Andean region (as they became synonymous). It has since been broadly applied to human rights activists, journalists, those criticizing the government's counter-terrorist policies, public university students, *familiares* and victims, and indigenous people. This made possible and justified the indiscriminate use of state violence against those involved in (or around, and even those outside) the armed groups, and different racialized communities defending their territories against exploitation by large mining corporations.

In the post-war period, a new term – *'terruqueo'* – emerged to contest the uses of the terrorist discourse as a strategy to discredit political opposition. It has been helpful to denounce the overuse of the term terrorism in Peruvian mass media and politics. Paradoxically, it also kept it alive, as many declare their non-terrorist status by denouncing an 'other' as 'the real terrorist'. In Peru, one regularly has to identify who the terrorists are to gain a space of enunciation.

The ubiquitous 'terrorist' can also be understood as a renewed figure in the imaginary of the internal enemy with a longer history that is 'constitutive of the modern national project', playing a role in 'reinforcing and normalizing a project of rule that operates against the population' (Drinot, 2023). In the present, these can be seen in the mobilizing of the 'terrorist' figure in political discourse, the use of the concept of 'apologia for terror' against human rights activists, and the 'anti-terrorist' legislation born of a counter-insurgency campaign that has expanded to criminalize protests against neoliberal policies. Indeed, Méndez's (2021) genealogy of the 'terrorist' label in Peru argues that any history of terrorism must also be a history of who claims the power to name/designate who is and who is not a terrorist, alluding to its political nature and appropriation by the state. The way it works, Rojas-Perez explains, is that:

> [t]his temporality of unfinished pasts is internal to the work of state power in that it produces both the kinds of new threats against which the post-conflict state can legitimize its violence and the grid of affects, such as fear and shame, necessary to establish its control over suspect populations. (Rojas-Perez, 2013: 152)

The centrality of the 'terrorist' discourse to both political dynamics and the state project more broadly has played out at different, albeit connected, levels for the HIJXS group. Their participation in formal political life has to reckon with the systematic deployment of the terrorist grammar during electoral campaigns. For instance, while such accusations had previously been levelled against the (successful) presidential candidate Ollanta Humala (2011), in 2016 the media turned on congress candidates to delegitimize the left coalition. Among them, a member of the HIJXS group ran for Lima with a focus on representing the marginalized neighbourhoods: *'los barrios al Congreso'*. The HIJXS mobilized around this campaign as a collective matter and received their share of vitriolic criticism, where the stigma of 'children of the terrorists' was relived. They had new compromises to make and new troubles to deal with: problems with their families, their work colleagues, their jobs, their parents' *compañeros*, the militants in the left coalition. The 2016 electoral campaign left in its wake exhaustion, divisions and guilt among the group. It also reminded us that the politics of fear have never gone away and are being strategically used to contest opposition in general, and particularly a right to political participation for specific groups.

These constraints and threats meant that disclosing the HIJXS *testimonios* involved personal safety risks for them and others (myself included). We had to carefully weigh them, and decided against making the *testimonios* public until recently, when a wave of texts from other 'uncomfortable memories' emerged to challenge and change the way we understand memory and violence. The slow but constant emergence of books started by *Los Rendidos* (2015) by José Carlos Agüero, and *Memorias de un Soldado Desconocido* (2017) by Lurgio Gavilán, have created an opportunity to break the boundaries of what is known, what can be publicly discussed, and what can be learnt from the war and its aftermath. This book is similarly animated by what Denegri and Hibbett (2016) term 'dirty remembering', those memories from forgotten/problematic areas and silenced actors in the war. It provides an opening and affirms a public disposition to listen to troubling stories and, most importantly, to change whom we can learn from.

Methodological companions along the journey

This work can be simultaneously described as narrative, ethnographic, action-oriented, critical pedagogy, life-long learning, co-construction and activist/militant inquiry. Its methodological pathway connects narrative inquiry and activist/action research (Pushor and Clandinin, 2009), in particular by paying attention to 'ways of negotiating the space between researcher and researched' (Speedy, 2008: 55) that produce particular genres of writing within (and on the edges of) academic writing. Most importantly, this book's motivation is to contest universal truths about *testimonio* and established narratives of the internal war in Peru.

As a result, the reading of this book requires a particular disposition. Move beyond traditional research criteria, such as replicability or generalizability. Instead, practise a collaborative reading, embrace Helene Cixous' idea that learning 'cannot be generalized but it can be shared' (1993: 7) and follow Jane Speedy's proposition of diverse 'judgement calls' paying attention to the 'liminal space for resonance and for the co-creation of our own stories as readers' (2008: 53).

This book is the result of a decade-long collaboration with its protagonists narrated as an inquiry journey (see Chapter 2) which also had companions along the way. I refer to the authors and theories I kept going back to as 'methodological companions' because we have been in conversation and I learnt alongside them throughout this journey. The amplified voices and visibilized knowledges that the inquiry facilitated are non-generalizable truths that aspire to resonance of the stories and of the process of producing located narratives with a particular group.

Narrative inquiry became influential to this project as a perspective that engages narratively with stories and their production, and is ultimately retold as a narrative (Clandinin and Connelly, 2004). It also connected me with methodological perspectives from feminist research and indigenous research based in storytelling. I was inspired by Tuhiwai Smith's *Decolonizing Methodologies*, and became methodologically concerned with 'the context in which research problems are conceptualized and designed, and with the implications of research for its participants and their communities' (2012: ix). Indigenous methodologies proved valuable to open up spaces for other possible knowledges in repressive contexts. As the context of this inquiry shows, working with a small community under threat demanded such a stance.

These companions allowed me to overcome the barriers to explore other possibilities for 'knowing and understanding' that academic institutions and other forms of institutionalized knowledge represent (Tuhiwai Smith, 2012: 223). They also led me to Gloria Anzaldúa's (1987) work, to play with her *Borderlands* as a metaphor with which I travelled from one world to another – border-crossing, exploring the margins created by binary categories, and inquiring into the in-between spaces – where I felt more at home. Patti Lather (1997; 2007) was my other companion in this journey, more as an attitude that permits *Getting Lost* and engaging in a 'troubling' stance to use certain categories while poking holes in them, making them problematic so I could continue using them productively. Both authors pushed my writing to be more engaged and break my previous sociological mindset.

My work also shares borderlands with oral history and memory studies from Latin America, rooting this inquiry within Latin American knowledge production in the context of state violence and 'memory struggles' (Jelin, 2003). I locate it at the intersection of both fields because, in their origins, both have strong connections with critical pedagogy activism and explicitly politicized work related to violence that asks how we can learn from troublesome histories of violence and their legacies.

There are epistemological and methodological reasons, which is to say political reasons, that turned me away from traditional analysis as it is presented in most qualitative research in social sciences (the classical 'findings' followed by 'discussion' chapter). Instead, I placed this book in the borderlands of social science and humanities. I moved from 'research' to 'inquiry' to describe this work, driven more by the protagonists' stories and the knowledge therein produced in the process of making them, than by categories pre-established in social theories, more as an art through the use of writing and creative writing to establish connections between stories, theories and literature, rather than a systematic (two-dimensional) approach to knowledge tamed by coding, dissecting and expert interpretation that fixes meaning over stories. The book is thus positioned as an engaged political inquiry that explored, through different movements of writing, the process of producing *testimonio* with a group actively struggling for recognition.

Working with the protagonists meant working with the textual representations we co-produced and working with the conversations sparked by our memory work (storytelling and activity-led conversations within a critical pedagogy framework). It resulted from an inkling of the epistemic and political gains to be made when working *with* and not *about* the stories. The process of writing sometimes involved struggling against 'writing-about' the stories which would position me as an expert, with the pretence of being outside; from an external position that was impossible for me to assume, given my complicated belonging to the HIJXS group. I was writing *alongside*, on, through, inside and under the stories, owning an epistemology that acknowledges that we as researchers are not only part of the world we research, but we are also actively making it; in this particular case through the ethnographic encounters and the writing. Hence I experimented instead with writing in different modes, sometimes a realist mode, sometimes using dialogic methods and creative writing, and sometimes using writing as a method of inquiry, all while I searched for a 'methodological rhythm' (Tamboukou, 2008: 116) particular to each of the three movements.

At the same time, it was also impossible to forgo some form of analysis given the academic position from which this inquiry was written. In those borderlands, of somewhere in between the activist/practitioner and the academic/researcher, I produced these texts in cycles of inquiry more than traditional analysis. Traditional analysis pretends to be a systematic application of sets of categories onto the data, in processes that dissect, classify and provide explanations. During my inquiry, I was not only complicating the data-analysis dichotomy by revisiting the *testimonios* five years later in another location, but also through using creative writing to re-represent some of the tensions encountered in our testimonial work. Complicating 'data' was part of 'troubling' as methodology, because I found it always already complicated and difficult to separate what is understood as descriptive versus analytical; the data from the analysis.

I relied instead on what St. Pierre called a 'nomadic writing' (1997); that is, writing as becoming. Contrary to starting with a clear path of systematic processes (albeit not less rigorous), this was a process of writing to help me 'think differently', to further inquire, while 'plugging in' encounters from the field with encounters with theories and literature, and ultimately with myself (Jackson and Mazzei, 2011). This was a process of making connections evident, always through the use of writing as method (Richardson and St. Pierre, 2005). Many times, I was writing against the mainstream knowledge and available categories of the Peruvian internal war and the testimonial tradition. This was a writing that came from the messiness of lives that experienced violence, state repression and clandestine lives since early childhood.

While pursuing an ethnographic rendering of our messy process of producing *testimonio*, I encountered ethnographers who consistently argue for ethnography as theory (Biehl, 2013: 583). For me, this resulted in the three different movements of writing, each with its own strategy, a different methodological rhythm, which in turn demands different reader dispositions.

The first movement is within the tradition of testimonial writing where texts were crafted from recorded conversations and 'plugged in' to archival research, suitable for the activist desires of the HIJXS to intervene in the public sphere. The second movement is an ethnographic rendering, reconnecting with the protagonists to revisit our memory work using dialogical methods which are later 'plugged in' to creative writings as well as the available academic literature. The resulting text provides glimpses of changes over time and space while I was exploring themes such as space/place and silences. And the third movement is more reflexive on the writing process itself and from there is 'plugged into' the ethnographic encounters as well as encounters with theoretical constructs, problematizing then the method itself, the writing, the troubling, and some existent categories to understand the context in which these encounters unfolded. The final epilogue explicitly draws the argument for *testimonio* as pedagogy by focusing on learning from testimonial as both process and content.

Researchers from South America invite us to pursue a writing intertwined with imagination to push the limits of language and to break away from established grammars that end up (re)producing oppressive power relations (Biehl, 2013; Gatti, 2011). To this, I add a form of writing that problematizes itself and the established analytical tools, such as the generational divides that the 'post-memory' category brings about. All these result from engaging with how the far messier and changing lives contest the existing analytical categories.

Generational divides, often used in sociological analysis, typically derive from group self-awareness or identification as belonging to a shared collective consciousness at a particular time (Andrews, 2007). In memory studies, the use of a generational approach gave rise to the concept of 'post-memory' to understand the process by which memories were inherited by the second generation of Holocaust survivors (Hirsch, 2008). This inquiry also works to/with a second generation, those whose parents were actively involved in the internal war. They are 'the children of'. Yet sustaining the clear-cut distinction embedded in the concept of post-memory proved impossible. For example, should one read the testimonial accounts of torture of the HIJXS' relatives as inherited post-memories, or were these accounts of their own experiences (as children) of the torture of their relatives? In different instances, the HIJXS drew attention to the difficulty of drawing such generational lines, and even of defining the ownership of the stories. Which ones were their stories and which their parents'? Which memories were inherited and which ones experienced? Was it possible to demarcate where one life began and the other ended? There are no easy answers to these questions or to their implications for testimonial writing and memory work. The HIJXS are constantly changing positions related to how to deal with such stories while doing *testimonio*, a constant movement between acknowledging their legacy while creating their own politics. This is one example of a category that becomes problematic and how the clashing against it in a reflexive practice of doing memory work will be explored along this book.

The questions raised about my relationship with the HIJXS, the tensions between individual and collective lives, the role of places/spaces in the stories possible, and the presence of silences and secrets were important results of the two fieldwork phases. Moreover an important question was raised about the relationship between real and fiction, how we relate to both when we engage in testimonial memory work, and ultimately what a realist mode of *testimonio* provided and what a creative writing mode could bring upon.

The metaphor of borderlands running across this book is borrowed from Gloria Anzaldúa. Instead of the border as an artificial line that divides one space from another, she put forward the image of a whole territory in-between. These are understood as creative spaces where tensions are productive and repression carries the possibility of becoming transformational. 'This is my home / this thin edge of / barbwire' (Anzaldúa, 1987: 3), she wrote.

A reading guide through different writings

The reader will encounter a series of strategically used writing devices throughout the book with specific aims, namely, *postalitas*, footnotes, languages, text boxes and locations.

Postalitas (little postcards) are brief re-presentations of moments and conversations that stayed with me infused with creative writing to crystallize them and further (playfully) inquire into them. They are an in(ter)vention resulting from the multiple translation acts containing their own layers of interpretations and negotiations that offer a way to deal with a context of repression and self-censoring mechanisms. *Postalitas* not only denotes smallness in size but also affection towards these texts, which became endearing objects to me; it is in Spanish that the term resonates as affective to me. They are signalled with the name and age of protagonists (real or fictional), location and year.

Similar to postcards, *postalitas* are static windows into their lives as seen by me: brief, fragmented, personal and registered at a specific moment made open to others for a desire to communicate. Methodologically, *postalitas* draw on the ethics of fictionalizations from the field in social research, as they make it possible to portray what would otherwise remain silenced (Banks and Banks, 1998; Clough, 2002; Sparkes, 2002; Speedy, 2008).

While based on our testimonial work, the *postalitas* have a life of their own, keeping specific words in Spanish to highlight that the resulting text comes from conversations in another world. As creative writings these artefacts produced a concern over 'manipulating data' and being 'unfaithful' to the recording (Clough, 2002). They are a creative form of the *testimonios*, one that includes me and others who could not be there. They bear witness to our testimonial work and attempt to affect others in ways that allow me to rethink our/my work.

The *postalitas* provided *a way out* of the initial problems of safety and finding alternative modes of re-presenting the *testimonios* by taking threads that have stayed with me from our work during the encounters. At the same time, the *postalitas*, as devices somewhere in-between data and analysis, are not an end product but working tools, *a way in* to revisit our memory work once relocated in Peru. The aim was to open the door for creative writing which could be useful for testimonial work by disturbing its disciplining aspect and cultivating a questioning of the hegemonic discourses that also inhabit us, opening our imaginations to other ways of political action and of making a life.

Instead of focusing on what was lost (and consequently using more technologies and devising more procedures to capture or reduce what could be lost), I turned and tuned my attention to what was being created, embracing creativity as a possibility for further exploring what is being produced. These provided space for questions to become evident the more involved I was in the group to the point of belonging to it. My image of them changed from the initial victim-stories to more contradictory and fluid storied beings – not as fixed as they seemed from the initial encounters.

Footnotes provide additional information and context without overshadowing silenced voices. In the first movement, they offer archival research and context clues, in the second, additional literature, and in the third, reflections that interrupt the direction of the writing.

Languages: words in Spanish appear un-translated and force readers (and writer) to acknowledge this text's roots in another language/culture. It interrupts the reader out of a too-comfortable position to prevent an easy appropriation. It is also an act of protest that bears witness to the untranslatability of the HIJXS' lives and our *experiencia*. Beyond multiple

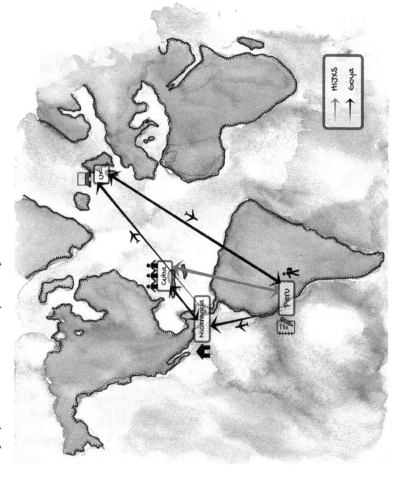

Figure 1.2: A map of the inquiry locations illustrated by María Jesús Viviani

translation acts from Spanish to English, oral to written, lived experience to academic research, it is about the language in which such experiences were reconstructed and the language in which we made sharing them possible.

Text boxes contain my reflexive voice interrupting the text on the sidelines. They display the multiple voices running throughout the inquiry and re-present dialogical layers of storied realities. They open the space for other possible stories and/or readings of them.

Locations: our inquiry travelled from its first encounters in Cuba (2007), where we recorded our conversations, to Peru (2012–2013) where we revisited our work. And it was affected by my movements from Peru when my family left for Nicaragua where I became a sociologist, a feminist and a popular education practitioner, and later to UK academia where the inquiry took its doctoral research shape and is now published (see Figure 1.2).

2

The Story of the Inquiry

This chapter tells the story of the inquiry in chronological order by tracing a series of encounters with the protagonists and with academia over ten years across three countries. It details the journey as a series of movements and the different understandings they produced: from the troubles with *testimonio* to the troubling of *testimonio*.

The account of that journey introduces the reader to my inquiry as a methodological challenge, where each new encounter triggered changes in the way I, and the HIJXS group, engaged with our memory work. Throughout the text, I introduce the ongoing arising of questions that led to the inquiry route, and how we went on addressing, producing and in some cases sustaining the questions in each of the following sections. The purpose is to display a book that is written narratively as the unfolding of a methodology.

A beginning for the story

I would like to start by telling the story of this research, although I am unsure about where it begins. We first recorded the *testimonios* in Cuba in 2007, where the protagonists met while pursuing their university studies, and I was undergoing health treatment. But perhaps I should explain how we ended up in Cuba. We were all born in Peru where the armed confrontation between two groups and the state forces during the 1980s and 1990s spiralled to an unimaginable scale. That, due to the political violence and state repression, my parents left Peru for Nicaragua in 1991 while the parents of the participants in this inquiry were labelled 'terrorists' and killed, exiled, disappeared or imprisoned in that same decade. That story could also be about my movements, how I was born in Peru, grew up in Nicaragua and later joined my parents in Cuba, only to find a way back to Peru.

This story should be, perhaps it is too, about my recovery from illness, learning to live with partial disability and managing chronic pain, returning to work and later starting a full-time PhD programme, in which *testimonio* began to play an ever larger part. It was never my intention to include what I call 'my arms problem' in the inquiry journey. However, the aches and pains were and still are very much part of the journey, and inspired by ethnographies from Isbell (2009) and Behar (2003), I included them.

But it is not about any of that, and yet all of it at the same time. I want to make it about the story-making that happened in the middle of it, the stories themselves and, most importantly, the people involved in listening and telling and crafting those stories about violence, identity, absence, loss and justice. Acknowledging at the same time, that it is also about reconnecting with my own history through others. I go back and forth: Is this about me or them? Both? Neither? Maybe something taking place somewhere in-between, produced in our 'bumping against' each other's stories (Clandinin and Connelly, 2004), and against those larger stories about Peru's internal war and where we came from.

Encountering the HIJXS de Perú

The participants in this project were young Peruvians who met each other while on university scholarships in Cuba, just two years after the Peruvian Truth and Reconciliation Commission (TRC) report in 2003. They organized themselves into a group called H.I.J.O.S. de Perú, a move inspired by the Argentinean H.I.J.O.S. which started in 1994, a decade after that country's dictatorship ended.

'H.I.J.O.S.' is an acronym translated as 'Sons for Identity and Justice, Against Oblivion and Silence' that also reads as the Spanish word specifically for 'sons' and generically for 'children of'. Some of the Peruvian group's members write 'Hijos e Hijas de Perú' or 'Hij@s de Perú' to make 'sons and daughters' explicit and ultimately use HIJXS.[1] They only entered into contact with the Argentinean group in 2010 when they discovered it had slowly sparked other groups, first in Latin America's Southern Cone (Chile and Uruguay), later in Europe and Canada (mostly children of exiles from the Southern Cone), and lastly in Mexico, Guatemala and Colombia.

All these groups belong to the International Network of H.I.J.O.S., which held its first gathering in Mexico in late 2010. There they produced the following declaration:

---

[1] For the purposes of this work, I use HIJXS. I have also adopted their differentiation of uppercase letters (HIJXS or H.I.J.O.S.) to refer to those organized in similar groups, and lowercase 'hijxs' to refer more loosely to 'the children of', those of the same second generation (sons, daughters, nephews or nieces) who had links to any of the armed groups fighting against the state in Latin America, but not necessarily participating in H.I.J.O.S. groups.

We are sons and daughters from the same history.

We are men and women who share experiences of state repression, although linked to different political processes: military dictatorships in Chile, Uruguay and Argentina; the war and the political, social and armed conflicts in Guatemala, Peru, Colombia and Mexico; the latter together with Spain and France as countries receiving exiles and at the same time offering refuge for agents of repression.

But it is not only the horror that binds us together; we are also sons and daughters of the struggles of Latin American *pueblos* and we are committed to working against impunity across our borders.

We are subverting pain into struggle and sadness into rebellion.

Because breaking the silence and denouncing the state terrorism implemented in the past and which continues in our countries is, for all of us, a way of working for a more just world where the inequality and injustice advanced and driven by imperialism using repressive methods, no longer exists.

...

We ourselves have lived the cruelty of state terrorism. We have experienced the pain and impotence of the forced disappearances, extra-judicial killings, murders, persecutions, tortures, exile, massacres, genocide, appropriations of children, imprisonment and crimes against humanity for political reasons. That pain runs through our bodies and was designed to isolate, silence and paralyse us. But it did not succeed in defeating us. Not even the cruellest crimes have taken away our spirit and will to struggle for a better world.

...

WE DO NOT FORGET, WE DO NOT FORGIVE, WE DO NOT RECONCILE. (H.I.J.O.S. International Network, 2010)[2]

Debates about membership were not uncommon among H.I.J.O.S. groups. In Argentina, the issue was whether to include only children 'directly affected', that is, those with parents disappeared or killed, or to widen membership to hijxs of exiles and ex-prisoners. Their dilemma stemmed from the language of human rights organizations at the time, which only considered those 'directly affected'.[3]

---

[2] My translation from H.I.J.O.S. International Network, Mexico City, 8 October 2010, www.hijosmexico.org/index-encuentro_internacional_de_h.i.j.o.s.html

[3] Elizabeth Jelin (2012; 2014) argues the problem arises from the adoption of the human rights paradigm to understand political violence. She criticizes the pervasiveness of such paradigm to understand political struggles and state violence because it moves the discussion to victims (and what was done to them) instead of what the struggles were about and the state's role in dealing with political opposition.

These internal discussions highlight an important difference between the H.I.J.O.S. groups. The Argentinean H.I.J.O.S. were united by their status as victims of state violence, which generated little contestation in the legal arena.[4] Their Peruvian counterpart came together through their parents' militancy in a specific armed group, the Tupac Amaru Revolutionary Movement (MRTA). Although the Argentineans marked their distance from other associations of families of victims by explicitly reclaiming (*reivindicar*) their parents' political activism, armed militancy remained a taboo (Tello, 2012; Jelin, 2014). In Chile, the H.I.J.O.S. initially reproduced their parents' division by political parties, informally separating into sub-groups. Only later did they work through the inherited distrust with practices of '*funa*' (Bondarevsky, 2003), their version of the '*escraches*' pioneered by the Argentinians.

Escraches were a public 'outing' of people involved in the repression during Argentina's dictatorship. The group would stage public local events to mark the houses of repressors and involve the neighbours in denouncing them. While *escraches* were performed as a challenge to the impunity enjoyed by perpetrators of state violence (that is, amnesty laws), they may have constituted a form of justice in itself ('social condemnation') as well as a public demand for legal justice ('legal condemnation') (Cueto Rúa, 2010: 139). The *escraches/funas* quickly became the trademark performance protest that gave the Argentinean and Chilean H.I.J.O.S. groups a sense of direction and a vehicle for public activism.

The Peruvian HIJXS group, however, is a different story. They were not connected by a shared identity as victims of state violence but by their parents' former MRTA militancy. Peruvian legislation does not recognize that the legal category of victim applies to the relatives of MRTA or Shining Path. Members found each other through the *familiares*, broadly encompassing the family networks of those imprisoned due to their MRTA involvement. Some HIJXS met in Peru while visiting their relatives in maximum-security prisons. Their scholarships to Cuba, where the group coalesced, resulted from the efforts of the *familiares* association. Thus, the HIJXS' lives are linked to the internal war through their parents' involvement in the MRTA and Fujimori's dictatorship. Following the defeat of the armed groups and the 'transition to democracy', they carried the stigma of being considered the 'children of terrorists'. They also have the shared experience of studying in Cuba.

The founding document of HIJXS de Perú did not specify membership terms. Still, a challenging question while in Cuba was whether to include

---

[4] Access to justice remains an ongoing struggle in Argentina affected by changing governments. Still, in contrast to Peru, Argentina had no legislation specifically designed to exclude the hijxs from the legal category of victim.

hijxs of Shining Path. Their first impulse was to restrict membership, concerned about trusting the newcomers, and wishing to preserve the strong affective ties that such a small group with a shared history typically creates. Yet, they were wary of reproducing the very stigma that they experienced. Unlike other H.I.J.O.S. groups in the region, the Peruvian group had limited opportunity to construct their collective identity through the human rights discourse of victims of state repression. Rather, they mobilized to challenge the inherited stigma and 'terrorist' label assigned to their parents by the official discourse, including post-TRC discourses and human rights organizations.

These (at the time) young adults grew up surrounded by a mainstream discourse, a story about widespread terrorism and the country's struggle against it. This official story was lived differently within their families, not with one counter-story, but with a myriad of stories told, silenced, half-told/half-heard, or heard once but never repeated. It was the 1990s, the time of Fujimori's dictatorship, which expanded a violent repressive regime by invoking the 'fight against terrorism' as justification for introducing neoliberal economic reforms.[5]

In this context of political violence and economic hardship, where their parents were persecuted and their organization defeated, university studies were not always economically possible or politically desirable. Universities were feared as the 'cradle' of radical groups and 'terrorists' and therefore under close state surveillance (and even military occupation). Cuba had offered university scholarships to Latin American youth as part of its foreign policy. It started to target scholarships at young people from low-income families linked to communist parties, social movements or a 'leftist background'[6] and continued institutionalizing scholarships through government agreements for low-income students without party affiliation. For the HIJXS, accessing scholarships meant the opportunity to train in professional occupations and also a temporary escape from a hostile environment at home. For their relatives, Cuba offered a way to 'keep them out of trouble'.

In 2007, I was in Cuba for a different reason, to receive treatment for a complicated and unusual health problem. This was when I met the HIJXS. A son of a friend of my parents from 'back then' told me about HIJXS and

---

5   During the Fujimori regime, Peru abandoned the Inter-American Commission on Human Rights, declaring that it no longer had jurisdiction over the country.

6   According to 2007 United Nations Educational, Scientific and Cultural Organization data, Cuba was the second biggest host of Latin American students abroad, after the United States, with 14 per cent of the total. The Cuban scholarship programme started in 1999, with approximately 10,000 students, and later strengthened when Hugo Chavez added funding to the Latin American School of Medicine.

I asked him to introduce me to the group. At this point, I had no intention or plan to engage in research but was simply looking for a community to whom I would feel connected. At the time, the group had between 15 and 25 members. I became curious to understand what my own story might have been, had my parents' decisions been closer to theirs. As it happened, they also provided me with 'a way back' that I did not even know I wanted.

Later that year, I asked the group if they would tell me their stories. Despite some doubts, we started recording them. Why did we do it? I guess it was in part coincidence, and in part out of necessity. They wanted to tell their stories and I felt drawn to them. I desperately needed something to do besides doctors, herbs, needles and physiotherapy. I could not type or write due to my 'arms problem', but I could listen. The group took my interest as an opportunity to articulate their stories for themselves as they had never done before. For some, it became an experiment in making their *testimonio* public as a form of political action in some undefined future, a 'coming out' sort of thing, their own act of denunciation.

My previous research-oriented thinking had been anchored in my experience as a sociologist and feminist in Nicaragua. Becoming physically unable to write transformed how I engaged with this project. I had no explicit research goals or research questions to pursue. In this initial stage, the work was personal and interpersonal, we talked and spent time together without any written accounts; only some one-on-one conversations were recorded as *testimonio*. My listening was embodied. It was also an escape from bodily pain. It was absorbing.

Looking back, I think there was also some guilt on my side, because my parents left Peru right before Fujimori's dictatorship; that is right before the HIJXS' parents were prosecuted, imprisoned, tortured and/or killed. I had my own problems with moving to Nicaragua, dealing with my parents' unacknowledged exile, living my own contradictory attempts and resistances to fit in, and figuring out what to do next after all connections to future plans and extended family were severed, but I was safe and my parents were alive.

In this liminal space, the HIJXS agreed to record our conversations and I unilaterally decided to store the audio files. No one ask me for their recording, as though an unsaid feeling that they posed a risk and were potentially harmful had already started creeping in. By the time I returned to Nicaragua in 2007, I had 40 hours of recorded conversations with 15 of the HIJXS, one page of notes for each participant, and memories of many hours spent joining in the group's activities and daily life. I later learnt that this engagement with the group could be retold as ethnographic, a 'deep hanging out'[7] mode of work that, drawn forward in

---

[7] The term is attributed to Renato Rosaldo during the 1994 conference *Anthropology and the Field*. Rosaldo's idea of deep hanging out appeared in published form in Clifford

time as a key element in my narrative inquiry, was enriched by 'engaged listening'.[8]

During those first years in Cuba I referred to our work in recorded conversations as 'life histories' while they called them '*testimonio*'. At one point, they asked why I insisted on the term life histories and I realized that these were different practices and we had ascribed different meanings to the same action of storytelling. Lines of contestation were drawn, lines which would become the methodological issues that make up the main threads of this book.

Upon reviewing our practices of recording conversations, I realized I was uncomfortable with the term *testimonio*. It felt heavy, outdated. I invested in it all that belongs to a former generation. During the years of armed conflict across Latin America, *testimonios* were a form of realist writing from and by 'the oppressed', framed by a leftist rhetoric of the 1970s and 1980s, and driven by an urgency to denounce oppressive systems (Beverley, 2004; Detwiler and Breckenridge, 2012). Within Peru's post-war transition after 2000 (or post-dictatorship transitions in the rest of the Southern Cone in the previous two decades), *testimonios* had the weight of legal and formal truth-telling, performed either in a trial courtroom or in the public audiences set by the TRCs. Neither of the two fitted, in my view, with what we were doing.

The heaviness and borrowed character of *testimonio* clashed with what I felt intuitively closer to: life histories, which had (for me) a stronger sense of ownership, turning the focus onto our lives. Besides, I was influenced by a feminist action research background and principles I kept close to my heart, such as 'the personal is political', hence the inclination to reclaim life histories as sites of knowledge production and political action (Andrews, 2008). Particularly after times of larger stories and big words such as 'structural transformation' and 'revolution', I felt (hoped?) life histories provided a shift, maybe a narrower yet crucial look at small particular stories lived within those larger ones.

I wanted to engage with the HIJXS in a collaborative project, but I was missing something about the significance they ascribed to *testimonio*. They had a sense of urgency, an interest to connect with those larger stories of the country, and held to an ideal of truth-telling with a strong denouncing texture and a political desire to work together to distort the private/public boundaries and defy the larger stories of the war/post-war and the social

---

(1997). It is also attributed to Geertz (1988) who described it as 'immersing oneself in a cultural, group or social experience on an informal level'.

[8] Engaged listening as ethnography was coined by Forsey (2010), suggesting the need to expand ethnographic tools from the well-known participant observation to an engaged listening with 'ethnographic imaginary'.

stigma they produced. Their use of *testimonio* also sought to define the boundaries of how I, and possible others, were to engage with their stories.

The 15 recorded conversations with HIJXS varied in length between two and four hours. In many cases we held two separate sessions, mostly because that was the only way to continue a conversation they were not ready to leave. Continuing them also depended on how the first conversation shaped our relationship in terms of trust, closeness and connections between our stories. In all cases in which we held a second session, it provided the space for further elaboration and being more reflexive about the previous conversation. The resulting 40 hours of audio files became our testimonial artefacts and I have travelled with them (not without some fear) from Havana to Managua to Bristol and (back) to Lima.

Encountering academia

The origins of this project are relationships and a 'working together' among a group of people that pre-date traditional research beginnings. This started as an experience with a collective of young people getting together to record conversations I reluctantly agreed to call *testimonio*; a name that would ultimately prove to be a challenging field of inquiry in itself.

The work we started in Cuba in 2007 only took shape as research in 2009 when I applied to the University of Bristol doctoral programme. There were two main reasons for moving in this direction: the possibility of having dedicated time and a safe space to develop the project; and an interest in learning other possible ways to continue it. In my explorations of approaches I was captivated by narrative inquiry, mostly the type of narrative work that places people's stories centre stage.[9]

It was important for me to be attentive to what was at stake in our struggle over naming this/our work. It became evident during the inquiry that there was a struggle over establishing boundaries for my role and theirs: How was I to treat and handle our recorded conversations? What type of listening and, ultimately, writing was I allowed with them? I decided to engage with the group's decision to use the word *testimonio* within this inquiry. This was possible for me only by challenging the boundaries of what counts as *testimonio*. Thus, I considered that the possibilities of engaging in a collaborative project with HIJXS involved understanding our recordings as becoming within the borderlands of *testimonio* and other life narratives; that in-between area of their and my meanings of what counts as political and

---

[9]   The School of Education at University of Bristol had a creative community of narrative inquirers and I was able to meet its lead professor, Jane Speedy, who became my first supervisor until her forced retirement.

as doing politics in the fuzzy territory of memory work. I was inspired by reading Patti Lather's book *Troubling the Angels* to move towards a testimonial inquiry by 'troubling' *testimonio*, that is 'to interrogate a commonsense meaning' (2000b: 289) for an activist inquiry into the space in-between the 'truth telling' dimension of *testimonio* and the 'after truth' turn in the social sciences.

By engaging with *testimonio* not only as products but as practices, I reconsidered my research text in itself as testimonial: bearing witness to the entangled process of producing *testimonios*. Situating myself 'as witness giving testimony to the lives of others' (Lather, 2007: 41) was followed by considering *testimonio* as pedagogy. That is, a continuous wondering of how to bear witness to the practices of producing testimonial narratives from a disposition to collaborative learning. How not to exclude what surrounds such efforts and what is provoked by them? How to account for what followed once we all relocated over those years? How to research an ongoing process that appeared increasingly slippery?

Nevertheless, beyond the ethical stance of not slicing the testimonial narratives up into categories, the initial work with the testimonial conversations produced a series of dissatisfactions. The first one was precisely about all the other people and stories that populated the recording moment. How to account for the more complex and rich encounters that took place beyond the limits of the voice recorder? This, in turn, hinted at an issue that would persist during the inquiry: that the act of transcribing and writing (editing) those conversations was insufficient.

Additional issues made me uneasy and slowly drove me away from the initial envisioned process of producing *testimonio* as a linear process whereby we would record → transcribe → revise with participants → edit, and *voilà!* Such a process was considered straightforward, as we see in Randall's *Testimonios: A Guide to Oral History* (1985), a work produced in the context of the Nicaraguan revolution where she uses *testimonio* and oral history interchangeably. I was inclined to follow this method due to my previous experiences in popular education with women and youth organizations in 1990s Nicaragua.[10]

The un-recorded individual and group conversations made me look beyond what we encountered during the recorded conversations and turn

---

[10] My family moved to Nicaragua in 1991, where I finished high school and studied sociology in 1993 at the Central American University. Starting my second year I worked with marginalized urban youth groups in a non-governmental organization active in the Central American Network of Popular Education. My early work experiences were heavily influenced by popular education's 'dialectical methodological conception' based on Freire (1996) and rooted in the Nicaraguan community praxis as well as my involvement in the women's movement throughout the 1990s.

my attention to the constraints that the testimonial practice put on the stories possible. How to communicate not only the experiences of violence, clandestine lives and state repression, but also the other things that were happening during our conversations? Things like the rawness of emotions, the changing tone and volume (and even accents) in the voices, the careful avoidance of certain words and names, the navigation through several emotions, the use of irony and dark humour, the normalized lightness with which some awful experiences were retold, the repetitions, the suspicious glances at the recorder, the inquisitive staring at my reactions, the efforts to remember and retell every little detail, or the confusion/frustration when they could not. And these are only the things I can name; there were plenty more for which I have not found words.

There was also a fear of saying something 'wrong'. This occurred at two distinct levels. First, saying something that could be misunderstood or misinterpreted, or worse that might be used against them, and saying something that, upon reflection, they would have said differently, or that possibly did not belong to the public sphere. The second was about accuracy. The anxiety of saying something they were not completely sure happened that way, they could not recall with precision, or was more of a 'borrowed' memory, or even made up. This was made explicit with expressions such as: 'Wait, no, that was before, or no, it was after … I'm not sure.' 'Now that I'm telling you this, I wonder if I was really there or if they told me that.' 'Well, no, that doesn't make sense, I couldn't really remember that, could I?' 'Actually, that was in the other house, because I was already … so it can't be in our first house.'

Such concerns and fears are closely related to the validity of their accounts, which can also be seen in expressions that, from the beginning, framed the *testimonio* as tentative or (perhaps) provisional. This took the form of a disclaimer at the start of the recorded *testimonio* or beginning of a story: 'I have a bad memory', 'I can't remember well', 'I was too little at that time', 'It's all jumbled up in my head', 'I always get those mixed up' or 'It's like everything happened that same year', acknowledging some form of unreliability in their accounts, hinting at *testimonio* as flawed and memory work as also frail and unstable. For Pilar Calveiro (2008), precisely these characteristics make *testimonio* a more honest discourse regarding historical accounts of state atrocities. In its effects of truth, *testimonio* always already contains a declaration of its limits from its own uncertainty and incompleteness.

However, I was disconcerted by a certain mode of policing oneself, enforcing a 'true' account, that was triggered by the testimonial recording. Here, I found it troublesome that the much-celebrated emancipatory effect of testimonial production could also bring, as a counterpart, an oppressive performing of stories in a particular shape with certain silencing practices. Within the testimonial context, there was no room for contradictory/messy feelings, blurry/messy memories or complicated positions towards their parents' politics. The space for doubts or open accounts was further reduced.

In *Getting Lost*, Lather expresses her greatest fear, 'That I will kill them with my high theory, that I will eat away their stories' (2007: 51). Not 'eating away' the HIJXS' stories has certainly been a preoccupation of this project, and it foregrounded my decision to place as much of the *testimonios* as possible at the centre while paying attention to creativity as an escape. As a result, a tension runs through these pages produced by the movements between creative writing and sociological explanations. I seek in literature what theories cannot grasp of lives and in theories explanations that I do not get from literature. In my writings, I make explicit different voices that I find inseparable within myself, and try to intertwine them in a dialogical way, pushing them to start talking to each other. Engaging in such dialogue helps sustain the intricate layers, complex demands and multiplicity of lives within this text. The reader will begin to see these other writings, interweaving their voice and mine; narrating and reflecting.

> I couldn't figure out what to do with stories that resisted my attempts at dissection, classification, abstraction, analysis. I found myself isolating and carrying my limitations as a burden. Talking to others opened the possibility of academic research, to be away and discussing it in a 'safer' environment. A chance to think of what I want separate from what the group 'wants', because assuming we both want the same kept my purposes hidden and unchallenged. This, in turn, took me further away from the HIJXS, producing new challenges and uncertainties.

Yet talking (and listening) to each other is not a simple exercise. It is potentially fraught with conflicts that colour and shape the inquiry process. Three years after we held the testimonial conversations, one of the HIJXS said to me 'You have us in your hands.' This was a striking choice of words. Did he know that for years it had been precisely my hands that were not up to the task? I could not help but notice how precisely my hands, injured as they were, made it possible for us to coincide in Cuba and engage in those conversations, and how those problematic hands also enabled an exceptional listening and presence in those moments. But later, they made the next step of transcribing the conversations a difficult task that filled me with anxiety.

> Had I raised too many expectations? Added too much pressure by calling it 'the task' while disembodying it from ourselves, as something coming from above? Might that be my Catholic upbringing mixed with the guerrilla mythology of a destiny, with its

heroic narratives? And I thought I didn't believe anymore in such emancipatory-from-above language, because after inheriting defeat who doesn't remain suspicious? How can we create other ways of doing, embodied and in the present tense, embracing our continuous changes and contradictions, our lack of definitive answers?

Throughout this project, my chronic pain created a concern that my condition might worsen and I would be unable to finish. But there have been several layers of fears beyond that one. There is also fear of doing it wrong; of the consequences this project might bring for its protagonists. And a fear of confronting my own past; what Peru meant to me after I thought it was nothing more than a place with really good food where my grandparents used to live and where I went to elementary school. It concerns me how connected and disconnected from their stories I am now, and the directions my inquiries have taken me, closer/away from the HIJXS, closer/away from that country.

(Re)turning to Peru: revisiting

The post-war context and the TRC's construction of victim and perpetrator categories had wide-ranging implications for the members of the subversive groups, and for their children. Unlike Argentina's H.I.J.O.S., their Peruvian counterparts were denied the possibility of any access to justice or rights to reparations despite reports of state-inflicted torture, forced disappearance, extrajudicial killings and/or unlawful imprisonment. Furthermore, the transitional proceedings reinforced an already generalized stigmatization as 'children of terrorists', somehow conditioning their acceptance in society upon concealing their (parents') past. It denied them any space for political action without being seen as either suspects or defenders of terrorism, criminalized as 'apologia' for terrorism during Fujimori's regime and still existing in the anti-terrorist legislation.

Peru's context and its contrasts with Cuba, where the HIJXS spent between four and six years studying, created a unique opportunity to explore our changes over time and space, as well as the possibilities for *testimonio* production as memory work to be made public in Peru. Such explorations through 'revisiting' the first testimonial recordings after the return to Peru appeared suitable for a methodology relying on creative writing and collective methods for memory work. Yet it turned out not to be so.

First, the HIJXS rejected fictionalization. Most of them wanted to be named. One decided to abandon the project precisely because it was no longer safe to name their family. Even more crucial was how troublesome they found the idea of fictions mixed with the testimonial. Wouldn't fictionalizing cast doubts on the veracity of their stories and work against their denouncing purpose? What happens then with the facts, of living with their parents being killed, tortured and imprisoned? Wouldn't that render their stories un-real?

Second, the importance of my own relationship with the group and the country became clearer during the fieldwork. I could not hide behind the 'objective observer' position academics tend to assume and recommend (Denzin and Lincoln, 2011). In Peru, I came to see the impossibility of that stance more clearly. My fieldwork trip was also my first return to Peru in 20 years, and I carried fears about my own history: why my family left, how to explain my return, how much to disclose of my project, and how to explain it and the people it involved without being seen as 'suspicious' or 'someone to beware of'.

My initial plan to avoid getting close to the HIJXS' families proved impossible. I wanted to focus on the second generation and their stories, not on the older one. The problem was that their relatives sought to share their stories about the internal war. In addition, visiting the TRC archive in Lima gave me access to the parents' lives registered there (oral testimonies, newspaper clips and official documents produced for/by the TRC). The difficulty of drawing a boundary between the stories of the HIJXS and their relatives ultimately raised the question of why I wanted this separation in the first place. Lurking somewhere in the back was a mixed sense of curiosity and guilt, noticing the striking difference between the world of the HIJXS, their families and neighbourhoods with my own extended family.

Third, I was particularly stressed about 'conducting fieldwork professionally'. My personal involvement became somewhat problematic when I felt the pressure of producing 'research' and the haunting question in Lima was '*Is this research?*' The change from a collective project to an academic one was complicated not only for me, but also for the group. I was stressed about failed group meetings and individual cases when, despite agreeing, they were reluctant to attend meetings or relisten to the 2007 recordings. I felt (and transmitted) the pressure to apply my devised collective methods on the *testimonios*, but, as usual, nothing worked as planned.

It became evident that the HIJXS were busy with their lives and the difficulties of their own return, dealing with finding jobs, the situation of their relatives (illness, prison, trials, police harassment), and finding some form of activism that was meaningful for each. They were already struggling with finding their way back to Peru and constructing possible ways to position themselves in regard to their stories in the present, and the testimonial recordings intruded disturbingly into their lives at that moment.

After several attempts to get together, we held a couple of group meetings. Still, they were mostly filled with anxiety regarding the impact of the return on them and a bitter sense of having achieved little upon their return to a country that (still) felt quite repressive. I felt their lives were somehow getting in the way of my research! It was only when I gave up on the collective meetings that things started to happen, enabling me to see 'them' more than my research.

In a surprisingly reciprocal way, they became interested in a trip I organized for myself to Huancayo (central highlands), and some joined me. The trip turned into a collective attempt to approach other hijxs who had not previously been contacted. We also continued collecting stories, adding stories to our stories. It turned out quite significant to be there, bodily present in that place ... *hacer presencia* in that particular geographical space with a history (Taylor, 2020), where other stories we heard about as children took place.

The trip opened the possibility of visiting Molinos (a smaller rural town in the same region as Huancayo) and meeting the children of those massacred on those roads, buried in a mass grave and later exhumed only to languish in the dusty corridors of the local public prosecutor's office, never recovered by their relatives. It was an attempt to get closer to those stories in that place and how they influenced us. But the trip was interrupted by the death of the father of two HIJXS after a brief couple of months in and out of the hospital. Upon receiving the news, we rushed to Lima (the same group resumed the trip once my three-month stay in Lima had ended). This particular death had a profound impact on the group, not only because they all loved this person very much but also because he represented the hope of a life rebuilt after 16 years in prison.

In the midst of my fieldwork, I had thought how much life got in the way of my plans, but it was death, actually, that had a strong impact. I have never been to a cemetery as often as when I was in Lima, when I was with the HIJXS and their relatives, visiting dead people, and finding out how they died of cancer or chronic illness due to the long years of extreme prison conditions. Those stories affected me more significantly than I expected.

The more I shared the space in Lima with them, the more I understood the importance of place in this project, and of not having a single-method approach, but devising more dialogical methods (Frank, 2005; Sykäri, 2012), creatively proposing activities and conversations that would adjust to each of them (Reason and Bradbury, 2008). The adjustment considered two aspects: making available the links between our conversations about *testimonio* and their present lives in Peru and engaging in doing things with them such as visiting their families, participating in public activities, going to museums, visiting their dead, or simply going to their places of interest. This was only possible by being more attuned to their lives and the shared and not-so-shared difficulties of being in Peru.

One of those difficulties turned out to be openly discussing our testimonial project and the research around it with the academic circle working on memory in Lima. The first time I posed this question to the group I was seeking their advice on how to navigate the country and its 'minefields' of memory (Jelin, 2003), including the subtle differences of vocabulary used to refer to those particular years. The HIJXS were interested in my participation in the academic memory circles but concerned about being identifiable by associating with me. Whereas my problem began with how safe it was to be associated with HIJXS and *familiares*, the reverse was also problematic for them, as being seen with me would mean becoming identifiable as sons and daughters of MRTA members.

A second return to Lima: accompaniment

Fieldwork led me to establish an important distinction between the HIJXS testimonial project, which started before and continues growing in number of recorded *testimonios* and activities, and the research. The latter, although collaborative, required some narrowing down and focus.

By 2013 I developed an acceptance of how things worked, and grew more at ease about how to handle myself in Lima. This time I decided just to be by their side, suggest some activities, and motivate them to join me in certain visits or events such as the TRC archive or a public event on memory. I was more determined to join their lives and felt at ease visiting their houses. I still scheduled some one-on-one meetings to record our conversations, but they were unstructured and with no commitment pressure. This time, they insisted more on making sure we held those recorded conversations and were more willing to sustain conversations about working their way through positioning themselves in relation to their history while being in Peru in the present.

The key word during my second phase of fieldwork was *accompaniment*, which was my way to keep from 'eating away' their stories, and instead be alongside as a witness to their lives and what we termed their/our 'memory processes'. Such activities included going with one of the HIJXS to the Victims Register Unit for his father's case, joining another at her medical service post in a remote rural town where her father had been killed, attending the first public trial of the paramilitary group responsible for killing another's father (18 years earlier) and visiting the women's maximum security prison to meet three former MRTA members who remained there.

The expression 'the stories possible thus far ...' became central as we realized the existence of other stories over time and places. This is what led me to inquire into the story-making process and use creative writing, exploring a poetics of memory, to create spaces for other possible stories. The HIJXS, however, not always considered creative writing acceptable as a re-presentation of *testimonio*. How then was I to deal with their transferring of 'writing responsibility' to me and their expectations of what is considered appropriate for testimonial re-presentation and what is not?

In delineating the limits and scope of this inquiry, I worked with six testimonial narratives. While there were 15 to begin with, I decided to include in the first movement only the ones who participated in the follow-up recorded conversations in Peru. This was important not only in terms of the argument about change and the writing of *testimonio*, but also to keep the ethics and safety of participants in check all these years later. There were a few other potentially 'eligible' *testimonios*. While I recorded conversations with other hijxs outside the group, I excluded them as *testimonios* in the first movement because I could not offer them the support and continuity the HIJXS provided each other. Still, I draw from conversations with other participants in the second movement, sometimes I write them following the realist tradition, and other times move away, by using fictionalizations, creative writing and composite characters. And while I could claim representativeness in that six is almost a third of the HIJXS group I knew, I see the reason for six *testimonios* as that is just how it happened ... much like the whole story of this research.

The following pages are filled with the tensions and problematics of doing this work as research, and the particular difficulties of settling with one account. I have attempted a way out of the 'stuckness' that characterized the writing stage by raising questions more than answering them, and by telling stories more than explaining them:

> Stories go in circles. ... It helps if you listen in circles because there are stories inside and between stories, and finding your way through them is as easy and as hard as finding your way home. Part of finding is getting lost, and when you are lost you start to open up and listen. (Tafoya, 1995: 12, cited in Wilson, 2008: 6)

PART I

The First Movement: Testimonial Narratives

The first movement re-presents the initial step in our memory work, the construction of realist tales which involves producing the stories to be retold as *testimonio*. These are written based on the conversations during our first encounter with the HIJXS in Cuba 2007 as the raw material, they do not represent how the HIJXS feel and think today.

It contains the narratives produced with the collective from a traditional testimonial stance. By crafted as realist tales, I mean they are constructed rewritings based on the recorded conversations with the protagonists. They respond to the collective desire for *testimonio* at that moment in their lives, which constituted the original purpose of our working together.

The following six testimonial narratives perform as resistance texts and counter-narratives of the Peruvian internal war at that time of their lives.

3

Adelín: Political Prisoners
in the Family

Stories about my father

My father has been a political prisoner for the past 14 years, since 1993. 10 June 1993 was the day he was caught. I was 13.[1] I also have an uncle, an aunt and a cousin who were taken as political prisoners; three were members of the MRTA [Tupac Amaru Revolutionary Movement] and one of *Sendero* [Peruvian Communist Party – Shining Path]. Actually, most of my family has been imprisoned and tortured. One uncle was even killed.

My father belonged to the movement. He was a '*político*',[2] but during the Fujimori regime, they detained *militantes* and *non-militantes* alike, students, workers, teachers, anyone … it was all very arbitrary. The Peruvian prison population got huge.[3]

---

[1]   Adelín's initial statements in our 2007 first recorded conversation have been complemented with more recent writings by her.

[2]   Adelín's father was a labour rights lawyer working with unions. By '*político*', I learnt later, she meant he worked in the organizational aspect and the political front of the MRTA, which included contact with grassroots organizations, unions and political parties. Adelín didn't discuss his clandestine role in the MRTA. She may not have known it at the time we first recorded our conversation, as I learnt later that this type of information was not fully shared in HIJXS except in cases where the parents were no longer alive.

[3]   Amnesty International report (2003: 3): 'Although official figures are not always available … between 1992 and 1993 the number of detainees rose from 713 to over 4,200 cases. In total from 1992 to 2000, 21,855 people were detained on charges of "terrorism" in Peru. Of those detained between 1992 and 2000, 6,075 were released … because there was no evidence of them having had any links to the armed opposition.'

When my dad was arrested, they kept him in Lima a few months before sending him to Puno, near the border with Bolivia, where he stayed for seven years in the Yanamayo maximum-security prison. Yanamayo was a terrible place, at almost 4,000 metres above sea level with below-zero temperatures, it was known as a *cárcel tumba*, 'tomb prison'. The cell was two-by-two metres with concrete beds only 1.5 metres long but my dad was 1.8 metres so his legs hung over. For those seven years, he was locked up practically 24 hours, only half an hour in the yard and that was organized to have no contact with others. Some cells were shared, but he was alone.[4]

He was moved back to Lima in 2002 or 2003 after the Fujimori regime came down. Before that, the Sendero and MRTA prisoners took over the Yanamayo prison, an *enfrentamiento* with the guards, and some people died. Most of them got transferred and separated, and my father was sent first to Challapalca, another prison near Puno but much farther away, for a few months before they brought him to Lima.

And then came the TRC [Truth and Reconciliation Commission] right after Fujimori fled the country and the transition period started. Then, several people got released, those 'wrongly' imprisoned, people who were just in the wrong place at the wrong time, no evidence, nothing. Under Fujimori, it was all about showing as many as possible wearing striped prisoner uniforms on TV, everything televised, like a reality show.

After that my father was sent back to Lima, to the Canto Grande maximum-security prison. Not so far from home.

Learning about my father's arrest

We found out because someone brought a note to my mom, that she should go inquire at DINCOTE.[5] Everyone who was caught was kept in DINCOTE for 15 days with no communication; that's when they were tortured, beaten and kept in 'the hole', some even got killed in there. And for those 15 days we couldn't see my dad, they threatened him with killing his family and said a nephew ratted him out; it was a very disturbing time.

My mom told me and my brother all these things. But we already knew this kind of stuff. We knew our father had a semi-clandestine life. He still came home, wasn't completely cut off from us, but we knew. I remember we missed him a lot … but there was this certainty that he always returned home.

---

[4] Yanamayo prison was inaugurated in 1994 by Fujimori. The Peruvian National Police together with Peruvian Army personnel were in charge of the internal and external security of the prison.

[5] Dirección Nacional Contra el Terrorismo (National Anti-Terrorist Unit).

Since I was little our family reunions were always outside of Lima, my dad would arrive from one side, my aunt from the other side, and my uncles from another. I always found it strange, and leaving was similar, taking turns, different directions. But we always had those get-togethers, no matter what, until dad's arrest.

My father never told me about the MRTA, like in a conversation, nothing like that. It would come up in grown-up conversations. … Also, we saw he was careful coming home, using different routes, or we'd meet him somewhere else. But nobody talked to me about the MRTA. It is only after my father's detention that my mom told me he was in it. Later, I even learnt that he took me to some of his meetings when I was a kid, but I didn't know until people I met in prison said they knew me. And I learnt more things once my brother entered university, and there people approached us and told us stories about Dad. So, I started to get to know my father in those stories, through others outside the family.

Still, I wasn't taken by surprise when he was accused of being MRTA. What surprised me was to see him on TV. I was returning home, just walking in and I saw the screen with my dad's face and the striped prisoner uniform with those numbers on his chest. That was shocking, those headlines in the news, calling him a terrorist. Only because I had no idea of what would come after. I was 13 and at that age I thought this kind of thing, like prison and being far away from the people I love, would go by quickly. I had no idea.

No one told me but I had an intuition, I knew they were doing something, and that we had to be careful, all those 'security' things. With my aunt, *La Negra*, we'd go out, like to rent a movie and she'd be Diana or Carmen, and I'd ask why … and zap! a slap on my wrist, no explanation needed [laughing]. It was clear that they had to. It became normal and also something to keep quiet about. The same as when I saw her with her looks altered. Somehow I learnt it; I guess it's how they educated us.

Maybe from all that hushing, we knew not to tell those strange details in the house, like my dad coming home sporadically, months without seeing him, he was 'travelling'. It wasn't like a normal household. Even at school they asked about my father, but I'd say my parents were separated, I think my mom told me to say that. For my elementary school graduation in 1991 I knew my dad shouldn't come, that it wasn't safe. But he wouldn't miss it. This was one of the few times we were together in a public celebration, maybe the only one.

Before the arrest

When Fujimori pulled off his coup, I was too young and had no idea of politics, but I came to understand what could happen. Still, I wasn't prepared for my father's detention, even knowing it was possible because a cousin was detained for being in Sendero. I remember feeling very sad then, not shocked but sad.

Nothing compared to my uncle's arrest, he was caught in the San Martin region, *la selva*. I recall my dad coming home unexpectedly one night, after a while. That night he said he would turn himself in the following day because they had caught my uncle and my brother was with him. He would exchange himself to get my brother.

I was right at the table with them talking to each other. And I heard my mom saying no, that she'd get my brother. She would bring her son back. Even today, it still impresses me how determined she was. Such a fantastic moment, my father surrendering for the love of his son, and my mother's love making her step in, not willing to lose either of the two. At that moment I saw them really together, they shared something unknown to me. I imagine that was one of their toughest moments, knowing they had your son and that it was because of you; Abel was only 13, or 14.

I couldn't even sleep after hearing my parents' conversation. By that time my mom had already imagined they were captured, because she had dreamt about it … like she knew. A part of me was very sad. … I kept imagining they could kill my brother.

My mom went to *la selva*, and after a few days, she came back with Abel and my cousin, because the military had detained my uncle, together with his son and my brother, there at the base. They tortured my uncle and made the two boys watch. I know because my uncle wrote a letter to his son with everything the military did; I remember reading it. Very heavy stuff I can't erase from my head, but even more terrifying is the idea of my brother, so little, being there.

After Mom brought Abel home, it was two whole years, where he would only talk about being at the base, witnessing all sorts of things. He remembered every detail. Whatever we were doing he'd interrupt to tell me again and again, and once he started it was as if he couldn't stop, like being possessed or something, it was scary. I thought he was going crazy with those memories. I didn't know what to do. I was also a child and it was horrible stuff. All I thought was not to tell anyone, to keep it between us. Even now I worry about him. I remember feeling shaken by his stories. The damage is already done, it's already inside us.

After the arrest

I remember *las visitas*. Mom would take me and my brother every couple of months. We got *soroche*, the altitude sickness, and the cold was horrible, although I didn't suffer as much as my mom and brother.

After such a trip, we'd see him but we couldn't talk like we're doing right now, we had to use *locutorios* that kept us like a metre away. The whole visit was monitored by at least one guard. We couldn't bring newspapers and even though we were children the guards searched us, removed clothes, with hands everywhere. Anything we brought was checked, the letters were read and some undelivered.

La visita was exactly 45 minutes. Imagine reducing all I had to 45 minutes, and through those very tight metal *mallas* between us, so I couldn't see my father's face, eyes, mouth … all form disappears … we couldn't hold hands, kiss, hug or even touch. It was frustrating, talking was shouting actually. And then, saying goodbye, after those 45 minutes, just like that, trying to imagine your hand reaching the other side. … That's how we got to spend birthdays, Father's Day, Christmas Day, New Year's Eve. No day was special, they were all the same. And the years passed like that. Seven years, until I turned 20.

It wasn't all about being sad; I was also angry. *La visita* made me angry each time. I remember my mom chatting with the guards to ask favours, because rules changed arbitrarily. But I couldn't be friendly, it made me furious, and I always ended fighting because I knew those same people kept my father incarcerated. … The thought of them hurting my dad and the others enraged me … that they beat him, that anytime there was a problem the guards entered to repress them heavily. I knew it. Even my family was tired of me being so angry in those years he was in Yanamayo.[6]

And that was the point, it was also *our* punishment. The *carcelería*[7] was also ours. The point of sending them to a remote prison was to isolate them by

---

[6] 'Yanamayo [prison] was built to break their will. It was not the first time the idea arose: the *altiplano* as a territory of exile. In the early twentieth century, the island of Taquile, in the heart of Lake Titicaca, was the target of the most stubborn opponents. In the eighties, Yanamayo was designed to eliminate all the factors that had facilitated the conquest from within the prison space. Twenty-three and a half hours a day locked in two-person cells of one and sixty meters by two and thirty meters windowless, with temperatures below the freezing point, nearly 4,000 meters above sea level, ensured a complete control. Prevent any kind of group activity was a key objective' (Rénique, 2003: 94–95). According to the Peruvian Ombdusman Office (Annual Report 1999–2000): 'The regime to which the inmates are subjected in the Yanamayo prison is at odds with our constitutional requirements, international standards and human dignity, and suggests its suitability for such rules, without involving endangering the safety of society. Particularly important is the urgent need to review the hours of confinement in cells, the visits system with *locutorio*, and the illegal practice that forbids access to any information.' (My translation from Peruvian Ombudsman Office, 1999: 15–16.)

[7] '*Carcelería*' is related to prison (*cárcel*) and even forced imprisonment. In spite of being rarely used in Spanish, the term is used quite often by Adelín, and others in HIJXS. I heard it for the first time with Adelín. What surprised me was the use of a word encompassing how the prisons affect people both inside and outside (the children, and the relatives in general). It is used also to designate the time served as in '*el tiempo de carcelería*'. The term was new to me, and it interested me for this broader meaning beyond how the imprisonment is lived 'inside' but also how the relatives 'outside' lived it, and particularly how then the visits are so charged.

discouraging relatives from visiting. The International Red Cross provided like six bus tickets a year, so we'd go on the weekend, when they allowed visits, Friday to Sunday. But we couldn't afford a hotel for three nights, so we visited two days max. My family wouldn't give up, but very few families visited. Most couldn't because you needed two days to get there – it was incredibly difficult, travelling through the highlands with landslides and detours through nameless paths – then two days to visit and two days back. Where could you get a job that gives a week off every other month? And we never had enough money, so we were tired and sick and hungry.

The thing about *carcelería* isn't only the time in prison, but mainly the conditions people were forced to endure there. I'm unsure where the word *carcelería* comes from, but it's the relatives' word for all the things everyone lived because of those prisons, including what we had to put up with. Even now it isn't over. True, it's now less complicated than at first, now that he's in Lima. Things have 'calmed down', but my father remains in prison.

I hope he'll be out in five years but I don't understand the legal stuff. First, under Fujimori with the military judges, they gave him a life sentence but a new trial and a 30-year sentence came with the transition government. It's almost the same, but in a couple of years he can fight for his release. That's what the lawyers say, but who knows if it's true. Even if it is ... time has already been lost. We've been hurt already. The family, he, us ... for not having him, for being subjected to abuse and police harassment, for having to go through all the *carcelería* with him ... and seeing family losses because of the harsh conditions relatives had to endure to visit ... having to go through all that shit.

We would never be able to undo any of that. Even if we do have our lives, carry on like normal and laugh and enjoy life like regular young people ... that will never be erased from my mind. Already the time in Yanamayo, those visits, is indelible: we'll never, ever forget that, not me, not my brother.

It's more than that, because that's only what you directly lived, but it's also knowing all the stories from other *compañeros* ... what their families endured, or so often how their families abandoned them, or they couldn't see their children; how do you explain to little kids that their dad or mom is in prison sentenced for 'terrorism'? That's how they said it in Yanamayo, we'd be queuing and they'd shout: 'The relative of *terrorista* X!' Another guard might say 'political prisoner', but very few. It was difficult for me, but I had to concentrate on seeing my dad no matter what. I could see kids scared and crying, kids who didn't want to be there. Many times I didn't want to go either; Mom said I was being difficult. I had to think of my dad and his life in there to really push myself to actually go. It was hard to see children there because it was very damaging for them, psychologically. Well, probably also for us, don't you think? It did affect me, and maybe later on some of the effects will surface.

Now that my dad is in Canto Grande prison, I no longer go to Yanamayo, but the other *compañeros* are still in my mind, those who stayed there or were transferred to other prisons, because over all those years their families became my family. One thing I gained from that place was a larger family.

Police harassment

We organized as *familiares*, relatives of 'political prisoners', after Dad's imprisonment, still under Fujimori's regime, the toughest times. They didn't let us organize, detaining our family members and 'searching' our houses to intimidate us, so our group kept shrinking even though political prisoners kept increasing. And because my mother was coordinating the *familiares*, we were constantly scared but never let her know our fears, because we knew her work was important, that no one else would do it otherwise; besides, I doubt she would have changed her mind. I had great admiration for her and the role she took on. She was brave. It was tough work: she got arrested, beaten up and threatened several times. Before that I don't think we knew she had it in her because before that she was Dad's *compañera*, but wasn't involved.

They met when very young; she was a factory worker in an auto-parts company then became the union leader and my dad was a law student working on labour rights. She always resented quitting her political activism while dad continued, because he didn't let her go when she was invited, particularly after she got pregnant. She was at home with the family and he worked with the unions.

I've heard her questioning him about why he didn't make her part of his political life, why he kept her away; he didn't say anything. I think he just assumed she would be in charge of their children because if something happened to him she'd have to take care of us. And she did have a vital role in our upbringing. I don't mean just the mother thing, I mean educating us with the same values, and doing everything in her power to sustain our relationship with Dad. So she became active again only after his arrest. And she took care of everybody, the *compañeros* and their families. She was very committed.

The first time they arrested her was without any notice or explanation; they accused her and other relatives of working for the MRTA and held them at DINCOTE for a few days; it was reported on the news, calling them terrorists as well. I remember they said she had 'terrorist propaganda', because of a stupid drawing I did in her agenda. It was my fault, for scribbling.

One night my mom was brought home handcuffed in a police truck and the police searched the house, *la requisa*; it was really frightening. Even though there was a blackout in the neighbourhood it was like daytime in our house, and the police took lots of stuff, even personal letters. This was during the MRTA's takeover of the Japanese Embassy when the government had everyone under surveillance, targeting the relatives … to punish us. Months later, when the relatives organized a religious mass for those killed by the army, the police picked everybody up outside church; my whole family was there.

And those were the 'official' detentions. Other times, after 'visiting' prison, they would just beat her up on the streets, steal her things and threaten her. She received phone calls with death threats. We were terribly scared. I remember my grandma telling her to stop visiting but that was exactly what the Intelligence Service wanted, to isolate those imprisoned and intimidate and silence their family members. They kept watching us, they knew our steps, they always knew.

There was fear

The whole system operated by instilling fear. Even my mother's family kept their distance. I can't blame them, they were scared; but they left us on our own, and we were just kids. One side of the family was imprisoned or persecuted, and the other just stayed away. Only my grandma took us in. There was a lot of fear in the air, and most people appeared to be too scared to reach out, just in case. I had a schoolmate whose family, as union workers, actually knew my father very well, but during the whole five years of school they never once asked me how he was out of fear, pure fear.

It was only after Fujimori's fall that things seemed to calm down a bit. Some people stopped denying they knew those imprisoned, they were friends or colleagues, and even more. By the late 1990s, people would approach us in university and talk to us about our father. They even organized visits to the prisons. That was a whole new discovery for us, we could be more open. Once when we went to workers' *barrios* where they knew my father; those people hugged us and apologized for they would have liked to be closer, but feared for their lives. There I didn't have to wonder what to say. They asked about my dad and the rest of the *compañeros*, and told me the kind of stuff about my father that I wanted to know.

Yet, the fear is still there; some people still call my father a 'terrorist'.

And a sister …

There's something else I learnt about dad's life. I have a sister. She's 14 now, exactly his years of imprisonment.

We didn't know about this sister. My mother found out when she went to DINCOTE asking about him. From that moment on she was deeply hurt. Mother suffered a lot and couldn't believe it … but she loved him very much. They weren't separated, she assumed his absences had only been about his political life; it never crossed her mind that he had someone else.

In my case, I felt cheated and hurt, not when I heard I have a sister, because I love my little sister, but that he cheated on Mom. When it was revealed, it came as a shock, especially after seeing how it affected her because we had to deal with both things at the same time: my father's detention and that. I didn't expect it to be as hard, I didn't know it was going to be such an awful thing for so long.

And it was complicated because I feared for him; I kept thinking what if they torture him. At the same time I could see Mom was deeply affected by his doings. I was upset but there was no one to be upset at, because Dad was taken to prison. Afterward I tried to talk to him about it, but he just told me he's regretful, that there are things which can't be explained, that even he can't understand about himself.

My mom just identified herself with the problematics of those being imprisoned and their relatives, and against the regime's injustices, so at the end she didn't pay much attention to Dad. She couldn't really, because there was no time to talk or be sad. You have to understand: it was like suddenly it was time for her to be in charge, to take on the task … and that left no time to 'discuss their relationship' or sit down and talk it over or yell at him or hit him, maybe. … There was no time. She did what she had to do.

It took my father by surprise that she was there for him; he assumed she'd leave him for sure. Mom took an even larger responsibility on herself. She told him she was doing it for all of the *compañeros*, not for her husband. I know she's still resentful, because there hasn't been time to deal with it. Everything happened so fast, we had to keep going no matter what, just keep going.

It's only now, after his transfer to Lima, that he's trying to win her over, when they have more time to see each other and sit down and have a normal conversation. I think Mom loves him, but it's not easy to forgive.

One thing I want to make clear is that this should have been a private, family issue, but somehow it was used against us. The fact that we couldn't live it as private, but instead had to live it with all the complications of imprisonment and the generalized fear complicated everything. It all kind of felt stolen from us.

My aunt

My dad's sister, *La Negra*, was arrested in 1995, and I don't know the reasons, but they moved her from prison to prison around the country, mainly ones for men, so she was kept isolated. Because visits were restricted to immediate relatives, we couldn't see her so she had no visitors. Her parents had died, her brothers were already in prison, her two children went into exile and her husband, well, he was persecuted.

One day when I was showing my papers to visit Dad, they asked if I was *La Negra*'s sister. I was surprised, because I didn't know she was there. I said yes, that I had come to visit her. And when I got to see her – well I couldn't actually see her because of the *malla* – I told her it was me, and immediately afterward my dad entered right next to her for his own visit time with Mom. It was the happiest moment ever, because they could hug and kiss. It was very brief, because the colonel entered abruptly and started shouting at me, and well, they kicked me out. I couldn't see my father that time. I was very nervous but it was very exciting as well. We always remember that as a happy anecdote.

The daughter of ...

Being the daughter of a 'political prisoner' has meant really good feelings with many people, receiving a great deal of affection from people who have approached me because of him. I learnt about my father after his arrest, and I cannot express how wonderful it was when a group of union workers invited me to their houses and told me 'This *barrio* belongs to your father', because he was by their side in their struggles for the land. I find that just beautiful, to learn about his commitment to workers' rights; I can feel how proud those people feel to be now talking to his daughter, and I feel the same.

So, if you ask me, it's wonderful to be a political prisoner's daughter, but it's also sad, and terrible.[8] The things we had to go through as a family, as a daughter, needing my dad but not having him by my side. Although I can't say my father's decisions weren't a problem for me, I never felt abandoned or anything. I've always admired him and how brave he was, but not just him, also my mother, and several people I got to know who faced even more terrible things for being involved in the MRTA.

I think my father's choice wasn't completely illogical ... it was almost a natural thing; I can see him in it. He grew up in a very poor family,

---

[8] Adelín was reacting to my question about using the term political prisoners. A term that is rejected in Peru to refer to those imprisoned under terrorism charges. She refused to discuss it and sent me to read the definition. I found Amnesty International defines 'political prisoners' as those whose case has a significant political element. This may include the motivation for the prisoner's acts, the acts in themselves or the motivation of the authorities in imprisoning them. The term 'political prisoner' includes both prisoners of conscience and those who have resorted to criminal violence (or have been accused of other ordinary crimes) for political motives. However, it is only for prisoners of conscience that Amnesty International demands immediate and unconditional release (2003: 2–3).

his mother raised four children on her own, and he had to work by her side in the market. He lived that reality of poverty and inequality and it left a mark that pushed him to work for labour rights, to stay close to the working class. That's where he met his future *compañeros*, he comes from that side, the unions. So, it's no surprise that at some point he decided to try to change the country's reality. That's how I explain his life and then our life to myself.

All that brought us together as a family; like other families remember stories of their childhood, we remember '*la visita*' … all its crappy things or when we tried to sneak things in or when they kicked us out. It's all funny now, these are our family anecdotes … and there's always a new story, something we didn't tell before and we all laugh, even at the harshness of it all. I think the whole experience made us closer, particularly with my brother, I can't forget those long journeys, such a stunning landscape … it would have been beautiful if only we were tourists.

The thing that stays in my head is the time lost … because no one will give us that back; there's no way to recover all those years apart. Imagine, I was only 13 when they caught him, all my twenties he remained in prison. And time keeps passing.

When my father was in Lima I've only visited when I travel to Peru, because now that I'm studying here in Cuba I can't afford to go every year. We communicate by letters but not always because the guards still monitor communication, so you can't really be too personal or talk too much. And that's … it's not private.

Last time I saw him was a surprise visit, he wasn't expecting anyone so he hadn't shaved and was all dishevelled. The moment he saw me, he just broke into tears and cried like a little child. … It was awkward. I'm not good at seeing people cry, my mom and my brother cry very easily but I don't. And he's getting old now. … I saw an old man, thin and frail. Everyone who spent time in Yanamayo has all sorts of ailments, they get these *tumoraciones* in different parts of their body. My dad has it in his mouth, others in their heads, arms. I've consulted with doctors and they think it's very likely to be intoxication, possibly from chemicals in the water, and there were rumours from the International Red Cross that they were slowly poisoning prisoners. And this is beside the back and joints problems they all have from the extreme prison conditions. Some problems are only now surfacing, and we know probably more will come later, the *secuelas* from Yanamayo.[9]

---

[9] In 2013 Adelín wrote an updated statement: 'My father was a political prisoner for 16 years from June 1993 until 2009 when he got his freedom, only to die of a widespread cancer a couple of years later, most likely an effect of his imprisonment conditions.'

4

Miguel: Experiences of Exile

Growing up in several countries

I lived in Lima until I was four years old with both my parents, but I can barely remember anything about Lima. Well, probably because I was very little, but mostly because my memory has never been good. Then, I was sent to Colombia to live with my mother's family. Mom would come for one or two months at a time, but she wasn't living with me. My father's in Peru, in prison at the Callao Naval Base since 1995. … Now my mother and little sister live in Cuba and so do I. In between Colombia and Cuba we lived in Chile.

In Colombia I lived on my grandmother's farm which was full of animals, but we later moved to the capital of La Guajira,[1] with uncles, aunts and cousins all living a few streets away. So, I was always surrounded by extended family, which brings me very nice memories of Colombia as a beautiful place. I stayed there until somewhere around 1995 or 1996, just a bit after my father was arrested.

I remember my dad was very loving with me … but I really didn't live with him much, because of my dad's history, their way of living, and everything that happened. All I remember is playing with dad and waiting for him at night. Despite the little time we had, all these vivid memories of being with him have stayed with me.

We never lost contact with Dad. His letters have been a constant in my life; he's great at writing letters, full of stories. Even now, we continue writing monthly. We have a very strong relationship; closer than with my mom, who together with my grandmother raised me. With her it's more a mother–son relationship, whereas with my father it's more a friendship as well as a father. He's someone I can talk to about my stuff; we have a certain trust.

---

[1] La Guajira in north-eastern Colombia, a peninsula divided by the border between Colombia and Venezuela.

A televised arrest

When my father was arrested[2] I was nine or ten, maybe 11, I can't remember. The very day of the arrest we watched it on the TV news with Mom, and she turned to me ... and explained it all. I don't really remember much of what she said. I remember the arrest on TV, just when my dad and his *compañeros* handed in their weapons and themselves. I didn't watch the rest of it, starting with the whole *enfrentamiento* with the police, who surrounded their house all night long.

I remember it was a lot to take in. ... Many things rushing through my head and my mom telling me that my father was involved in the movement.[3] She said: *cayó preso*, there was an *enfrentamiento* ... there would be a trial, and I shouldn't worry. That's what I recall, but I don't remember much about those days. I think my brain has erased most of that part of my history. I can't remember it.

What I do remember is having my whole Colombian family going through that with us. There were so many things to be arranged, everybody doing something. *Cayó preso* ... Now, what? At that moment, it was as if Lima was some remote place.

My mom had been staying with us but left to arrange for us to move to Chile, although I don't really know that because I never asked. Chile was closer to Peru than Colombia, so we could have more contact. It was actually in Chile that I learnt more details of my dad's arrest, and watched the Peruvian TV video of the *enfrentamiento* and capturing of my father.

Learning about my father

I learnt about my father in the MRTA when he was arrested, although I probably already knew but didn't quite understand. My family would always tell me, your father is this ... and I would go, 'Ah, OK.' End of conversation. It was like he was a hero and I thought it was cool. It makes me laugh now

---

[2] Miguel Rincón Rincón was arrested on 30 November 1995, in a Tupac Amaru Revolutionary Movement (MRTA) urban base in La Molina, where the group was planning to take over the National Congress and negotiate the release of MRTA prisoners. It became a shoot-out with the police that lasted all night, until they surrendered to the police at dawn. The event was televised. Between 17 and 21 people were arrested and several injured (one policeman killed).

[3] 'The movement' is one of the several ways the HIJXS refer to the MRTA in their *testimonio*, others use different words such as the organization, or *la guerrilla*, the armed struggle, or 'the M' (probably inherited vocabulary), or more indirect references '*aquello*' (that). They rarely mentioned MRTA directly, and neither did I.

that I think about it, but in a way it was that simple for me. I had so much family around me that it never felt … like something was wrong.

I also had an uncle I was very close to, who treated me like a son. He talked to me about Peru's situation, people suffering of hunger, the striking poverty, how the economic conditions led to people's desperation, and that my dad was struggling against that; that's how my uncle explained it. So, there were always these explanations. They never concealed the truth from me, although it was in very broad terms, with no specifics on the MRTA; in fact they never mentioned it by name. It was only with 'The Embassy' events that I started paying attention. I guess my family mentioned the MRTA in their conversations, but it didn't mean anything to me.

I already had an idea of 'la guerrilla' because I always had a fascination with that from the books I grew up with; stories about Sandino and la guerrilla sandinista, Chiapas and los zapatistas, el Ché and the Cuban revolution, I thought of my dad like that. That was my idea of the MRTA, a group fighting for their people, for something better.

Now I know my dad's involvement comes from his own history, he is from la sierra, and grew up seeing the injustices from the hacendados, how they treated people, and when his family migrated to the capital, they lived very harsh times, and once in university he got into history and took a stand against that reality. It must have been a tough decision, one many made then in different countries, se lanzaron. Of course, not everywhere had a victorious end, like in this case. And yes, people made mistakes, major ones, things that shouldn't have happened; people died but that wasn't their way of doing things. And yes, maybe they should be judged for some of those things, as crimes during the war. But right now, we have a state that only condemned the armed groups and doesn't recognize state crimes, which weren't isolated events, but instead part of a policy to systematically exterminate opposition, or the poor, indigenous, the expendables. That's because the state won, and it blames those it defeated.

If asked about my father, I tell them he's in Peru, imprisoned for being in la guerrilla, but I don't say more. In Colombia my friends kind of already knew. In Cuba telling wasn't even an issue. But in Chile, quite the opposite, I never ever mentioned anything to anybody, people didn't ask and we wouldn't have told anyway.

La Embajada

We lived for three years in Santiago de Chile, from 1996 until early 2000, when we moved to Cuba. I remember Chile as difficult, toda una época difícil even economically … and because of the whole situation. It was the time of the takeover of the Japanese Embassy, remember?

La Embajada started in December 1996 and ended 22 April 1997. In fact, that was really difficult, there was a constant worry. Those were a very tense five months. Well, same for the whole country probably, but for different reasons … such a long period.[4]

I'm trying to remember the things going on in my life at the time, but I can't. … I remember the end of it, when they killed them all … and it was over. That, I do remember well. We were at home, monitoring the news on the TV … and boom, it happened. That was a serious blow, it hit me very hard. It was the death of all the *compañeros* right there, in a few seconds, all gone. And my mom talking to me, explaining … again.

What I don't remember is what Mom said that day, only that soon afterward we moved to another house. I guess it wasn't safe anymore, or maybe to avoid any harassment. Or it could easily have been for economic reasons since we moved to a cheaper place. I do remember her explaining why they took over *La Embajada*: because of the situation in Peru, you know, *los pooooobres* and all that, and also that they did it for me, for my imprisoned father, for all those in prison. They gave their lives … *por una causa justa*.[5]

I think I understood that, because it wasn't the first time my mother explained it. We always talked about things, and I think I understood … but still … it affected me very deeply. … I kept thinking, OK, but what next? I was a closed person but that day I cried … because of everything. Later I calmed down and it was normal again.

I didn't know other people in Chile, even in school I wasn't close to anyone. I guess it was hard to share what I was living, so it wasn't easy to make friends. Only my mom was there. If I'd been in Colombia, things

---

[4]   After the failure of the National Congress plan, an MRTA group took over the Japanese Ambassador's residence in December 1996. Although it wasn't the Embassy itself, the event became known in popular memory as 'The Japanese Embassy' or 'The Embassy'. While other people say 'the Embassy assault or kidnappings' HIJXS uses '*la toma*' ('takeover'). Hostages were high-ranking government officials, military, religious and business men, all people with influence in the country and diplomats from other embassies. After releasing women and the elderly (including Fujimori's mother) during the first days, the MRTA kept 72 hostages at the residency for four months until the army stormed the residency 22 April 1997 killing the 14 MRTA members. This was the last known armed action by the MRTA, after which it was defeated.

[5]   This part of our conversation was very slow, Miguel made several pauses in between sentences, like gathering his thoughts, choosing his words, or actually trying to find the words to describe that period. *La Embajada* is a key event in the HIJXS narrative: marking the end of the MRTA, and watching death televised that breaks the 'revolutionary' tale, a failed action, death also of hope. The TV showed the bodies, Fujimori parading around them, a success story for a regime already in decline, and for the military rescuing almost all hostages alive. The illusion of freeing their imprisoned relatives vanished. This was the second attempt; the first was the failed plan where Miguel's father was arrested. 'The Embassy' was considered their last resort.

would have been easier, more of a shared thing. But, it was just us in Chile. I don't like Chile, but it's not Chile's fault, it's everything we lived through there. In those three years, I went to three different schools; we moved every year. A big change from a small tropical town in rural Colombia to a big cold industrialized city in Chile. It's also where I first felt class differences, seeing dire poverty on a daily basis. Only in Chile did I experience that feeling of being in a foreign country, feeling completely out of place.

Vacations visiting the naval base

It's not easy to explain all the feelings my dad's situation causes. I can say my dad's in prison and every time I say it, a voice inside me asks, for how long? I keep wondering if he'll be free when I graduate; it's always in my head. And the feeling grows stronger with time, to share the streets with him. I understand how the system is and how it works against those who oppose it, so I know my dad won't get out of prison; in his latest trial he was sentenced to 25 years. Another trial is coming up, and it may even be worse for him. He's now 60 and has been inside 12 years already. That's a very long time.

I started travelling to Peru while living in Chile, still in elementary school. Every vacation I went to Lima to visit my dad. I'd go for a month, and be at the base almost twice a week, like five times total.

My mom couldn't enter Peru because we didn't know if they'd open a case against her, at least until Fujimori left. She didn't get to see Dad for 11 years. Every year prior to *la visita* is always difficult, dealing with lots of legal stuff, papers and permits to travel and to enter the naval base, wondering whether the International Red Cross would cover the airfares.

I can't exactly remember the first visit, but it's almost always the same. First, you enter the base and there you go through *la inspección*. Then you have to wait 15 minutes to half an hour; there is a lot of waiting in *la visita*. First the guards check your papers, then call the small armoured van to pick you up. The van is completely enclosed, you're locked in there, with no view of the outside, only a tiny dim light … and you stay inside until it starts moving. There are two more check points before you arrive to the detention centre, which has several huge iron gates, each one closes behind you before the next one opens. You get a *sensación de encierro*, the feeling of being locked in. It's the creepiest place.

The detention centre is surrounded by high walls, with barbed wire everywhere and a minefield … and then there's the prison. We stop at another shielded door where they check our special visitor's ID cards, then another door opens and there is the *lugar de visitas*, the command centre, and some offices, all are full of navy guards everywhere. In the *lugar de visitas*, they separate us into different rooms, *la revisión*: checking bags, food, newspapers and letters, and each of us, shoes off and all that … you must leave your wallet, phones, keys … and finally, we enter a room where we wait until we see my dad entering. He enters, and we hug a long hug and then just hang out.

In spite of all that, it's always nice to get there. It's not hard to explain why I have a happy memory of the *visitas*: I was going to see my dad. The place is awful, but still I don't remember it as being as bad as it is, maybe because I still have to go there. Inside the visitors' room we're alone, with one table and four chairs, and a two-way mirror through which we're watched all the time. My grandmother brings food and that's the best part, sitting together to eat and chat, like a family. And that's how *la visita* is … the two hours end, my dad re-enters the prison.

My sister was very little, just three or four years old, and she wanted Dad to get out, to leave with us. I had to explain that he was imprisoned, that there was a trial, that we had to be patient … same things I was told. That seemed enough for her, like she understood, or at least I think she did. I also had to explain the dangers of the base, not to run off because of the land mines and barbed wire, be careful not to talk to the guards. I had to keep her calm each time until Dad arrived. One of the hardest things was trying to explain to a little girl the things I was just starting to process myself.

Anyway, she enjoyed those visits; it was fun, at least until we had to leave. She was always upset at the end, lots of crying. She never knew Dad outside that place, only inside. Leaving was hard for all of us; apart from her crying, it was a very silent exit. The whole thing was quite awful, a creepy place full of armed military men. So, I imagine that it affected us a bit, because it wasn't a very normal place to spend vacation with your father.

Years later, it slowly started changing; a little bit more 'freedom'. We went to the patio and met others: two of my dad's *compañeros*, and a couple from Sendero [Shining Path]. My little sister was the only child going at such a young age and she lightened up the place; they enjoyed a bit of her childhood. That was nice, because my impression of those people isn't the same as what you get from the media. I don't know them like some inhuman monsters; I know them mostly as people severely affected by years of a harsh imprisonment regime, people with various chronic illnesses, old and ageing fast.

During the visits my dad organized things to do, always slightly nervous. I remember once the authorities didn't let my grandmother enter with us. That was one of the worst visits: seeing my grandmother on the other side felt wrong … like for a moment I wasn't sure who the imprisoned was. … My little sister didn't take it well, Dad explained to her about the laws there and also that they did it to mess with people, *pa' joder* … there's nothing you can do.

Once, I saw my dad's cell: two by one-and-a-half metres and three metres high. It has a *rendija*, a hole at the top with bars, from the early times when they built cells with just that opening. The rest was completely enclosed: no doors, no windows, just the hole at the top – literally an underground concrete tomb.

They have these thick steel armoured doors on each cell, with a service hatch to get their food. There is a small patio for jogging and doing laundry, and a workshop area, a small library, a radio and a VCR. It was a radical improvement after Montesinos[6] was imprisoned, but my dad's against it, because things changed only when the dictatorship's right hand was incarcerated. So, my dad keeps using cold water, although he should use the hot water during winter, but he is like that. And maybe he's right, maybe it is unacceptable.

Within my family, Dad's politics was never a forbidden topic, I knew what was going on, and also how things were while we weren't living in Peru, *la época de la violencia*. Dad himself told me about the history, but mostly about his trial and the conditions at the base. Our conversations were never directly about the MRTA, more about history and the current political situation, because that's my dad's work, he writes about Peruvian history and international politics.

I never learnt that much about politics from him, and my sister hates any conversation remotely linked to politics. I learnt more the human side of my parents' politics, about how to feel affected by others: less about my dad's views about the country than about his values. A very strong value system. You have to understand our communication wasn't free, every conversation inside the base is totally invigilated. You're always conscious of where you are. I don't say sentimental things; they could use them against Dad to break him. People in prison can't show their weaknesses, there's a constant psychological pressure.

Last year, Dad and others went on a hunger strike to contest the prison conditions, demand their rights. When we arrived, we weren't allowed to enter, they took away most of our visit time to punish him, but it was like they were punishing us. Two weeks lost; I never forget that.

I understand that Dad is a political prisoner, because of the Peruvian situation, the Fujimori regime and the repression that followed. I also understand that he took that different path. I don't think I have any problems with him as

---

[6] Vladimiro Montesinos played a critical role in the Fujimori regime. He led the intelligence service and was Fujimori's main advisor. His wide-scale bribery of congressmen and media owners became public in 2000, leading to Fujimori's resignation. Afterwards, he was convicted for embezzlement, corruption, drug trafficking, arms trafficking (including deals with the Revolutionary Armed Forces of Colombia) and extrajudicial killings, including the notorious Grupo Colina death squad.

I understand what he did. I am proud of how he faced the consequences, when I think of him in the trials. I saw him once and I think it's cool how he faces that with such resolution, such dignity. He has been able to sustain his principles; after all the repression, he's still standing. He didn't let them corrupt his soul, *no dejó que la represión lo apagara*, nor kill his mind. He didn't just stay there as a prisoner, he is reading, writing and painting, making things.

For now, in the next couple of years at least, nothing will change. They won't change on their own, but they have to change. Who knows how long it'll take; for now it's time to wait … see what happens. My dad and his *compañeros* continue expecting the close down of the base; it was a requirement of the last judicial sentence, in the *megajuicio*, but nothing.[7] They expect to be transferred every year, even knowing things could be worse for them in another prison, especially at the beginning, more isolation. That's their goal, to get out of such an ugly base, where everything is designed to damage your humanity.

Now the frequency of visits has increased to once a week but only direct family can visit: parents, siblings or their children. Others have to request a special permit, but no one wants to do that. Going to the highest security prison centre in the country is pretty heavy, you're marked after that and people get intimidated; they may visit once but never again.

I know that in the future, I would definitely have to be involved in politics, no way around that. First of all, because my father won't get out of prison if no one does anything from outside, *si eso no se mueve, solo no se mueve eso*, and they will all die in there.

HIJXS

HIJXS for me is *una cosa bien bonita*, my way to encounter Peru beyond my once-a-month affair (visiting Dad at the base); it strengthens my links with Peru. … Once we watched the *Alias Alejandro* film,[8] at one point he asks why his father had children if he was in the armed struggle. That's a question we could all ask our parents. I think that if you're risking your life, there is an instinct to leave a sort of legacy, and it gives you strength.

---

[7]   The legal sentence explicitly stipulated transferring civilians out of military prisons (naval base). Regardless, that sentence has not been implemented. The legal battle for the transfer continues, with the media strongly opposing it by equating the transfer to being released, and stressing that this would set a precedent to free Abimael Guzmán, the former Shining Path leader who was imprisoned in the naval base until his death in 2021.

[8]   A 2005 German-Peruvian documentary by Alejandro Cárdenas-Amelio, it tells the story of the filmmaker's journey from Germany to Peru to meet his father, Peter Cárdenas Schulte, former leader of the MRTA imprisoned at the naval base until 2015 when he finished his 25-year sentence.

It's a controversial issue, but I never asked, because I totally agree with their decision to have me [laughing], even considering I didn't have my dad next to me. For me taking up the political struggle doesn't mean you say fuck the world; it doesn't mean you don't believe in life; a child is also a way to surround yourself with life in the middle of a war, something to live for, to dream on. Of course, I wanted to have my parents staying with me. I remember crying every time Mom left. But, now I like the family I've got. Especially as a grown up I say all that happened is OK, obviously not that my dad's still in prison. ... Things turned out the way they had to, and that made me who I am, and I like myself. I became an open-minded person who makes an effort to understand other worldviews, which comes from living in different places.

Me? An exile? Where I'm from ...

That ... that was very weird, and fun as well. Knowing new places was nice but moving was strange.[9] Leaving people and places behind was tough but also nice for the new. I don't regret it. Such a life leads you to know a little bit of everything; at the same time you don't know much about anything. It's great to know different countries but you also lose something, like your country's history, which is your own history. Things like the national anthem, which you can't learn later on ... if you don't get it in school, it's just a bit of a ridiculous song.

It only gets complicated when people ask where I'm from. Sometimes I say I'm Peruvian, another times Colombian, sometimes both. Otherwise it's normal: I feel both Colombian and Peruvian, not one or the other, and I live in Cuba. I don't feel Cuban but I love their way of living, the parties, the solidarity, the loudness. ... It's where I've stayed the longest ... like a home.

When I came to Cuba I wasn't very sociable, a very introverted kid, but this place opened me up. I had a Cuban adolescence, I learnt to live and talk like them. And being here meant a place where communism and *revolución* weren't bad words. It's all around you. Suddenly I could say anything and that was liberating. Here I refer to my dad as *guerrillero* and political prisoner.

Peru isn't the same. I only go there to visit my dad, but I don't know it. And Lima isn't a nice place to live, it gives me allergies and it's a grey city, almost of a yellowish colour. My links with Peruvians started in university with those who came to Cuba on scholarships. It was weird, because during high school I was *El Peruano*, but to say I was Peruvian in front of Cubans

---

[9]   Miguel never used the word 'exile' to refer to his experiences. I asked him how he felt about being an exile, and he refused to use the word, and answered with a question that became the title of this section.

was one thing, while in front of other Peruvians … for them I'm more Cuban or Colombian.

Plans for returning

Leaving Cuba behind will be tough after these eight years living here, but once I graduate I'll go to Peru for a while … maybe even stay there. Although I'd rather live in Colombia, but I have to be with my dad, be closer to him. Peru is where I'm meant to be, *donde me toca*, and I should be there. But I'm still not sure where I'm going. For now I think it's Peru … not moving there permanently but in the short term it's the place that makes sense the most. Once in Lima, I can visit my dad even every week with the new regime at the base.

Living in the Cuban system, it's hard to imagine how things work in Peru. I don't know if I can get a job, and there everything depends on money. I don't know if having a degree from Cuba is a good or a bad thing. I don't know if having Dad's surname would be a bad thing. So far, what I have lived is solidarity here in Cuba.

But I'm slightly afraid of Peruvians, because I know those living in Cuba, but Peruvians in Peru aren't the same. I didn't experience people referring to my dad as '*terrorista*'; no one ever said to me 'your father is a terrorist'. Although regular people don't usually talk about that. Still, I've always been afraid of that.

5

Iris: Growing Up Visiting Prison

A mom in prison

I call both my aunt, Armida, and my birth mother, Lucero, Mom. I only add their names when I talk to others because they get confused. For me it's normal. Since I was five, I lived in Puente Piedra[1] with my mom Armida (actually my dad's sister), her three daughters and oldest son, as well as my grandma, until she died.

My mom Lucero has always been present in my life. I've been 'visiting' her ever since I can remember. First, once a month for half an hour at the naval base in El Callao. Then, twice at Yanamayo, the prison in Puno. Then, more often at Huaral, outside Lima but closer. Then far away again, at Chorrillos, on the opposite side of Lima. At first, she was with common prisoners in Chorrillos, because she was the only MRTA [Tupac Amaru Revolutionary Movement] prisoner. Recently they moved her and other *compañeras* to the maximum-security area, but by then I was already in Cuba.

The first memory of her is from when I was three. I remember the feeling of running as fast as I could and then my mom's tight hug. After that, I'm six and all my memories are from prisons.[2]

---

[1] At the Northern Cone of Lima, Puente Piedra is one of the oldest districts created as commercial and industrial poles of Northern Lima. It is now dedicated to commercial services, multiple wholesale markets, large commercial organizations and countryside restaurants.

[2] In October 1987, Lucero Cumpa was first imprisoned while pregnant. In June 1988, Iris was born during her mother's time in Canto Grande prison and handed to the care of her father's family. In July 1990, Lucero and 47 MRTA members escaped Canto Grande through a 300-metre tunnel dug from the outside. In March 1991, she was briefly arrested but later 'rescued' by an MRTA operation in which three policemen were killed. In May 1993, Lucero was caught in the Amazonian rainforest, where she commanded the Frente Nor-Oriental, and remained for the next 30 years in maximum-security prisons.

I remember the first years at the naval base, the strict routine of the *visita* in that eerie, depressing place, with soldiers guarding. Why can't Mom come out? First question to my grandma on arrival; she never answered. Either she or my mom Armida took me to the base, but they'd hand me to my mom's sister because only immediate family was allowed. I have this image of immense walls with menacing barbed wire, countless gates and a huge *portón*, then a small room for just me and Mom, and a colonel with a voice recorder watching us. My aunt stayed on the other side of the glass, *el locutorio*; they talked and we played.

Mom always made me feel like nothing else mattered, like it was just us in there; she was very loving and amazingly happy. I remember her always with these outbursts of laughter. She taught me to play chess and every birthday she gave me a book, which I didn't understand at first but I caught the reading bug. A last fleeting memory of the base was walking past this dark room I thought was a storage room but it was her cell.

Then came the time of The Embassy and they didn't allow any visitors. I couldn't see Mom for Christmas or New Year's … even past April; she was cut off from everyone. Next time I saw her was in Yanamayo, and she didn't look well. She was skinny and haggard but smiling non-stop as always. … They had a harsh regime; I remember they read the letters in front of me, like a humiliation. I was furious, and even more when they said I could only see her for one hour, after such a long trip and sick with *soroche*, only one hour! At the base, at least I could touch her, but in Yanamayo with *locutorios*, no touching allowed.

The second time in Yanamayo, around 2000, we went by plane, I was very excited because it was my first. That visit coincided with a protest by the political prisoners against such a restrictive regime. I entered alone because they wouldn't let my uncle in, but I wasn't scared. Inside, everyone who saw me went 'Ahhh … Lucero's daughter' and guided me through. Everybody says I look exactly like her. One of the *compañeros* took me to see her, but at that moment they started banging the bars and making loud noises. It frightened me to the point that when I saw my mom in the yard I almost jumped off the balcony. Later she came and we hung out with the *compañeros*, and there was this beautiful Puno song with drums, which I'll never forget; it reminds me of that feeling of camaraderie.

My mom Armida is a tough, hardworking woman, *una luchadora*. She raised four children by herself overcoming all obstacles. She was involved in the *familiares* group and spent nine months in prison for that. All I could think of was that I didn't want my sisters to live what I did with my mom Lucero.

There was very little talk about Dad at home; I only knew he entered the clandestine life at 17. I have no memory of him, only two photographs. In one he's very young, and in the other I'm in his arms. As a child, I made it my daily routine to look at his picture before leaving for school. I saw him as a handsome guy but that was it. Still, I dreamt about my dad my whole childhood, mostly that he was alive. Once I dreamt that he showed up at the door, but I never saw his face, he entered the house and later left again, and the next moment Grandma is telling me he was killed. It wasn't that I missed him but that I missed having a father in my life.

Even today I feel the need for a dad. Maybe it's an ideal, but it saddens me that I didn't have one, even knowing he'd also be in prison. I wish I had a memory of him not only the dad of the photographs.

A religious school

I went to Catholic school. At the end of elementary school we received a very special medal of Virgin Mary and I gave it to my mom Lucero. Only much later did I learn she was atheist, but she still wears it.

I told one schoolmate about Mom, but when we got into an argument, she told others and one girl called Mom *una loca terrorista*. I cried, my faced buried in my desk, slowly becoming so infuriated that I slapped her with everything I had kept inside. I got into trouble, but no one said it again.

When I was 12, after I defined my position about my parents, it became easier to tell my schoolmates I disagreed with what they thought. Once in a class the teacher talked about the war; it was very unusual but she said Sendero [Shining Path] fought for their ideology while the MRTA were drug traffickers. I got very upset and quoted the TRC [Truth and Reconciliation Commission] saying the MRTA was responsible for only 1.5 per cent of the deaths.

I consider myself a Christian, but I don't believe in church. I have my beliefs but don't like religious rules: how can they condemn non-believers? Many people I know are atheists and it seems exaggerated to send them to hell. I believe in a God that accepts rather than condemns people. Once I tried to 'convert' my mom, right? She said she believed in the scientific and the real, but that if God was about love, then we were in tune, and that should be enough. I was shocked: wow, to believe in nothing? Throughout my life, faith helped me a lot. Now we respect each other's ways.

My mom Armida and my grandma are Catholic. I decided to read liberation theology, like Frei Betto, 'the real Christian is a communist without knowing it, and the real socialist is a Christian without believing it'.[3] I learnt to value Jesus as a revolutionary who in a context of imperial repression argued for the poor and equality … the first socialist.

---

[3] Brazilian writer, political activist, liberation theologian and Dominican friar, famous in the 1980s for his book *Fidel y la Religión*.

The economic situation

The economic situation wasn't easy growing up, and it got worse. Still in school I had to work at Mom's market stall selling chickens. I got there at five in the morning wearing my school uniform to receive the load and continue selling. In my final school year I barely made it to class, too busy working at the market or crying at home. Well, I also read a lot at the market, the books Mom used to get me, and some cheesy romantic novels I got.

After finishing school I couldn't continue studying because there was no money, so I had to work slaughtering chickens with a machete all day long. That came as a shock; suddenly I was one of those people who couldn't afford to study and everything was so real, end of school, off to work, no dreams. My mom Lucero felt impotent because she couldn't give me what others give their children. That made me aware of the pain I could cause her, how despite never showing it, she also hurt, so I wanted to be by her side, *acompañarla*. She doesn't deserve all these years in those prison conditions, suffering the loss of her mother and mother-in-law without saying goodbye.

My mom's reasons

'Mom why don't you get out?' I asked bluntly one day. She talked about her desire for a better world for me and all the children, a world without poverty and hunger where everyone could be happy. So, my childhood explanation was that Mom was in there for being good and the president was evil; he was keeping her locked up in there.

Over the years we had several conversations, mostly prompted by my questions ... but I don't remember things getting any clearer. I do remember asking, why not the legal way? Her response was that they had no other option but to take up arms; the legal way was no longer possible. I don't think I understood but I didn't ask anymore. ... And my mom Armida never told me why Mom was in prison until I was 15.

Age 12, when things started to change

I've had my private doubts ... all of us have, we know that in HIJXS. If everyone called our parents '*terroristas*' then maybe there was some truth in it. *Les dudábamos, calladito.*

I did have doubts but never about my mom Lucero, because I look up to her. She's my ideal, the best thing in my life and the most good-hearted person in the world. But I had doubts about her past.

The age of 12 was a particularly hard time. I was constantly reminded my life was nothing like that of my friends or my cousins. And when Grandma died everything felt worse. I adored her; we lived in the same room, and losing her was quite traumatic. I kept asking myself: Why is nothing nice coming into my life? How much more pain can I take? Why can't I have a 'normal' family?

I used to cry lots out of frustration for not having parents with me. Life felt lonely, as if no one could understand me. So, I embarked on inquiring about Mom; I was determined to find answers. First, when I was around nine, I thought maybe if the *compañeros* are in prison, it's because they're bad and deceived Mom into joining them. Then, with Mom's talks, I understood more – that the media, the government, the system was deceitful. The second doubt was born around age 12; I wondered if any of it had been of any use, really. Everything Mom went through and did only to end up in prison? Her sin was to fight the system, have the will to change it for the people, and now 'the people' call her *terrorista*. Is that what she fought for? I thought maybe Mom had the best intentions but if 'the people' don't care, then why uphold those ideals, why be so stubborn?

Slowly I started changing that train of thought and realized it wasn't true that everybody was against them or called them terrorists; most people simply didn't know about the MRTA or my mom, and the media was in charge of instilling fear, using it against them to accuse some of terrorism, instil fear and keep everyone else quiet. I know some won't accept what they believed, but others were supportive, others did agree and still want to try to change things by other means.

I found reaffirming strength in learning other cases. Once I learnt our history as something beyond my own, it made sense. Before, I just lamented, why this life? Now I don't even want to think what I'd be without this life. I take great pride in it and feel honoured and proud to be Lucero Cumpa's daughter. I admire how she withstood such brutal repression without giving up her ideals, without hatred, *sin rencores*. She entered the MRTA well aware of what could happen as a woman, a repression that hit her with all its power.

She taught me another way of understanding the world; where I used to see an ugly place of too much evil, she showed me beauty and strength. I learnt things can be changed; there are alternatives. From then on, I've walked with my mom's history before me, telling friends up front who I am. The doubts had their moment, but I no longer have room for them. Now, all the people in that struggle became my family.

But with the doubts came rage, and it had its different moments. When I was little it was against Fujimori; I detested him as if he was the personification of evil. Later on, the rage was about everything that having my mom inside brought: against the traitors, the lack of justice, those who called her a terrorist. But she told me 'Rage never leads us anywhere, it only destroys you, *te va joder*.' Today I know the real enemy isn't the people, it's the system. I'm against that oppressive system and those who promote it. It conceals the real culprits, makes us believe things are better and we're the problem. That's what our parents struggled against, what made them take up arms, and we must find new ways to struggle against that same system.

As I got older, I developed a feeling for Mom's *compañeros* because of their presence in my life through her stories, my prison *visitas* and the relatives I met outside prison. It was through them that I now have some references about my dad. He got killed in Cusco, during a clash with the police; when he turned back to recover his *compañero*'s body, he got shot right in the head, dead in an instant.

When I turned 15, the *compañeros* made a birthday tape where they retold stories about Dad. And I started to construct a dad. They say he always had a picture of me on the wall, and that created this certainty of my presence in his life, that he loved me; it was quite something for me.

The *megajuicio*

When the life sentence was annulled, Mom got a new trial, a civilian one this time. It was the *megajuicio*, a mega-trial for members of the MRTA leadership[4] that lasted almost two years, with the sentence handed down in 2006. I thought justice or at least some sort of justice would be done, at least a bit.

I felt inspired during the hearings; it was a learning experience. They revealed everything, even their own wrongdoings. They discussed what the MRTA was with such dignity, standing up for every one of their actions: 'we did that, for this and that reason'. It made me angry that the media only showed the opening (as a morbid spectacle of seeing the accused) and the final sentence, but none of what the MRTA was all about.

The day of sentencing was the longest; I spent it all in there from two in the afternoon until late at night. I started out calm but slowly got nervous, it didn't seem to end! Their argument was to challenge the 'terrorist' charges and instead be judged for 'rebellion', which is within Peruvian law.[5] This

---

[4]   *Megajuicio* refers to the trial combining the cases against the MRTA leaders. It took place after the transition government to fulfil its commitments with the Inter-American Human Rights Commission. Previous sentences dictated under military trials during Fujimori's regime and its anti-terrorist legislation were overthrown for violating legal guarantees established in the Inter-American Convention on Human Rights. Peru left the Inter-American system during the 1990s and returned in December 2000 under the transition government. In spite of not abolishing the anti-terrorist legislation, changes were made regarding revision of sentences, failure to provide due process and military trials for civilians. The *megajuicio* lasted 15 months until March 2006 when MRTA leaders were sentenced to 20–30 years of imprisonment plus monetary 'civil reparations' to be paid to the state.

[5]   This was the argument in the trial and writings by MRTA leadership. The HIJXS inherited it as a framework to understand the MRTA actions.

wouldn't have meant freedom but I was hoping Mom would have no more than three or four years left. Finally, when they read the judgment and I heard 'terrorism', I froze.

Right after that, I heard my mom sentenced to 28 years ... I stifled a scream, *ahogué un grito*. It hurt as if each year was falling upon my head, one by one. At that moment a previous dream came to mind: I was returning from Cuba and Mom was waiting for me at the airport with my little brother by the hand. ... I realized it was nothing but a dream, 28 years ... and the tears started rolling down silently. My mom Armida hugged me and started crying like I've never seen her do before, muttering '*es injusto*'. Yes, I thought, and cried next to her. I told her to stop crying because my mom Lucero could see us, but she couldn't and neither could I.

I was gutted. She's already spent too many years inside. I felt impotent and wanted to scream, 'Again! What are you doing? Repeating the same thing. Why can't all those years, my whole life, be enough!?'

But then something happened that took me by surprise and really lifted me. Each of the accused spoke up in the closing argument, and it was amazing to see them reject the judgment, asking for annulment, expressing disillusionment with Peruvian justice, regretting having believed the regime had changed, and stating that they would appeal. They looked at us and made the victory sign. ... We all applauded non-stop; I remember my hands burning. It was as if they were telling us: we still haven't given up, so don't you all. They displayed such strength and intensity. Their internal *tupacamaru* came out.

When it was Mom's turn, I remember her adding, 'I never have been, am not, and never will be a terrorist'. Those words still resound in my mind. I made my best effort to draw a smile before saying goodbye to her from the distance. But my face was so revealing that when she looked at me, her eyes went watery, almost crying right there. ... I felt terrible. ... I tried to smile, to show her 'everything will be OK'. My lips with a big smile, but my eyes with big tears. ... Mom put her hand on the glass wall and smiled back, as if saying 'forgive me'.

I didn't understand; like she felt guilty for everything that has happened to me; it was despairing. I didn't know what to do because Mom was on the other side and I was on this ... she was feeling bad and I couldn't hug her. ... I was the source of her pain. She had been so strong, *tan digna*, and suddenly she saw me devastated and broke down with me. I hated myself for being weak precisely at that moment. ... Why couldn't I be strong when she needed me? My weakness was what made her feel bad. ... And that only made me cry more.

I left like that and outside everyone saw me. People who knew Mom were hugging me, people I didn't even know, and with each hug I felt more devastated, like they were offering condolences. I wanted to scream 'She's not dead!' I couldn't stand them. I was desperate to get away and scream at the top of my lungs until I lost my voice.

All I wanted was to go home and sleep, and next morning visit Mom and spend the day laughing together. But all the press was waiting for me. All these lights on me, the journalists surrounded me, 'Lucero's daughter!' Everyone pushing, flashing, microphones shoved to my face, the journalists shouting 'What do you think?' I was in shock … and barely muttered 'It's unjust.' And worse shouting came, 'How about the people your mom killed?!' I made a crooked grin of rage, *como con cólera*. I wanted to call them out on their ignorance. How could they say that without even having listened to the arguments during the hearings? But it was as if I was at the very bottom and they were all above me. All I could hear was 'Your mother is a killer, killer! terrorist! terrorist!' I couldn't get hold of my thoughts, I just cried and cried, even worse for being unable to control my weakness. I kept repeating to myself, 'fuck, stop crying!' But I felt as if I was going down and down, them shouting, and each time I was closer to the ground.

Somehow I got away and to a corner where I found my mom's lawyer. He grabbed my arm and told me, 'Your mom wants to see you hold your dignity and strength.' It was as if those words were so strong that they lifted me. And I laughed, thinking why didn't he say that before? I wasn't crying anymore; I was done with that. Some journalists were still taking pictures but I didn't look. I approached my own people, the *familiares* who were hugging each other and still crying. I was again thankful we were there together. A few were being interviewed by the media, and some mothers were shouting 'My son is no terrorist.' I just stood by their side, but soon got caught in the mood and was chanting with all of them together: the TRC said 1 per cent … 1 per cent … 1 per cent …[6] Then, my mom Armida got me into the van. I sat there feeling nothing, when I saw a camera by my window, I thought my mom is no killer, I have nothing to hide, so I showed my face

---

[6]   The TRC established the MRTA was responsible for 1.5 per cent of the victims. The number has been repeated by *familiares* and sometimes by HIJXS as well (especially earlier on), to emphasize a difference with Shining Path. *Familiares* and lawyers mobilized the '1.5 per cent' to highlight the disproportionate reaction by the regime towards MRTA members who were punished with same (or worse) repression and *carcelería*. Although the HIJXS supports this point, it is considered a problematic discourse, as '1.5 per cent' reproduces the same discourse from the Fujimori regime and military forces: 'We killed less' was the (in)famous quote by Fujimori allies after the TRC report. Moving away from such discourse is crucial for HIJXS, and what became more complicated within the group is how then to mark the difference between MRTA and Shining Path, and if that is actually desirable. Few agree with emphasizing their differences as an argument, particularly those who also had relatives in Shining Path, or those who consider it important to move away from the 'terrorist' narrative to make other conversations possible. The discussion is ongoing.

with a big smile and made the V sign. Every time I remember it makes me blush; it was impulsive, straight from the heart, I was 17.

Then we left, some crying and some yelling angrily. Me and my mom Armida were quiet on the journey back home. I kept picturing my mom Lucero. When we got home, we watched the news and there I was, my first time on TV and what an image of a crying baby! [Laughing]. The media complained that the judges hadn't decreed life sentences, that 'they went soft on the terrorists'. Again, the same shit.

Next day, I went to my mom Lucero's, but it wasn't sad. The moment we saw each other with those huge puffy eyes, we burst into laughter. And we chatted and laughed the day away, well, at least *la visita*. She showed me that everything was fine, nothing was lost, and that we'd continue struggling, *seguíamos en la lucha*. And I was fine for one day. Then not so well. I was just numb, working at the market stall, everyone asking what's wrong. I couldn't laugh; I was neither happy nor sad, but that wasn't normal! I didn't say anything at home, or to anybody for a while. And we were at the peak of the presidential campaign, so Fujimori supporters came to the market, giving away pamphlets, chanting 'Bring the Chino back! Chino for President!' I got furious, shouting, machete in my hand, without even controlling my words. It was such a primal reaction. Other market stalls joined in, calling Fujimori 'thief, murderer, liar!'

That's how I found relief, and learnt to distrust Peruvian justice and see that this 'democracy' only works for some, not everybody. They appealed the sentence fully knowing a worse outcome was possible. But I was prepared for that, knowing it'll punish us for it. We knew the District Attorney requested life sentences again, the Supreme Court was under enormous pressure given the electoral year, and the media was against us. I know there's no such thing as independent justice.

Right before the *megajuicio*, the news showed all these distorted images of the MRTA, pure propaganda, adding more pressure on the judges. A lot of people, in the government and the army, came out looking bad over the course of the internal war, and those people won't let the MRTA obtain reduced sentences; they'll do the impossible to get the maximum punishment. I know that now. I have to keep a cool head without becoming a cold person. I couldn't even if I tried! [Laughing] I just have to be prepared so it doesn't affect me.

It bothers me every time I remember the *megajuicio*, because it was my first experience in a legal trial and with the media. No more faceless judges; I could be there. I expected not only the procedure to change but the outcome as well. I expected much more from our democratic transition, as they call it, *la transición*. The media harassment continued for a while, but it wasn't the first or last time. There had been police harassment before as well, against my mom Armida and my grandma. Constant phone calls, death threats, all that was very common. We all knew they had my mom Armida under surveillance; even my grandma was arrested and beaten in a police station, but that was long ago. I didn't live all that, I only heard the stories, but I knew. And again within the *familiares* collective, it wasn't that we were paranoid, we knew.

Cuba

Coming to Cuba was very exciting but wasn't an easy decision. I worried about not seeing Mom. In Peru, I could see her once a week or once a month, but not here. More shocking than not seeing her was how it gave me time to reflect how much she's suffered, and every time it saddened me, as if I'd left her behind. But after a while I realized she isn't some poor little thing to feel sorry for; she knew what she was doing, and she faces it all. Every time she was beaten under torture or things got worse; she has known how to face it with dignity. I know more bad things will come, worse things probably … but she'll know how to rise above it.

Mom always told me about Cuba, and the more she told me, the more I fell in love with the idea and wanted to come here, and have my own experience. When I was in secondary school Mom told me about the scholarships, and I went quickly to sign up; it took more years but I made it. At first, I didn't think of studying medicine. I wanted to study law, of course. My uncles on my mom's side would warn me, you don't want to end up like your parents, do you? But I had it fixed in my mind to get Mom and all the others out of prison.

But the scholarships were only for medicine, so I had to. Mom instilled in me a humanistic aspect that I took in with my Christian faith, to give without expecting anything in return, to help others in need. Here in Cuba, I learnt to be amazed by how the human body works and the importance of health as a basic right. Here medicine isn't about money; it has a strong sense of justice. A doctor is a key to changing the world. And you don't learn medicine like this in Peru or the US. So, here I finally found my place.

More like her

My mom Lucero always has a smile on her face, and they say we share the same loud laughter. From one laugh to the next, that's how we spent our visits together. I inherited her infectious joy and stubbornness. And later I learnt to pursue what I set out to do, because I used to be shy, barely speaking; only recently started to speak out. I wish I was more like her.

I could never feel my mom abandoned me, never; she made an effort so I'd never feel abandoned. I'm my mom's joy, and I've taken that up as my task.

When I think about the future, I try to imagine my life, but I can't. For too long I've thought making plans was senseless. No one can guarantee things will work out, so I'd rather not have plans; I don't want to be disillusioned. I'm now studying medicine in Cuba and want to finish, but better not to have fixed ideas about the future. I do have dreams, like Mom getting out of prison, my little brother living with me, me becoming a doctor and travelling to each little town in Peru where there are no doctors, being able to make people understand their right to a healthy life, and the need to struggle for our rights. … Those are dreams, not plans.

On the other hand, I know I'll be in politics, because it's already in me; I was born in that world. Being politically active erases either stress or pain from my life. That's the only certainty about my future, because I'm not even sure about children. I don't know if I'd have the dedication, and it can get in the way of other things I want to do, although I do like the human side of it. I think being a mother must be great, something about creating life making you more human. But I also find it scary, too much responsibility.

When I was little I wanted a 'normal' family, but not anymore. People ask me about negative effects but I can't see them. I mean, there are negative things like my mom's continuous imprisonment, the pain we have to endure, the lack of justice and the impunity, *el engaño a la gente*, that's the negative. But I want to recall and use the positive things I learnt, everything I lived, having two moms and this extended family beyond bloodlines, embracing ideals, learning to toughen up. It's true the HIJXS had to grow up faster, because of what we lived. But luckily I had a mother who was able to compensate things, so I can't say I had no childhood, no adolescence. I did have a childhood, although I grew up faster … maybe even a bit more mature? [Laughter] It's true; we were forced to catch up with our circumstances. But I didn't lose that much, not on the emotional side; I had my mom Lucero's happy and loving way of seeing life.

Every time people tell me I remind them of her, I get excited. I wish I remembered all the stories I've heard from her, because they're amazing. I could write them down, from a daughter's point of view, or maybe write about myself, but writing about my life is writing about hers, because her life is very much inside mine.

6

Rafael: Living under Silence

17 April

Saturday, 17 April 1993. That's when my father died. It was a turning point in my life, like an earthquake that shook everything out of place.

We all said he died in a motorcycle accident when the question came up. There was some truth in it; he was on a motorcycle the day he was captured. But it's not that simple anymore. Too many things got entangled, like fighting against the impunity in his case, and learning about a history kept hidden, even to myself. I only recently started talking about it.

My dad was murdered. And tortured. It's an ugly death, just to say it sounds ugly. But it also has its heroic edge, and that helps take away some of its ugliness. If my dad had talked he might have saved his life, but many people would have gone down. So people remember him for that. But the fact that he died can't be understood only from the mystique surrounding his death, because I suffered his loss, as did my mom, and his family. Even my stepbrother, who was born the day after his death. I want to at least tell him his dad's history, so he can form his own idea, but we must wait until he turns 18 to look for him.

The very same day

I was nine, and was staying with my dad and his family, because my parents were already separated. I remember there was a strong earthquake that Friday night. My dad had left that day and didn't say when he was back. Nothing strange, he'd always travel without notice.

I even argued with him that morning, because he was pushing me to drink milk, or something, although we made up right before he left. … It created a trauma, because I thought that if I hadn't … I was a believer in destiny, so for me, if I hadn't had that fight with him, he would still be alive.

Mom picked me up from school the next Monday and told me to take her to Dad's. I refused because no one was supposed to know his house. Mom insisted that she had to … I sensed something must be wrong for her to ask me to break that rule. When we got there, Mom told a girl there to take me off to buy whatever I wanted. I asked the girl, 'My dad died, right?' She denied it, but my mom confirmed my suspicions. I remember crying my eyes out, but also calming myself because I secretly didn't believe it. I even refused to go to his burial. I was 16 before I fully assimilated it.

You know, I thought I was over this, but talking like this chokes me up again. There is something about the abruptness of his death … when one day you had them, the next day you had them dead.

My dad's brothers and cousins got angry, kicking doors and screaming awful things, because they were very close to Dad. Maybe that's why it hurt and enraged them so.

A day or so later, we were in the car and Mom had bought the newspapers. They reported that Rafael Salgado Castilla, an MRTA [Tupac Amaru Revolutionary Movement] *militante*, died at DINCOTE premises, at such hour, that the autopsy reported his corpse displayed bruise marks on his face, head and body consistent with torture techniques. A photograph was included. Mom hadn't said … I guess she thought it would be too brutal to tell a nine-year-old boy his dad had died after an entire night of torture, *demasiado crudo*.

The police report said Dad was injured because he fell attempting to escape on the motorcycle, got sick once he was in DINCOTE and died on the way to the police hospital. But that doesn't coincide with the autopsy report. Luckily a reporter saw him entering the DINCOTE building, followed the morgue report, talked to the family and published the story, including Dad's photos.

There in the back seat of a moving car is where I learnt what my dad was involved in: *MRTA, torturado*. Maybe I already instinctually knew but wasn't fully conscious of my knowledge. I know I wasn't surprised when I read that Dad was in the MRTA; it was a logical explanation of everything else. Mom wouldn't tell me about the MRTA until I was older, and insisted. She had limited her own political activism once she had me; she joined in protests or meetings but nothing more. If I'm alive and well now it's because she opted for us, not the organization, and I'm very grateful for that. She dedicated her life to keeping us safe.

In conversations later about my own life choices, she encouraged me to focus on my career. I agreed, but there are more important things, like helping your people. I can't see my life centred on career success. No, being conscious of injustices means doing something, not just enjoying my privilege, disconnected from our reality. I'm interested in my professional education for political and social reasons, to contribute to the *campesino* struggles against the transnational mining companies, which get communities displaced and create massive damage to the land, destroying people's livelihoods. I do understand we need the resources but question how to build a more sustainable and just way of using them.

My family

I'm my parents' only child together. For me our family is only my mother, her parents, my half-sister and brother, my stepbrother (who I still have to meet), and well ... Mom's second husband, with whom I've lived for almost 14 years now.

My parents raised me within their values; they taught me that solidarity is a core value and that equality for all was a matter of justice. I learnt about socialism later on by reading. I remember asking Mom why socialism was good, and she said I had to find that out for myself. When my questions didn't stop, Mom and her husband dug a hole in the patio and I discovered, astonished, the books they'd kept buried there for years. I recall the precise moment like a ritual. It was like an inheritance gift for me. I devoured those yellow-paged old books, which I didn't understand, but treasured.

For a long time I wondered whether my convictions were just an extrapolation of my parents' ideas, that maybe the mystique I created around my dad had led me. Am I simply repeating their ideas? Of course there's an inheritance, but I'm not going to do the same with my life as they did, because that would mean we haven't learnt anything from their experiences. I want to believe there's a lot to learn, and I hope I can hold my convictions like they did. Both my parents came from *aprista*[1] families; my grandfather was in the teachers' union in Chimbote, which led one of the strongest strikes, and as a secondary student my mom rallied support for the protests. They inherited the indignation, then added their own.

When I was little

My parents were students at San Marcos University when I was born and they lived in a small rented room. When I was only four months old they were both out of work and couldn't support me so my mom's parents, who lived in Chimbote, stepped in. I only stayed with them six months, but we got very close. My grandparents found my return to Lima very painful, so every school vacation I visited Chimbote, religiously.

The life Dad chose forced us to move often but in 1989, when I was six and ready to start school, we moved to Pueblo Libre and stayed there for

---

[1]   *Aprista*, belonging to the APRA party, the American Popular Revolutionary Alliance – Peruvian Aprista Party (Alianza Popular Revolucionaria Americana – Partido Aprista Peruano).

three years. By that time mom had a job in an NGO [non-governmental organization] and we lived more comfortably. That house was full of friends, family reunions and stability, although Dad was gone a lot, sometimes for six months travelling. … I assume he was already involved. But then they separated and the hard times started. Still he came to see me every time he was in Lima.

One time when I was staying with him and his new *compañera* in what I later realized was a 'safe' house … there were rooms I wasn't supposed to enter, but I opened a door and there was a full arsenal on the floor, pamphlets, weapons and ammunition. I was stunned. When she walked in, she was so scared of his reaction she told me not to tell my dad. I never told anyone.

El barrio

Ever since high school, even before I knew about politics, I was sensitive to the injustices … because I'd always been close to them. While I had access to material things most people don't have, Mom's work with the NGO meant going with her to marginal neighbourhoods. The children I played with lived in houses made of reed mats so I saw their fight for survival.

But I knew it as an outsider until my dad's death, when the discovery of his involvement even cost my mom her job. With that I shared those people's reality. Mom had to work in a factory: very hard, badly paid, long hours. She counted every cent, and there were constant fights in the house. From a house in a nice middle-class neighbourhood we had to move to one in the slums with no roof, no toilet, no electricity … *el barrio* in San Juan de Lurigancho.[2] It has taken us almost ten years of struggle to improve it. It was a form of forced displacement.

That drastic change was one of the hardest things we had to face after Dad's death, because we were alone. His family kept their distance. It was a tense time and my little sister was born almost immediately after we moved, and the problems didn't stop until she was five, around 2001. That move changed everything for me. It was a whole different culture. The kids there were used to being in gangs, pickpocketing was a children's game. Mom had never even bought me war toys because she rejected violence; I didn't even know how to fight.

---

2   San Juan de Lurigancho (SJL) is a district in the Eastern Cone of Lima. SJL is the most populated district of Lima (and of South America) with more than one million inhabitants resulting from large migration waves that increased with the internal war from the most affected provinces. It concentrates the largest percentage of people living in poverty and houses two of Peru's largest prisons, Miguel Castro-Castro (also known as Cantogrande) and Lurigancho.

It was hard to make friends because I didn't even go to school with them. Mom sent me to the same middle-class alternative school (with a scholarship and sometimes Mom sold food in the school events). In the two-hour bus ride from San Juan de Lurigancho across Lima every morning, I could see how the houses changed as I travelled to an environment where I didn't belong anymore, then returned to the *barrio* where I didn't belong either.

My teachers knew about my dad and even mentioned it once in a morning speech. I guess it was a way to talk about the regime's impunity but I just remember it was awkward. When I was in high school and went through a '*Ché Guevara*' period, my teachers got worried that I was becoming 'too radical', living in the shadow of my dad's history. But I didn't even know what I was talking about.

One positive effect of all that was a stronger relationship with my mom. And also my sister, because I took care of her when Mom and her husband were at the factory and once she entered preschool, I took her on those long bus rides across Lima. But during my adolescence Mom and I fought constantly. I turned very rebellious and she was the target of my resentment. I didn't want to be at home and I blamed her for everything. Later, I could see she had a tough life as well, so we were able to return to our conversations, share our problems and even become friends; she's the closest person I have.

I think that was somehow a result of all the changes I was forced to live. I was always a friendly, happy little boy, joking around, making conversation with everybody, but after my dad's passing, I stayed aloof and became quiet at school; at home I was resentful, angry, in a bad mood all the time. Only in university did I start to open up again, but still keeping an introverted side, self-involved in my existential trips.

You know, I still say things like my dad's 'passing' by force of habit, I guess. … I couldn't say he was killed, because it was an 'accident', remember? But also saying he was murdered, or the day my dad was killed sounds more painful. The most upsetting part is that I don't even dream about him.

The legal case

Some things might never heal, even if there's legal justice. Trials punish a person or a group, but they won't make the victim feel good, whatever the outcome, nothing will restore your loved one.

My dad's family didn't want to pursue the legal case. They were too scared. My uncles say the police harassed them, they received threatening phone calls and one was detained and interrogated. So they got rid of all the evidence they had, including the photographs taken at the morgue. Fear is a very paralysing force. I don't judge them, but I do wonder why they didn't fight past it. Even today, when I tell them I'll continue seeking justice, they look the other way. I've stopped trying with them.

Mom didn't have money for lawyers at the time, so she couldn't do much other than *la denuncia*. Two years later, in 1995, the Fujimori regime passed the amnesty law to release the state forces from all responsibility during the conflict,[3] so there was nothing else to do.

When the TRC [Truth and Reconciliation Commission] started around 2001, Mom suggested we approach them. But there was something between fear and the fact that I never talked about my dad and how he died. So, I didn't know what to do. I thought reparations were for people who suffered more, people in need, the victims ... so I didn't go. I was also discouraged by not knowing how to proceed. I asked around but no one paid much attention, probably because my dad was in the MRTA.

A couple of years later, the TRC published 47 emblematic cases to be further investigated by the Attorney General's office ... my dad's included. His case represented a clear violation of human rights by the state, because he was a young student who entered DINCOTE alive and next morning was dead. Even though they tried to hide it, he made sure they couldn't, because he entered DINCOTE shouting 'I'm Rafael Salgado Castilla, a San Marcos student', stuff like that. The news report and later the human rights organizations clearly proved he was tortured as reported in the TRC.

As soon as the news of those cases, *los judicializables*, reached the papers, we asked a human rights organization for their support, but they told me maybe I was confused and it was somebody else's name. I left feeling shocked, angry, upset and powerless, *indignado*; that was my father! They said they would contact me later on, but nothing happened. I knew it was because my dad was in the MRTA and that makes people keep their distance. Later, I went back and, with some help, directly contacted the coordinator, who offered to take on the case.

When the trial started, only the Attorney General and the defence lawyers for the accused could be in the courtroom, not us. It was the first case against the state and the judge found the defendants not guilty! I was again discouraged but when we got the news that the Superior Court judge didn't uphold the sentence and a retrial would be needed it encouraged us to continue. But things moved really slowly, which I found upsetting. The human rights organization said they didn't have enough lawyers to cover all cases, and would rather not draw much attention to ours to avoid the media coming out against them because of my dad's *militancia*.

---

[3]   On June 1995, Congress controlled by the Fujimori regime passed an amnesty law, which ensured that human rights violations committed by agents of the state since 1980 in the course of the counter-insurgency war will go uninvestigated and unpunished. The law also cleared the records of those already investigated and/or convicted.

Our generation grew up in a 'media dictatorship' in which all we heard was '*terrorismo*'. But some friends I later told my dad's story to started questioning those stories. That makes me think there may be a role for our stories, so others can question what they've learnt. There's no recognition anywhere for someone whose father was a political prisoner or was killed. We're not victims or perpetrators; there's no place for us.

I finally got tired of all that and contacted another lawyer involved in the mega-trial. We stayed with her and are now waiting for the legal paperwork to approve our participation in a new trial that should start soon. But now I'm in Cuba, so my mom will continue with all that.

Visiting prison

I think I always knew about my dad, but was only certain after his death. There was this knowing that my dad was up to something, but I never had the dimension of it. I only learnt about him once I met his *compañeros*.

When I was little there were all these things … like he told me once, 'If anyone calls asking for Bruno or Emilio, you say he's not here'. And I thought wow, he uses other names. He also taught me when I was very little that if the police ever asked about him, I had to say he worked in so and so, travelling, then just say I didn't know. He taught me to record these automatic answers in my head. He even tried to teach me to use another name for myself, but I never learnt that one. Once we went to a football match at the national stadium for a meeting. My dad instructed me, 'Say your name is Camilo', but when this person asked, I said my real name. Of course, Dad got upset, but I was a child.

Dad apparently used to take me to many of his meetings with his *compañeros*, because when I met them in prison, they all asked if I remembered them. I remember one clearly, because once when we were at home watching TV with some relatives of Mom's husband, he appeared on the news screaming while being held by the police. I blurted out, 'Look that's Dad's friend!' Mom pinched me so hard. … It was 1992, which I later understood was the beginning of three years of the toughest repression and I could see people on TV being caught all the time.

The first time I went to the Canto Grande prison was 17 April 2004, if I remember right. The *compañeros* had organized a commemorative event on the anniversary of my dad's death. Maybe that's not accurate, but I like to remember it like that. It was a very emotional and unforgettable moment, a mix of pride and sadness. The scene filled me with awe; it was like a whole world just opened in front of my eyes. Luckily they didn't make me talk because I couldn't have said two words.

That day I was able to grasp the meaning of my dad's life, almost touch it: the importance of his actions, the consequences of his life decision.

I learnt his trajectory, how he had worked with the people in the capital, then was sent to the central highlands; how he wanted to train in the 'people's army', *en el monte*, but ended up in the special forces, the urban guerrillas. All that I learnt by listening to his *compañeros*, and feeling how much they appreciated him. They were so happy to see me; everyone had a story to tell about Dad.

There's no one specific reason I decided to visit prison, I like to think several signs pushed me in that direction. But after the first visit, I kept going back to Canto Grande and to Chorrillos (the women's prison), eager to hear more stories about Dad. Those prisons worked as a space of freedom for me. Adelín's dad was friends with him, Miguel's dad even wrote a poem after he passed away, Willy's aunt was arrested together with him, and it was my dad who organized Iris' mom's rescue in 1991 when she was captured by the police in Lima.[4] You see? We're all connected. There are so many stories about how even in the toughest moments my dad managed to keep his positive energy and a characteristic spontaneity that put everyone at ease. I can still picture him like that.

Before I used to live it more as the death of a father, but after visiting prison, it became the death of a hero as well. He gave his life for a cause they all believed in. But then his death became more entangled in others' histories, and complicated with my country's history. I just wish I could ask him about it, I have so many questions for him, as a father and as a revolutionary. But we never had those conversations, there was no time, and I was too young.

Consequences

I wouldn't say visiting prison is problematic, but it's complicated. My stepfather doesn't want me to go for safety reasons. Each time you enter you are registered, stamped and marked. The *familiares* don't see the problem. They think the war is over and nothing happens for visiting prison. But I'm not so sure. Repression is still on, and heavy surveillance is part of it.

That's probably what led to my name being broadcast on the news. I was part of a collective in Lima, which was organizing a two-day encounter with other regional collectives that were part of the anti-capitalist movement. I was very active in the preparation, but only attended the event for an hour, and

---

4 'On 11 March, in one of the most impressive and violent actions carried out by an MRTA commando in Lima, Lucero Cumpa Miranda was rescued while being transferred to the Judicial Power together with PCP-SL [Partido Comunista del Peru – Sendero Luminoso] member Nelly Evans Risco in a van belonging to the Technical Police of Peru. Three policemen were killed.' (TRC, 2003d: 194)

didn't even speak. Yet over the weekend they reported the event negatively on the TV news and mentioned my name, focusing on my face, as the son of Rafael Salgado Castilla, MRTA *militante*, alias *Negro Bruno*, and so on. It was to remind people of the fear of terrorism, because they put my name next to two ex-prisoners – to remind us that we're under surveillance and carry a stigma. How did they know my name?

That's another reason for my decision to leave for Cuba. Visiting prison brings consequences, but it wasn't a mistake. All the mechanisms at the entrance are to deter visitors, but you have the right and it's important to continue, for them and for yourself. My mom worries a lot. When the news report was broadcast, she freaked out, crying that she had warned me about this kind of stuff, that I was supposed to be careful, that my telling her times had changed was bullshit. It made her relive the late 1980s, early 1990s when she watched her friends go down one after the other. ... She took it really badly and demanded I throw anything remotely political out of the house. First step, clear the house; I knew that one.

I could see the fear in her eyes when she shouted, 'I've been through all that already, my cousin killed in the jungle, his body never found; my first husband killed; my other husband imprisoned for months; another cousin in prison ... and so many more friends, and colleagues, persecuted, imprisoned; I will not go through that shit again!' She's very fearful.

That did it; she became a big supporter of me leaving Peru for Cuba.

Cuba

Actually, several reasons made me go. The first was my frustration with my university curriculum when I was studying environmental engineering. The second was that our economic limitations meant I had to work as well; the jobs meant having to skip classes and I was failing my courses. The third reason was my first steps into political activism, which I took very seriously (and also meant skipping class). I joined a couple of collectives and took on too many responsibilities because I was over-enthusiastic and believed in doing something. And the fourth reason was to gain some independence from my family, because while me and Mom became very close, we both knew I needed to break away and start over, and would never be able to do that living with her.

The first time they offered me the scholarship in Cuba, I refused saying that I didn't want to leave my country, too many things to do here. But I met a couple of people already studying here, and it seemed better. So I requested the scholarship with the '*familiares*'.

Cuba meant a better education both academically and politically, which means a lot to me. I can read a lot and also experience life in the Cuban system, learning from them, sharing daily life, listening to how much they can complain about the regime yet defend it all at the same time. I came here quite unsure of my decision, but it's been amazing. It would be a lie to say I came based on a political conviction, because for that I could have stayed in Peru and started building something from within, where the real work is. It's hard to get used to the distance, knowing I should be in Lima to continue pushing for my dad's case. That still troubles me.

Options

When your father is killed with such violence, there are two possible outcomes, you either embrace violence yourself, or you become really afraid of it, scarred for life. Strangely enough I find myself between the two. I know that choosing violence, however justified, even as self-defence, ends up with people dying, including loved ones. If someone asked me if I wanted to take up arms, I'd refuse. But … how to judge someone who does it out of necessity, like self-defence?

I believe in a revolution in terms of a structural transformation. Taking up arms was our parents' way of getting there, at very particular times under specific circumstances. I don't think it's the way. Nowadays, you can see the Venezuelan and Bolivian processes, which I don't know enough about to put my hands on the fire for, but they're interesting enough to pay attention to for the possibility of changes through other means. Like the Tupamaros in Uruguay who took up arms and later gained power in an electoral process. There are other ways now. We believe in change for humanistic reasons and there's nothing humane about war, yet we also know the neoliberal system is an inhumane one.

At the time my parents entered the armed struggle, most leftist groups believed in taking up arms to overthrow the government. It was their generation's option. The polarization of society had reached a point where people took sides, and many saw the war as a needed means to a better end, and in that process many wrongs were made. Although I don't justify them, I don't think they can be understood outside their context. My parent's choices push me to think things more thoroughly, because now we know what can happen.

Even now, talking about the consequences of my dad's decision, I don't think I could understand my parents if they hadn't taken that option, if my dad hadn't joined the movement. I wouldn't understand my own life without that. True, it's painful and difficult. But I never had that feeling of blaming my dad for what happened. Probably because at the time I couldn't say my dad belonged to the MRTA, knowing something but not being able to pronounce the words is quite a different story. So, who was I going to blame? I guess I blamed my mom's husband, an easy target just because he was there. As I grew up, I started to accept things differently.

Dad's death

The fact that my dad was killed and tortured didn't have as much traumatic effect, partly because I understood it within that larger story of political struggle. It could have caused an angry vengeful feeling, but it didn't. In a weird way the fact that no one ever asked me about it contributed to that; when you tell a cover story for many years you end up almost believing it; it becomes your life. Yet no matter what political convictions you may have in your head, they killed and tortured him, and it was horrible, and it hurts and it fucks with you.

Dad's *compañeros* remember him very fondly; people trusted him with their lives, and even took him home to meet their families in times when doing that was dangerous. And everyone called him Rafillo, as you'd call a little kid, not a grown man, a fighter in an armed struggle who led *recuperaciones* and kidnappings, who was in the 'special forces' and had a strong political education. They called him that for the great deal of affection he inspired.

7

Abel: Knowing More than You Should

Memories of my dad

Fundamentally my family was my mom, my sister who's a year and a half younger than me, my grandma, me ... and my dad. I mention my old man last because he wasn't always with us, like a couple of years yes, another year no, *por temporadas nomás*.

It was my elementary school graduation, when I was ten, that I more or less realized my old man wasn't ... how can I say it, a normal dad. ... Although he said he'd make an effort to attend, I wasn't sure he would. Same story for my sister's graduation two years later.

1990 was the year I saw Dad the most, when Patria Libre, a legal political movement, was created. Because he was its organization secretary, he led a normal life ... at home. I was 11 at the time. Patria Libre had its local base in Lima's historical downtown. I went to the inauguration event in this big hotel. First there was a huge march with young people, students, women ... *gente de barrio*. There was a struggle with the police, but at the end we all returned to the hotel, and it was full. That was the first time I saw my dad speak in public, talking politics. I kept staring ... mesmerized.

We had already started talking about a few things a year earlier, and I had started reading a lot. Many books were kept upstairs, thick, fat books on Marx, Lenin, Mao. ... I had already read about Nicaragua, and Cuba and *Tania la guerrillera*.[1] So, one day, thinking of myself as a grown-up, I took Marx downstairs and showed it to Dad, like I'll read this. He looked at me,

---

[1] *Tania, la guerrillera inolvidable* (1970), the story of Tamara Bunke, an Argentine-born German involved in the Cuban revolution who participated in Che Guevara's guerrilla in Bolivia. It was iconic in our parents' generation, creating an almost mythical figure of women in guerrilla movements and espionage.

grabbed a package wrapped in old newspaper and handed it to me saying, 'Start with this. Leave Marx for when you're 40 or 50'. It was *Cien Años de Soledad*.[2] I caught the reading bug.

Also in 1990, before secondary school, we made a month-long trip to the southern provinces. Everywhere we went my old man would meet with people and hold long conversations. I remember getting so sick going from Cusco to Puno, puking with blood coming out of my nose and ears. Dad got really scared, but this old man gave me *mate de coca* to drink and saved me.

I more or less knew Dad was involved in something that had to do with Tupac Amaru, because I saw that name in stuff he left lying around. But on that trip his work became clearer. Words like *revolución*, the struggle, the base, the front and the miners ... have all stayed with me. I loved seeing him with others ... people would give him packages of traditional Andean food to take with us *pa'l camino*. I remember once we were in a rural house, with a dim yellow light, and I woke up in the middle of the night and went looking for Dad. There, *me asomo y medio veo*, in the next room was a formation of people, I think they were in uniforms.

Other memories are of Dad arriving home very late, after being away all week, and he'd spend Sunday with us. Mom would wake up, and they'd talk and talk, sometimes until dawn. He always arrived with some big fat books under his arm and his little black bag in the other hand. He'd lie in bed reading his books in a day. When it was time to eat, he'd come out and talk with us at the table ... then back to his reading. ... I'd always interrupt him by sitting by his side, until he'd close the book and talk to me. I picked up his habit, so during the week I'd lie in bed and take his books, *ojeándolos*, sometimes I couldn't understand squat, but I read them anyway. But for me it was always about having conversations those Sundays at home ... *toda la relación era dentro de la casa, in Comas*.[3]

Mom and Dad

I never saw Dad and Mom even raising their tone with each other; they were rather passive, with a rational approach to their partnership ... they talked things over, *conversaban mucho mucho*.

At first, they lived with Dad's family, but she pushed for them to have their own place so they went to the east side of Lima, a *barrio* of migrants from

---

[2]   *One Hundred Years of Solitude* by Gabriel García Márquez (1967).

[3]   Comas, a district of Lima, at the Northern Cone, that was made by several migration waves mainly from the northern provinces, currently with approximately half a million people (most second- or third-generation migrants). During its first decades Comas was considered a left-wing district well known for its collective struggles for land rights and basic services, evidenced in the names of the avenues and neighbourhoods.

Ayacucho who had taken over the land, *invadieron un cerro*, from an important Peruvian family. Dad was their lawyer in the legal battle, so they gave him a house. My parents learnt an even harsher reality there, because there was poverty everywhere you looked. We lived there till I entered school, when we moved to Comas with my grandmother. Mom was a factory worker and union leader at the time ... and Dad was supporting their union. He was still a student, but was in these struggles together with his brothers as defence lawyers fighting against the owners' lawyers in some 20 factories taken over by the workers, they were known by the people as '*los doctores tomas*'.[4] Mom says she knew Dad was already involved in that thing they called '*un proyecto*', which became the MRTA [Tupac Amaru Revolutionary Movement], but wasn't called that yet.

Where my name comes from

The CROMOTEX massacre was in February 1979 and I was born that April, which is why I was named Abel Hemigidio. My dad's friend Hemigidio Huerta worked at CROMOTEX, a textile plant, and was one of the leaders of a union takeover of it. Dad and his brothers were in the legal battle but also in the takeover itself, alongside the workers. Even my grandparents and my aunt, *La Negra*, were there supporting the workers when the massacre occurred. Six workers were killed by the police. I was named Hemigidio in homage to this *compañero*. Everyone in my closest family calls me Hemi, even now. I keep the meaning of my name close to my heart.

Many of the CROMOTEX survivors were arrested and sentenced for life, including Lucho's dad,[5] but an international solidarity campaign got them out that December. They even wrote a book afterwards,[6] which they dedicated to my dad's family, *por la entrega y eso*. We had it at home, but Mom's family burnt everything ... barrels of books ... out of fear after Dad's arrest, *cuando cayó*.

They even say I used to go with Dad to union parties at the worker-owned factories, but I can't really remember. I was totally immersed in school, went to bed at eight and woke up at five to feed grandma's animals. ... She had turkeys, chickens and rabbits on the roof ... a typical

---

4   In Peru lawyers are referred to as 'Doctor', and '*toma*' refers to a takeover of land by squatters or a workplace by its workers. The nickname means literally 'the takeover doctors' (which has a sarcastic tone).

5   Lucho is another participant whose *testimonio* remains unfinished. His father was in the CROMOTEX union.

6   'Compañeros, tomen nuestra sangre ... la lucha de los obreros de CROMOTEX' (1980), made of survivors' testimonies (Cromotex Sindicato Textil Industrial, 1980).

immigrant bringing the farm into the city. I loved caring for them with her, they thought I'd grow up to be a veterinarian; *La Negra* even bought me books about that.

Another memory I have is of Dad's family reunions at some picnic area outside of Lima. *La Negra* was always the last to arrive, alone, never with her husband. At the time it was odd they weren't closer as a family. For example, when my grandmother died, Dad entered the house during the wake, greeted everyone and left ten minutes later. So did my uncles. Only *La Negra* stayed. I was shocked, because ... she was his mother! No one explained to me that they had to be careful.

Dad's family wasn't very close to me and Adelín, but I could feel they were 'concerned' because we lived in a marginal area, *un barrio popular de Comas*, not their middle-class neighbourhood. ... Again, *La Negra* was the exception. Some birthdays dad couldn't be with us, but she would always bring me something, a book on animals or science experiments.

By ten I started picking other books, because I was getting interested but at that age you don't really understand. ... Just some terminology, like 'the poor' and 'the rich'. I remember they used to tell me the CROMOTEX story and how now 'we continue struggling so they won't kill workers anymore'... 'so there will be no more poor people and no more rich people' ... words I then recognized from the books and that got stuck in my head, *que no haya pobres, que no haya ricos* ...

I was always inside because I was sickly, catching all available ailments. Only when I started secondary school and ventured into the *barrio* did I start hanging out with my cousins from Mom's side. Unlike me, they were always running barefoot in the dusty hills, playing in the streets. ... Everyone only asks about my dad's family but I picked up many more things from Mom's family. Learning to live in the *barrio* I started discovering another world and their struggles for water, sewage and streets.

1990

I only started hearing about the movement in 1990, when I entered secondary school. That's the year my grades started going down. It was the time of Patria Libre so dad came home more frequently. It was also the time of the Fujishock[7] and the letter-bomb attack against *Cambio* newspaper.[8]

---

[7]   The structural adjustment 'shock' programme implemented by the Fujimori regime. The measures and its effects, including sky-rocketing prices (for example, the price of gas rose 30 times) were announced on TV in August 1990.

[8]   A letter-bomb sent on 10 October 1991 to *Cambio* weekly newspaper (which published MRTA communiqués), killed 23-year-old journalist and editor Melissa Alfaro.

Things were further radicalizing … *nada bueno se veía*, and my parents' started telling us to be careful, insisting, *hay que cuidarse.*

Dad would come home with bodyguards who had guns they'd put on the coffee table, *track, track las desarmaban* … although never in front of grandma. … I was very curious, but not really surprised, because we'd already watched some videos together about the MRTA entering small towns in *la selva* … *las tomas de los pueblos.*[9] It was like the Sunday evening family film. … There were even other videos I wasn't supposed to watch.

I was still very tense about being the best, getting to school as early as possible, but around 1992 my old man disappeared and Mom told us we wouldn't be seeing him much because they were after him … *ya lo andan persiguiendo.* Dad returned once to tell us there was already an arrest warrant, that they had arrested everyone else in Patria Libre almost immediately after the coup.[10] I didn't know what a coup was, *el golpe*, but I did know something heavy was happening; Comas was filled with soldiers. If we met it was blocks away from the house.

My school

There were many people in Sendero [Shining Path] at my school, and most of the teachers. I knew because of the graffiti in the *barrio* with PCP-SL [Partido Comunista del Peru – Sendero Luminoso] or the hammer and sickle symbol. I remember telling dad about the things my teachers had us write in our notebooks: *Vamos por el camino de Sendero Luminoso.* Dad looked at the drawings and the slogans, all Sendero propaganda, and he said they weren't 'the good ones'.

We could hear explosions all the time … and blackouts everywhere. The next year people came screaming once while I was on a corner, and boom, a blackout, and boom, they blew up four banks near my house, and boom, *el cerro* behind my house started hissing … until Sendero's symbol lit up on fire, *la hoz y el martillo*, against the black pitch night … a spectacular show!

There was a teachers' union strike, but not everyone supported it, so Sendero blew up the school gates at six in the morning. After that nobody showed up to school. There were also cultural groups with the students and they would march and display red flags, and sing Senderista music. So,

---

9   A takeover of towns in the north-eastern *selva* from October until December 1987 was part of the filmed armed actions of the MRTA that were shown in the Sunday news.

10   On 5 April 1992, Fujimori, together with the military, announced the 'dissolution of the National Congress' and 'reorganisation of the Judicial branch', a *self-coup* as Fujimori was the elected president at the moment.

I gathered my friends and organized my own group, an Andean music group with a Quechua name, we played and talked about what was going on, since we didn't have classes anymore. I was mortified because I liked studying.

A trip to *la selva*

By the end of 1992 I was hanging out with my cousins and nephews in the *barrio* … again I was the youngest. … They were already experts in drinking, so I started … but once Dad showed up at home and saw me sooo drunk. The only time Mom beat me up. I was so drunk I didn't even feel it. … Even now remembering Dad's face gets me embarrassed again.

After that I never got to see him at home again. In January 1993, he took me to my uncle's, whose son is a year older than me. Then my uncle asked me if I wanted to go to *la selva*, and I was very happy to go. We got to Tarapoto in a truck, which they started unloading at night. It had so many secret compartments, and weapons kept emerging from each one. My older cousin was already living there and another woman with her three-year-old son, Toñito.

The first days, my uncle would leave early and come back late. Me and my cousins would play football, swim in the river and help at the store. Then, because I used to wake up early I saw some radio equipment, and the woman who used it, also people who came blindfolded to be transported elsewhere, others that changed their hair colour. In the process I lost the phone number Mom gave me to call a neighbour, because we had no phone at home. I knew she was getting anxious, but I was really happy there; I even met my first girlfriend there.

In April my uncle got us plane tickets to return to school in Lima. But just a few days before our trip, a friend of my cousin arrived at the house. He knocked and told us that on the road from Morales to Tarapoto, our truck was surrounded by soldiers along with another truck full of *arrepentidos*[11] that had been driving around the city. Me and my uncle went to look for it, but we didn't find anything … and when we returned, my uncle said 'Don't turn around, keep walking … we're screwed'. The place was full of soldiers with two huge lamps facing the house … *ya nos jodimos*.

---

[11] *Arrepentidos* refers to those subjected (voluntarily or not) to the Repentance Law. Created in May 1992, the Ley de Arrepentimiento No.25499 granted benefits to those who broke their links with the armed groups and provided information about them and their activities. In place between 1992 and 1994 it was used by an estimated 8,295 people (6,792 men and 1,503 women). See Manrique (2014) for an account of the complex politics of the 'innocent victim', the role of the '*arrepentido*' category and its discretionary use by state institutions.

The moment we approached, the soldiers grabbed us, pushing my uncle and cousin inside. They pushed me down to the ground and pointed a rifle at my head. I hit my face against a rock on the ground. They kept me like that for half an hour. ... Everybody on the street was looking, but all I could think of was my girlfriend watching from her house, I was utterly embarrassed. The soldiers raided the house and took the radio woman, Toñito and my uncle with them while they locked me and my cousin in a room for 24 hours. Every now and then someone came and asked us stuff, and we'd always say we knew nothing. At some point they separated us, and started using us against each other. This went on and on… while they literally destroyed the house, looking for stuff.

Next evening, they took us to the army base in Tarapoto. There I saw the *compañeros* who had been trained to take over the radio communications set in another safe house … all lined up, blindfolded, handcuffed, *enmarrocados pa'trás*. We were put next to them. … I kept trying to register as much as possible, but then they put us in some sort of cells for two days … then to the commander's house, inside the base, where they locked me, my cousin and Toñito in one room.

They let us out to eat in a hut across from the house. Every day before dawn they pointed flashlights at us and called our names … we had to say *presente*, and a picture was taken. … They even sent a woman who kept asking questions and slept in there with us … she said she knew my dad, but I told her my parents were separated; it was all I could think of.

Some ten days later my uncle appeared; he was literally shaking. … He said he was all right, that everything would be over soon, but I'll never forget the sight of him. He couldn't even stand up straight.

There was also this short man with spiky hair who would come and sit with us to eat and chat with us the whole time. Later on, talking to my uncle, I found out this man was his torturer. And he had eaten with us every day!

After we'd been on the base about 13 days, we heard a lot of movement during the night, trucks and big lights were on. I peeked through the small window and what I remember in my imagination is that I saw so many dead bodies … just lying there … *yo me asomo, y los veo*. I ducked back down and hid. Next morning, we heard they'd caught Lucero, Iris' mom. Not much happened after, except that daily routine of calling our names and saying *presente* before dawn … and that every day that short guy would come to eat with us.

Almost a month had passed when Mom came. Only after Lucero was caught did Dad get the news and figure out what happened; he showed up in disguise at Mom's food stand and passed her a note to meet later. She left almost immediately. When I saw her that morning, we just hugged a long hug. After filling out some paperwork we left the base that afternoon. Next day we were on a plane back to Lima.

I remember we went to the International Red Cross office to tell them what happened. They asked if we'd be willing to file a formal charge because they had no knowledge the army base held children to use against the detainees. But I have no idea whatever happened to that. I did learn how they caught Lucero, by threatening to hurt Toñito, they forced the radio woman to instruct Lucero by radio to go to a meeting place where the army had prepared an ambush.

Back at home

Back home, I talked non-stop about every little detail of that time with my sister, my mom. ... Maybe it was not to forget, maybe to test myself if I still remembered, or maybe to see if it would go away.

I was feeling almost sick because I loved my uncle ... and then the thing with my oldest cousin. It was all too much ... *fue muy jodido todo*. So, I contacted some people to arrange to meet my dad. But the very day I was going to see him, 10 June 1993, another *compañero* told me, 'They caught your dad'.

I ran home to tell Mom. It wasn't just my uncle anymore, it was Dad! When I got home, Mom had just received the news. She was in her little shop and she just cried and cried. This old drunk from the *barrio* who was there, Mrs Laupa, asked what was going on and Mom told her, all the while crying and saying she didn't know what to do. The old woman, who was already an expert in arrests and prisons, said 'Don't worry, give me the food. I'll take it to DINCOTE and make sure he's there.' She wasn't even our friend, but she was the first person to offer help; she lifted our spirits.

Mom's family and friends stayed away ... out of fear, of course. But Mrs Laupa took care of us, because we ran out of money. She'd take Mom to the cheapest markets; she even fed us. And she'd go to DINCOTE with Mom every day; she even stopped drinking at the time.

But something odd happened: once the police in DINCOTE told her, 'You must be the third wife.' She didn't get until later that Dad had another woman and even a daughter ... that devastated her, *fue un golpe durísimo*. Then one day when we were finally able to visit Dad, a colonel came up to her and said, 'Is that your son?' And to me, 'You're the one who was in *la selva*, right? Don't play dumb, you know too much.' I was petrified.

We saw Dad only twice the whole month they kept him under investigation in DINCOTE. After that they transferred him to Castro Castro prison ... but first they 'presented' him. We were home that day and Mom's nephew was arguing about all the trouble and pain we were causing Grandma, and the danger ... when Grandma called us into the living room ... there was Dad on TV wearing the striped prisoner uniform. ... We froze, and started crying silently

... until Dad started speaking. ... He went on about poverty, and children ... that's what he talked about, the amount of children living in poverty in Peru.

That's when another life started, the life of the prisons.

The life of the prisons

I only had a year to go to finish school and already no one knew the whereabouts of many in my school. Some had joined an armed group in the provinces, others left in fear, others were disappeared. ... Then they took the school director and half the teachers and showed them in prisoner uniforms on TV. They said my civics teacher had been arrested in 1992 in an attempt to blow up one of the Air Force buildings. The whole school went mute ... you couldn't even remotely mention politics.

So I kept silent too. I was still going to school but barely studying. ... I wasn't interested. My classmates started organizing in gangs, and I hung out with them.

We knew my old man was in Castro Castro, but you could only visit the imprisoned starting a year after they were sentenced. That was the law. And his trial, well, he had several ... one by the Air Force, another by the Navy, and another the Army ... he got two life sentences plus 30 years.

Once the year passed, we were going to visit Dad, but Mom didn't want to go. We argued, we cried and talked about how painful it was about his other family, but also how many people needed us to go visit the *compañeros*. She was very hurt, and still is ... I'm still upset about it too; it's like trusting and being deceived ... realizing that he's not ... not *el Ché* [laughing]. ... Well, at that time I didn't know *Ché* had his own stories; that I learned later in Cuba. For me Dad was the perfect revolutionary, yet he had pulled all this shit in secret. ... It made me closer to Mom, and I always back her up more now in whatever she decides.

The first visit

My first time in a prison was in Castro Castro in mid-1994. I went with Mom. It was via *locutorios*. ... There was one metal grill on your side, with very tiny openings, and another on the prisoner's side. I remember the grills were freshly painted. ... I'll never ever forget the smell of that paint. ... I had to leave and I puked and puked outside, because of the paint ... or maybe the place or everything altogether. ... When I got back Mom had lit into Dad. She didn't even ask how he was; she just hit him with all her anger ... and a flood of tears. She kept asking why ... but he had no answer. It's been so hard for her. ... Same for me.

By the time I finally finished school, visits were every three months for minors. I think I saw him next for Christmas, after six months. That was one of the worst Christmases ever, same for Adelín. We were all tears, well I was, Adelín not so much. Most of Dad's family vanished, some imprisoned, one fled, and the rest kept their distance just in case. Only a half-brother brought us food and mostly encouragement. Apart from him and Mrs Laupa we were completely alone.

But Mom started making friends at the prison gates and she started organizing things ... the more you go, the more people ask you for little favours. In the following years that became Mom's thing, travelling around, knocking on doors, talking to the relatives, first the mom, then a sibling, even a cousin sometimes, *los familiares*, convincing them to visit. ... Some outright rejected her and very few actually went. ... In the hardest times, most *compañeros* had no visitors ... out of fear, or other reasons.

Soon there was a small group, *familiares*, who knew each other from the queue at the prison gates, even some children I watched grow up out there. But slowly over the years some started fighting, some didn't want to be associated with the MRTA, or regretted having been part of it. ... Mom, who used to be with all of them, watched the group shrink even more.

Yanamayo

Yanamayo started in 1995, after I'd already finished school. We travelled there three or four days round trip. Usually people got in touch to coordinate dates, because it was cheaper that way. The visit was monthly for adults but only every three months for children ... and only for 30 minutes. We'd go once a month.

Yanamayo prison was like an army base ... many gates, military people with rifles who treated the relatives horribly ... and so much waiting. We'd be at the gates by six in the morning, in such cold weather up there in the mountains, and wait until nine for them to open ... always five or six families, some Sendero, some MRTA. Once the gates were open, we turned quiet, relatives were forbidden to talk to each other in the queue.

Inside Yanamayo I remember Dad saying, 'Get closer when you pass me the stuff ...' and he'd stretch his hand through a little hole, and I managed to touch his finger ... in a prison like that, the touch of a finger can fill you. I really needed some hope, because I couldn't stop thinking about torture, about my dad suffering like my uncle did, with the shit they did to him. ... I feared for him, *que le hicieran mierda*.

But when I left Yanamayo I felt calm. Every time I saw Dad ... the long trips, the altitude sickness, the freezing cold, the cheap hostels, the bad food, the army soldiers, the waiting, the mistreatment at the gates, all their arbitrary rules, the hushing, the stripping for the check-ups feeling their hands everywhere ... none of that mattered when I saw him, even through the *locutorio*. We talked and he was surviving … it made me happy. Yanamayo was really tough.

By the end of 1995 they caught *La Negra*. I was 16 then. The next year, I started to withdraw *empezaba a desentenderme*. … I didn't want to visit Dad, hear from him, or write him letters. … I don't know why; I was more and more into the gang stuff. I wasn't even pissed off. … I just had no horizon, only 25 people armed with rocks and sticks fighting, defending our territory, drinking and living in the moment … *la vida del barrio*. They called me *loco triste*, or *el político*, because I talked shit when I was drunk or fell into sadness. Mom watched all that stuff horrified, because I'd arrive drunk and all bruised and cut … life didn't matter. … I was looking for a place to vent all the anger I think I had accumulated over those years [tearful] … and the gang was the perfect place for it [laughing], even fighting with the police; I got my skull cracked open when they dragged me down the hill by the hair … they took us to the local police station, beat us up … still I felt nothing.

The Embassy

I had this girlfriend, she was used to the drunkenness and the fights; I thought we'd have a family and stay in the *barrio*, like that was all there was to life. So I used to hang out in her house, and that's where I was when they took over the Embassy in December 1966, *tomaron la embajada*. I hadn't seen Dad that whole year. I only wrote him two lines, and he asked why was I so laconic. … I had to look up the word in the dictionary. In my last letter I wrote, 'Yes, I am laconic … sorry' but it was too hard to express myself through letters. I've never liked it; especially in our conversations I needed to see exactly where each comma and each dot fitted.

When the MRTA seized the Embassy, it was like going back in time … everything happening again … because there'd been nothing left except prison life, and that felt very passive and I couldn't take it. But watching the Embassy thing on TV … it was a wake-up call. Just a month earlier my mom, I don't even want to know how, had received a love letter for *La Negra* from 'Nestor', describing the immensity of his love for her … it was like things you sometimes think aren't humanly possible, that only exist in the movies, and moreover that these people couldn't be the romantic type, could they? They were tough and dealt with life and death situations, and yet …

So the night of the Embassy, I was at my girlfriend's house, and the person speaking to the press on TV said, 'This is *Comandante* Hemigidio Huerta speaking …'. Can you imagine? I ran home … gave Mom one look, and she confirmed: that's 'Nestor'.

Then, all that history started. … It was very strange because the first ten days people were very supportive of the takeover, they knew the hostages were Peru's rich and powerful, but slowly and heavily the poisonous media, controlled by the regime, changed people's minds, and by the end people were saying 'what's taking so long?', 'they should kill the terrorists', stuff like that ... that propaganda slowly won.

I started thinking more and accompanying Mom on her trips to prison again and then to human rights organizations in her desperate search for information once the prison visits were suspended and we had no idea what had happened inside. She was also getting anxious about the Embassy. I was still in *el barrio* world, but in that other world at the same time, resisting being sucked into the spiral. ... In my head everything was spinning, *Hemigidio Huerta*. ... I was reading the news compulsively.

By April 1997, when they took back the Embassy and killed everybody, I was studying for the university exam. When they broadcast the news, students celebrated, throwing their notebooks up in the air. ... I felt like I was dying in there. ... I ran to the toilets and cried and cried. ... Then I went home, but Mom was already out looking for the relatives, organizing to reclaim the bodies, get a lawyer to help them for no money ... see how she was? Pushing, not letting up, to get things done ... *detrás y detrás, jodiendo y jodiendo*.

The next day, 23 April, they buried Nestor in a hole far away on a hill at San Juan de Lurigancho.[12] That night after the burial, Mom was sending her friend off when armed men captured both of them right there on our doorstep, pushed them into a truck, blindfolded them and took them to the seaside, threatening them at gunpoint ... then to DINCOTE. So another trip there, this time for my mom. ... The next day they brought her home handcuffed and raided the house. That was scary shit. They found Nestor's letter and some other stuff. I think they could have sent her to prison, but they didn't, maybe there was no need anymore, or maybe it was as arbitrary as many things they did ... maybe it was her good aura. She was released after 15 days in DINCOTE. And every day we had to take food, just leave it at the gate with her name ... same ritual, now for Mom [laughing].

That's the year I started wondering what was I doing with my life ... and went to visit Dad. I was 18 then so I could visit him every month. He was like a huge ear; he doesn't speak much, but he knows how to listen. I think Mom had filled him in on my 'situation' but he never said anything.

The Truth and Reconciliation Commission

After the TRC started, I went to work to Huancayo, in 2002. There I felt like people were waiting for someone to arrive. The relatives had no chance

---

12 The Nueva Esperanza cemetery in San Juan de Miraflores, Lima, is one of the largest cemeteries in Latin America.

to denounce, because we were considered the perpetrators side, there's no one to listen to them. The *testimonios* were by ex–MRTA leaders who asked for forgiveness, reaffirmed their belief in the democratic system and renounced armed struggle. No one wanted to listen to the affected on that side. Many *familiares* didn't want to talk because they were afraid, only a few did, and many of them were living in such poverty, extreme poverty really … *una miseria*. But we managed to get them together and have a public say about *Los Molinos* case, and make the TRC acknowledge it.

It felt like a huge responsibility when people recognized me by my last name. I never liked it, because I want to be recognized for my own history, not my father's. I preferred to stay away from those who knew my old man, but many knew him because of his work with the unions. Although people have backed off now. … That surname weighed so heavy on me that I couldn't even breathe because whatever I do will always be compared to what he had done. … It still weighs on me, but now in a different way.

Cuba

I left for Cuba in 2002. Mom was probably trying to get rid of me [laughing] … because although I was in second year of university, I wasn't studying much. I had no time between … getting money by writing essays for first-year students and working at a fried chicken joint but most of the time I was dedicated to political activism with a collective I met in university.

HIJXS is hard to explain … maybe at another time I could, but at the end of this long conversation, I can't, because it's a more spiritual thing. … Feeling that you share the pain is good, feeling that you share hope, that's something else.

8

Willy: Remembering Torture

Disclaimer

I came to Cuba and got involved in HIJXS through Dad's family. They more or less attempted to create a better Peru, particularly my aunt Gladys, who has been in the maximum-security prison at Chorrillos for a very long time. I can tell you our stories as far as I know them, but I must warn you, the family is riddled with untold stories.

A complicated history

My family has a complicated history, conflictive even … with members on every side of the violence … and relatives whose deaths remain obscure. My grandpa died in unclear circumstances; he was a Navy officer and a violent man who hit his wife and children, and died in the house by gunshot in the head … officially it was 'suicide'. Then, my uncle was in constant trouble, went to prison for robbery and got sick with lupus. Aunt Gladys, the oldest sister, left her family to study abroad and returned to enter the MRTA [Tupac Amaru Revolutionary Movement]. My two other aunts felt abandoned and left the house as soon as they secured jobs; both had failed marriages. There's Uncle Manuel whose wife was shot when my cousin was little. My old man, who was a musician in the conservatory, joined the Navy, but always had disciplinary measures and constant problems with the family. And there's me, who moved out at 16, worked long hours and studied a technical night course, but was doing stupid things at work, showing up drunk at Grandma's house the off nights and always hanging out with troublemakers.

More relatives died in circumstances concealed from 'the children', *los chicos*. For example, Uncle Iker, in one of his street fights his face was cut open so he had an emergency blood transfusion and got HIV. My aunts said it was cancer, but I was working at a hospital so I knew that such care wasn't for cancer. Only after he died did I learn it was AIDS. It was tough to witness him die … we didn't know it was the end. I was very upset with my family for not telling the truth. … They always had their secrets and their cover-up stories 'for our own good', but it's worse because we always find out in a bad way. Grandma died immediately after Iker did, out of sorrow. … We scattered then, like she'd been the one gluing the family together. It's kind of sad now, everyone at their own place, dealing with their own stuff, holding resentments with no reason to get together.

Aunt Gladys has been in prison as long as I can remember. I was probably ten, but it's hard to remember because the family kept an airtight silence about her to other relatives, the children and neighbours, *nadie sabía nada*. In each strange situation they'd make up some minimal excuse, so we were left with our suspicions and stuff we overheard.

The whole family was somehow involved in the mess of the conflict: Gladys' brother Manuel on his own side, had his wife killed because of it, and my father who was forced to resign from the Navy. Officially Uncle Manuel's wife died from sickness, but I learnt it was in a shoot-out in some clandestine operation, *baleada* … my cousin was left an orphan. It all affected Manuel very deeply, but he never says anything. I've realized that even now you can never really know about anybody you're talking to in Peru, whether or how they were involved, on which side, or doing what. Everyone pretends they weren't touched by the conflict; it is always the others.

Aunts and uncles

Gladys is kind of the key story, at least the one I was drawn into and which brought me here. She was the only one who got a higher education. She was in a university in Lima when she got a scholarship for international law in the then Soviet Union.

The other two aunts didn't get involved, but have her similar inability to overlook injustices. A lot of people just swallow the bitterness of reality without complaint; not them. I was sometimes embarrassed by their temper (when I was younger), sometimes very proud (as I got older). I think it's in their blood, the same blood that caused relatives to take up arms. But my old man was the dissonant note among the siblings. He was in the military, as his father had been. He studied music then became a Navy officer although he continued playing in the band. But he resigned. He never told us why, but we figured he was under too much pressure because of Aunt Gladys.

Until I was 11 or so we lived in Grandma's house in San Miguel de Porres with most of them and I saw things there I wasn't supposed to. My aunts took care of us because my parents didn't have time; life was for them just long hours of work: Mom in a textile factory always doing overtime and

Dad first in the Navy and later as security officer doing night shifts. I barely saw them.

Aunt Gladys suddenly started spending periods without coming home, first a weekend, then a week, at the end up to a month. But we always saw her somehow. Those encounters were super weird, first because they weren't at home and sometimes because she'd change her looks. We just had to wait for her; she'd suddenly appear from nowhere but keep walking and we'd follow without looking, pretending not to know her, until we reached a point where she'd turn around and hug us. Then she'd take us for a normal day out, playing and running, and telling one of her million stories about Russia and Cuba, studying abroad.

She'd sporadically reappear at home; we never knew when or for how long. Every time she left she'd do this 'game' she taught us: open the front door's tiny window and look both ways before exiting. … She also taught us signals for when we met at the University Park, a very crowded public space. With all those little odd things we knew something was going on, but didn't know what, and she made it all playful.

All this distanced the family from the neighbours. The windows always closed; the curtains down. We didn't have many visitors, except friends of Aunt Gladys who would have endless conversations, always away from the children. We'd be playing in the house but the visitors never talked to us. I remember wondering why. … I grew very fond of my aunts; they were my caregivers because Mom would leave for the factory while I was still sleeping. And my old man was fair but also strict and never displayed any affection. I don't know how to describe better that sense I grew up with … that our family wasn't normal. It wasn't negative, but it gave you a constant feeling something mustn't be talked about outside the family; shit, even within it.

Gladys I

Aunt Gladys' first arrest confirmed the enigma of her life for me. I was in school when it happened, but I've collected the pieces over the years and can tell you this much. They came armed with assault rifles and brutally forced their way into the house. They shoved past Grandma who fell to the floor, hit my uncle with a rifle butt and searched the house, *registraron todito* then took Gladys away in a pick-up. When we got back from school everyone had bruises and was worried about Grandma. I have no idea how long they held Gladys, but she reappeared much later with no explanations. If we asked, she just replied with yet another story about Russia and Cuba … so we stopped asking.

None of us dared ask Grandma; she'd give you one look and you knew to shut up. According to her, those things weren't children's business, period.

Ventanilla

Sometime near the end of elementary school, my parents moved to Ventanilla to build our own place. Ventanilla was not only far from the city, but was just vacant hills and sandy areas.[1] At the time a large group of Navy families were taking over land and settling there even though there was no electricity, water or sewage. It was just a space and a half built of precarious material, *esteras y madera*, just our beds and some kitchen stuff. We had a light bulb, radio and tiny TV all powered by a car battery we periodically had to put in a wheelbarrow and take down the hill to a repair shop for recharging. As children, that was fun for me and my brother.

Those times were the closest we've been with my old man. Some of them were after the bad 'episode' when my old man quit the Navy and ultimately got a night job in security services. Not that he talked much or showed any affection, but he'd come home early in the morning and we'd work on the house until it was time for our afternoon school. I learnt a lot about construction. I can do everything in a house, but I was particularly into electrical stuff, setting up connections, repairing the radio or making little inventions for fun.

The 'episode' was that we were watching TV when three army jeeps drove up very noisily. These men stormed in and turned the little house upside down, tossing anything in their way, trampling all our clothes. They only took a couple of toy guns my old man got for us, which was so absurd that it makes me sad even today. It was terrifying because the whole time they had my old man at gunpoint against the wall, *encañonado*; we were all under threat. I felt a boiling rage mixed with impotence and frustration for being so little and unable to do anything.

It was just once, but the outrage stayed, maybe because childhood experiences mark you more or because it made me realize how powerless I was in the face of their violence. Perhaps even because it was part of the larger, overbearing military presence in the city, the constant sound of bombings nearby and the military sniping on the hills, since there was a Navy base nearby. Also because none of the neighbours did or said anything. It was as if the raid never happened. That's symptomatic of how people reacted to the conflict in the city. Also my old man never asked anything from the neighbours, all Navy families.

---

[1] Located at the Callao province it was created with an industrial orientation by the military government and thus its inhabitants were mostly factory workers in the military and naval industries. Originally designed as a satellite city it was meant to grow organized but this never materialized, growing instead to become one of the most impoverished districts in the capital, with the majority of inhabitants living with the most deficient access to public transport.

As usual, we didn't discuss it. I guess it was because of Aunt Gladys. My old man was literally caught between her and the Navy. One day he came home saying he quit. He said it was because of all the injustices, but I didn't believe him. The next period was quite tough because we lived only on Mother's minimum wage, with no help from anyone.

Gladys II

Meanwhile Aunt Gladys stopped going to Grandma's. By then she was a lawyer so first they said she worked 'far away'. Aunt Gladys was always vigilant about not letting anyone know much about her. But when you entered the house, the growing concern could be felt in the air, and I knew it was about Gladys.

It turns out she'd been arrested. I'd see Grandma returning home late, which was strange because she only used to go to the market. ... My cousin used to tell me bits she heard, but it wasn't until like 12 years later, only a year ago, when I finally visited Gladys in Chorrillos, that I learnt she'd been caught together with Rafael's old man.

There was a journalist who knew Rafael's dad and saw him there, I don't know if alive or already dead, but he managed to find the other person caught with him. That's how Grandma finally found Gladys ... who couldn't even stand on her feet; she was bruised and burnt everywhere. ... She was in a clinic where she got some medical attention, and Grandma was allowed to see her, but no one else.

Gladys told me how they had been arrested together and tortured separately, but at specific times showed each one what they were doing to the other to force them to talk. She told me so many details about the torture, about unimaginable levels of bodily pain and passing out. She has scars from it all over her hands and face, which she covers with extreme makeup. She also can't see very well and can only hear in one ear. It wouldn't surprise me if she was raped as well ... she implied it by saying they 'abused' her, *la ultrajaban*. She was embarrassed to tell her nephew she was raped so she said it in another way.[2]

---

[2] After 20 years of denouncing before the Peruvian Public Ministry there was no investigation and Gladys' relatives together with a human rights organization filed the case with the inter-American justice system (the Inter-American Commission on Human Rights [IACHR]). In April 2014 the case was presented at the Inter-American Court of Human Rights: Case Espinoza Gonzales vs Peruvian State. 'Gladys Carol Espinoza Gonzales was illegally and arbitrarily detained on April 17, 1993. She was taken to the DIVISE (Anti-Kidnapping Police Division) and two days later to DINCOTE (Anti-Terrorist Police Division). In both state facilities, she was brutally tortured for several days, through multiple and continuous bodily and psychological attacks, drownings, beatings all over her body, and repeated rape. Those acts were applied with such violence and cruelty

After that conversation I went home very disturbed, and for some reason I took the soldering tool I use for working with electrical equipment and used it like she described. I was trying to see how she'd felt. … I can tell you there's no bleeding but it burns like hell. It was stupid, but it made me wonder how someone could possibly do that to another person … again and again.

I can imagine what happened to her, but I didn't see her when it actually took place, so I can't imagine how she survived it. She has told me all the worst of it, nothing pretty. I think of how they couldn't break her even with everything they did to her. … It's hard to believe how each thing only strengthened her. I mostly want to remember that strength; it's what's contagious from her and contains my tears, *no se quebró*.

But when I remember it all and think what I was doing at the time … how oblivious I was of that reality, I feel a mix of rage and sadness, but mostly rage. Gladys thought she'd be left crippled … and that left me with hate. When I saw a police officer or an INPE officer,[3] I had this strong desire to beat someone up. I know they didn't actually do all that to Gladys, but it's

---

that Gladys Carol Espinoza Gonzales lost consciousness on several occasions and got to the point of begging her captors to kill her. What happened to Gladys Carol Espinoza was facilitated by the legal framework, which allowed non-communication of detainees and institutionalised the absence of judicial oversight, leaving the detainees absolutely unprotected and defenceless. As a consequence of the acts, Gladys Carol Espinoza was left with severe and irreversible damage which was not compensated by the State. On the contrary, six years after these grave acts she was tortured again in Yanamayo prison in 1999, this time by officers of the DINOES (Special Operations Police Division). Nor has this described sequence of violations been effectively investigated. Only after 2012 with the in-depth report by the Inter American Commission did the Peruvian State arrange to begin such investigations. So far none of the violations has been judicially resolved, nor have the DIVISE, DINCOTE, DINOES or Public Ministry officials or medical agents involved been sanctioned in any way. As the court knows, the acts were a replica of what happened in an important group of cases on the same issue already ruled on by the Inter-American System. The Court also knows that the acts were part of a context of generalized use of torture and sexual violence by State agents in the fight against terrorism. The goal of presenting this case to the court is thus not about new facts, context or judicial events. This case is brought to the court because the Peruvian State has not responded to the pressing need to provide reparations and justice to a victim who is now physically and psychologically devastated due to the unjustifiable malice and extreme violence perpetrated against her. The persistence of cases of this same nature presented to the Inter-American System is an indicator that the Peruvian State has not taken effective measures to respond comprehensively in terms of reparation and justice towards a particular group of victims of the armed conflict, people who had a real or perceived link with terrorism' (transcript of the case presented at IACHR, video extract from the IACHR website: www.youtube.com/watch?v=E0et6XKI9NI).

3   The National Penitentiary Institute/Instituto Nacional Penitenciario, branch of the Ministry of Justice in charge of the prison system. INPE officers are the prison security.

anger for everything that was done without ever considering them people. How can they torture to death people who had children, nephews, mothers, and feel no remorse? They don't see them as human … but as objects to be beaten. That really fucks with me. *Eso me jode.*

I don't know what I'd do if I knew who tortured her, that's the level of my rage. It wasn't just my aunt, just *guerrilleros* who were tortured, but many other people, which is somehow worse because they didn't do anything, didn't even have their convictions to survive. I think I've outgrown most of those feelings after talking about them, because even if I find those people … what next? Nothing would be solved. I can't reproduce what they've done, I don't want to become like them. And that's the thing with such horrific violence; it easily consumes you and if you're not careful it becomes you.

There's a legal case, and we must be patient. There's plenty of evidence of Gladys' torture; the family and the doctors have all seen her beaten up. This evidence would help her case, but the trial has stalled for years so evidence doesn't matter. Moving the trial forward is another thing altogether, and a favourable verdict is like, utopian. There's nothing to do about it, drawing media attention makes things worse because Peruvian society is against such trials; if you're a 'terrorist' you lose all human rights.

Sometimes I wonder about my dad, but I don't think he could do that given how much he supported his sister. … Maybe he left the Navy because it was too much … and too dangerous, for them both. Once he told me about one of the many times he was arrested. It was during the curfew and he was standing at the entrance of the Navy base with his assault rifle. Suddenly this guy was walking on the street. My old man's superiors were right behind him and they ordered dad to shoot. He aimed but didn't shoot. Instead he yelled *toque de queda!*, giving the guy a chance to run. His superior put a gun to his head saying, 'Either you shoot him or I shoot you!' But my old man didn't. He got arrested for a week. That was the kind of thing he had to deal with.

Outside of prison

The first time we went to see Aunt Gladys, we took a plane and they told us we were going to Arequipa. Only when we landed did they tell us we were in Puno and were going to see Gladys. Puno was by far the coldest place I've ever been. I didn't even wash my face because it was freezing. Yanamayo can be distinguished by the long lines of families waiting outside the gates for the visit. We joined the queue and bought stuff from informal sellers who have stalls there. They advised us what can be taken inside and what not.

But the guards didn't let me or my brother in. They said children were forbidden, but it was because we weren't 'direct' family. So, we stayed outside alone, looking at the families and the sellers. We were cold and hungry but there was just cold water. After three hours, my aunts and grandma came out. They still didn't say why Gladys was inside. I asked how she was and they said she was happy, while Grandma cried and cried ... I thought out of happiness, but Gladys later told me she couldn't even walk at the time because they had tortured her again in Yanamayo.[4]

When we left Puno, we landed in Arequipa and stayed three months on vacation with my aunts; I guess my parents wanted to get rid of us. I forgot all about Puno and Gladys. We never went back; only Grandma continued visiting.

Inside of prison

I was in Ventanilla throughout high school and didn't think much about Gladys, except when I visited Grandma's house or my aunts. I knew she was accused of 'terrorism'. My old man told me a bit, my other aunt another bit, and in the house you could hear about the trial, the visits and how the house was under surveillance. Maybe it was paranoia, but you never know.

When I finished school, Aunt Gladys was transferred to Huaral. That was my first real visit, and the first time inside a prison; my old man took me. Gladys was in maximum-security, and there I got the first stamp on my history of prison visits, each gate another stamp on the arm. I remember Dad telling me in the queue to show no fear, stand up straight and answer their questions calmly and firmly ... don't let them scare you.

Inside it was high walls and long corridors, pavilions and pavilions of prisoners. I was happy to see Gladys, but all I kept fantasizing was how to get her out. In Huaral we could enter all the way into her cell, unlike Chorrillos where you can only go to the yard. In Huaral each of them had their own cell, with mini TVs. Dad and Gladys talked and talked the whole time. I asked a couple of questions but mostly made her laugh and listened to her tell me about Russia and Cuba. ... She was somehow slowly convincing me of her ideals, to help others, focus on the collective welfare, complain against injustices; think for yourself, defend your ideas, fight for your rights ...

I only saw her twice there, and also met Iris' mom there; that was great because she was always laughing. Still, saying goodbye was the hardest part; it was terribly frustrating and infuriating to leave her in there, thinking why

---

[4]   Gladys was detained and tortured in 1993. After three months, she was transferred to Chorrillos prison and in 1996 to Yanamayo, where she was tortured during an inspection in August 1999. The IACHR found Gladys' precarious conditions of detention without medical attention over five years constituted cruel, inhuman and degrading treatment (IACHR Resolution, 20 November 2014, http://corteidh.or.cr/docs/casos/articulos/seriec_289_ing.pdf).

is she here? Why her? We had our silent four-hour journey back home, and later ... you just put those things aside and continue with your life.

There was always a reason not to visit more often, the money, studies ... but it was mostly that my old man didn't want me to get closer to Gladys, as if I could get 'infected' by her ideas [laughing]. ... Apparently, I did! No, I started working and earning money, so I left my parents' house for a small rented room, and started a crazy life, hanging out with friends. My only contact with the family was at grandma's house where I'd go to get news about Gladys.

Some years after Huaral, she was transferred to Chorrillos where she is now. It's closer to Lima, so I kept asking Uncle Manuel to take me, but he always said they had important things to talk about. A month before coming to Cuba I finally managed to enter Chorrillos and see her. I brought her some food and stuff she needed. I didn't know where she was, so I said 'political prisoner', and they asked which party, then the stamps and the gates and the searches. Then, I was sent to the yard to wait. ... She came very neat and fashionable as usual, with her makeup, high heels and tight clothes. She always had such presence ... but now, behind all that, you can tell the years and hard life have really hit her. In any case we hugged for 15 minutes. She was so happy I was coming to Cuba that she cried.

That was the first time we could talk alone, and the first time I dared ask about her life. She started telling me, piece by piece. I told her I was in 'familiares' and had met Rafael there, and she got very excited and added more stories, detailed ones. I never told Rafael everything Gladys said about his dad, because she asked me not to, she was afraid he might not know. So, me and Rafael, we both know but never talk about it ... maybe that connection is why we cry together when we get drunk. Ever since I learned that, I see Rafael through different eyes. Knowing all the things his family suffered and how he turned out to be a good person, a great friend, that's something.

Familiares

I don't remember how I got involved in *familiares*. Uncle Manuel told me about it but he didn't want me to get involved. I did anyway. We were a small but very active group. I hadn't been involved in stuff like that except in the student movement, where I was joining protests, but that was different. In *familiares* we did sit-ins in public places, cultural acts and distributed flyers about prison conditions. We also held meetings where we met others; only a few young people. Sometimes a lawyer or a relative talked; sometimes it was about *las visitas*, new problems, maybe a trial, a new worse law, or the scholarships to Cuba.

We knew the police kept the place where *familiares* met under surveillance; they also video-recorded any public activity and followed us afterwards.

There was always this fear of being caught, of being against an unjust but legal system ... a combination of paranoia and knowing what has happened before to others. You can't compare our activities to theirs, and still ... there was such tension. Those little 'games' I learnt earlier proved useful, like changing routes when going to the same places, looking to the sides but never back ... everything I was taught without knowing and was now doing almost automatically.

I told my old man about *familiares*, and he was pretty upset. I learnt there was this sort of agreement in his family that none of my generation would be involved in anything to do with politics. Actually, I was the only one interested ... not sure why. I think it started as fascination about Gladys' life, and a reaction against what's called 'normal' as a given, as if we couldn't change it. We see people and children every day on the streets starving, homeless ... and prefer not to think about it. Mistreatment has become normal; just because you have no money or influence you can be treated like garbage, forced against your will ... your dignity. That pisses me off. How people have a 12-hour workday and can't even see their children. That was our reality at home and it pulled us apart. That shouldn't be normal.

So, the whole idea of becoming a professional with ideals became appealing. When they offered scholarships to Cuba, I didn't think twice. I also kind of fell for the others in the group, like Iris, who has lived such difficult shit but still believes in change, and has this joy about it.

All that helped me form a different view of life, where change is both necessary and possible ... but through other means. My parents don't agree, they keep saying they don't want to see me in prison. It doesn't matter how much I explain to them. They keep telling me not to trust people, not get involved in politics ... 'Look at your aunt, in Chorrillos' they say to discourage me, but I want to prove them wrong.

The first thing is that I want to see my aunt free. I don't know how to get her out of there, but she has to get out ... and be with her family, back where she belongs, because it's completely unfair. I know she did things, but she has already spent 14 years in prison[5] while the police did all those horrible things to her and many others, yet nothing happened to them. The state forces killed and tortured people and they aren't in prison; even the very few who were punished got short sentences. State terrorism was legal, while the others who were fighting to change society are imprisoned as 'terrorists'.

---

[5]   That was at the time of Willy's testimonial, 2007. Gladys remained in Chorrillos maximum-security prison until she finished her 25-year sentence in 2018. She died of cancer less than two years after her release.

Terrorism

Gladys never told me exactly what she was involved in, but she did explain her reasons. 'We must change things' she kept repeating like an imperative. She told me that in our country's history things changed only by rebelling. … I think there was a dose of frustration in her words, like it was a last resource, because they all came from other forms of political action that failed and taking up arms was their only way. … She added, '[Y]ou'll come to understand it. It's up to your people to find your own ways to change things, but once you start, trust those around you and don't ever turn back, because that's when mistakes arise.'

I knew she was in the MRTA only because I overheard it after my uncle went to visit her. Around that same time my old man said Aunt Gladys was 'accused of' being a *militante*, but wasn't one. It became a certainty when I visited Gladys in prison, and heard them called 'MRTA terrorists' to differentiate them from Sendero [Shining Path].

I remember, as a child getting angry whenever I heard about those '*terroristas*' who were bombing 'us', so I'd say those shits should be killed. All I knew and that hatred came from the media and I just repeated what I heard on TV. Only growing up did I start to realize it was a distorted image … and my idea of who the terrorists are has changed. When the military searched my house, raided buses, denigrated people because they were poor … plus the killings and tortures … I started seeing them as the ones using terror. I also learnt the conflict was far more complicated: Sendero was against the state too, but there were also clashes between Sendero and MRTA. The only clear thing was to distrust the media and the government.

This became more evident with the Embassy, which the media portrayed as a successful military intervention to rescue the hostages, covering up all the evidence of how they killed all MRTA people in there, even when some surrendered. They didn't even return the bodies to their families for quite some time. The media changed the facts even during the takeover, never explaining what it was really about. It just became a simplified story of let's kill the terrorists inside The Embassy no matter how and make the army and the government the heroes of the story. And that was it.

I think about all that and Gladys. … I see the military people out and about while Gladys is in prison, and it just makes me frustrated. It really hurt my family not to have her with us; she was like a mother to my aunts, and also to me and my cousins. I have to remember her stories, her laughter and her strength … that's what keeps me going. And also knowing the trial against the state for her torture, which will be important one day … we just have to be patient.

Afterthoughts

There have been negative effects of growing up in that environment, not just on me, but also on my brother and my cousin, the only children around. It wasn't a normal upbringing; the family had a way of only talking about what was strictly necessary, hiding everything, not relating to others ... it was the family trademark. That affects you.

There's constant mistrust and the whole family lives a sort of dry isolation. There was hardly any show of affection, for example. You see other families kissing and hugging, and having conversations while my parents barely touch us and as for talking, inexistent. All that forces you to grow up faster. You see things other people your age don't notice. ... I think I also learnt to be always ready for something, always on guard, *a la defensiva*. In Peru, once you step outside your house you're in danger ... of being robbed or attacked. You learn to be alert and think out your moves beforehand. Now imagine how it is for someone who lived danger inside the house as well, when they broke into our house armed and threatened us.

Somehow, I never had many friends and became very selective about the relationships I established. But I don't see that as negative. The negative stuff was during my childhood and the years spent without communicating in the family. Now, my relationships have been unstable, because it's hard to trust myself not to hurt other people. I think this way of being kind of cold really affects others, people expect more from a partner. Like a barrier ... I find it hard to relate to others that close.

I hope I don't come out too strong and that my ideas don't affect my family because in practice they are closer to Gladys than to the rest of them. Not to repeat the same, but some ideas. The ideas I've learnt even in her absence, because there was a presence in her absence. I don't think my family likes that, and I do worry about affecting them.

PART II

The Second Movement: Politics of Memory

The second movement engages with the problems that emerged of/with the realist *testimonio* presented in the first movement and how they became more complicated over the years.

This movement results from the purposeful troubling of *testimonio* by revisiting the recorded *testimonios* during my next encounters with the HIJXS group in Lima between 2012 and 2013, five and six years after we first recorded our conversations. We called this movement 'the politics of memory', because it explores how narratives are impacted by the changes in their conditions of production including relationships between participants and places/spaces; and the shifting character of silences.

This second movement acknowledges the need for *testimonio* as realist tales. At a methodological level, realist tales provide the object of troubling, while they are also needed for political/activist reasons. Doing politics in a context of state and societal repression calls for *testimonios* as a means for political action and a necessary initial step for claiming recognition.

9

Spaces/Places: Working Out Testimonial Spaces

Troubling spaces/places

Spaces and places are more than the backdrop of memory practices. Their entanglement and complicity become apparent when researchers use them to visualize the memory struggles of diverse actors, when these actors/practitioners demand something from spaces/places regarding their memories, or when spaces/places may even 'talk back', transforming us.

Both fieldwork phases in Peru (2012 and 2013) posed a complex challenge as a result of a shift in place and space. Recording conversations – as a method for reflecting on both our changes and the testimonial work – did not work once in Lima. This time, in this other place, it was harder to set aside quiet time to re-engage in conversations about *testimonio*, and thus to produce a '*testimonial space*' as we had before. One reason was their absorption in their (new) busy lives in a large city like Lima between work, family, studies and the different forms of political activism in which most of them were involved (that is, political party, community-based work, professional union, university collectives, cultural/artistic groups, and so on). The other reason was a certain unacknowledged reluctance to bring painful memories back by relistening to old conversations, or engaging in new conversations about those memories.

In response, I decided to change from 'interview time' to *dialogical* methods during the second fieldwork phase (see Chapter 2). We talked about activities they were involved in that I could join, or I invited them to activities I was involved that might interest them (that is, photographic/museum exhibitions, book launches or research presentations, cemetery visits, family gatherings, meetings of their collectives or prison visits). It turned out that doing and talking about it was far more interesting than conversations in a secluded place. Maybe the artificiality of recording conversations in a closed room did not connect with their collective attempts to be more engaged with the country they/I had just returned to. Something about being-in-place and actively doing something was more appealing for us. Taking our conversations outside the 'safe' closed doors (Jones et al, 2008) felt somehow more daring and attuned with their return. Perhaps there was also an element of pushing me outside of my comfort zone by getting me involved in their lives and the surrounding spaces that the return to Peru had presented them with. An activity-led conversation brought the testimonial back home to inhabit the space they referred to in their first narrations. Such 'ethnographic doing in place', Luttrell (2003: 148) argues, is useful when there is less 'narrative urgency' about the past to make conversations flow, allowing instead a focus on a 'performance' of 'evolving' stories in the present.

I was aware that places played an important role in our testimonial project, in the sense that it took place in different spaces, first in Cuba (then the UK for me) and finally Peru. While our first conversations took place in Cuba, Peru was actually the place we had in our minds as the (im)possible 'stage' but also the one we were talking about, where the experiences narrated in the testimonial conversations took place. I also planned to explore how each place produced a different practice and a different writing because the spatial dimension of *testimonio* mattered in relation to how it affected the stories possible. Yet, I side-lined the entanglements between spaces/places and memory work, how spaces were being made of stories, and vice versa.

The spatial dimension of *testimonio* work became more evident during the second fieldwork phase in Peru (2013); it brought an awareness of the need to consider space as a distinctively relevant analytical category to think with. This led me to Doreen Massey (1992; 2005), who considers space as relational and dynamic, questioning dominant ideas of space as a 'surface' over which events happen, removing its links with time and its analytical contribution to understanding 'knowledge formation, social reproduction and the constitution of subjectivities' (Robertson, 2009). She and the growing literature on the 'spatial turn' (Lefebvre, 1992; Soja, 1996; Harvey, 2001) understand space as the product of interrelations, a sphere of contemporaneous pluralities, always under construction (and co-construction). Most important for me is Massey's proposition, 'perhaps we could imagine space as a simultaneity of stories-so-far' (2005: 9).

The growing literature on memory has highlighted the relationship between space/place and violence since Pierre Nora's work, *Les lieux de mémoire* (1984–1992). In its multiple translations as sites, spaces or realms of memory, Nora's work infused the Southern Cone practices of memorial sites regarding the recent past (Jelin and Langland, 2003; Sosa and Serpente, 2012). More recent literature asks how memory is inscribed in space, and how we are to understand the entanglements of places and memory; exploring how the state's violent crimes 'unfold in space and reconfigure it in the long term' (Colombo and Schindel, 2014: 1), how spaces in the present become haunted by the past, and what to do particularly when there are no recognizable locations or material traces of violence.

State violence relies on, and creates, spaces of exception where 'the rule of law' is suspended (Calveiro, 1998). Thus, Latin American scholarship explores the memory/space nexus as critical questions of how to institutionalize memory about violent states past (in Argentina, Chile or Uruguay) or present (Colombia). Furthermore, violent exceptional spaces are not simply confined to 'detention centres'/'camps' (Calveiro, 1998; 2008), but co-exist with and infiltrate 'ordinary spaces', even expanding beyond national borders. When infiltrating intimate spaces as they did in the case of appropriated children by the Argentinean dictatorship, they become 'superimposed on the everyday' and 'persist by haunting' the spaces where forced disappearances took place (Perez, 2014). Exceptional spaces can, however, be created by rebellious spatial practices that reconfigure their uses to 'alter and defy spatialities of power and subvert the given order' even in or precisely by ephemeral practices such as performances (Sosa, 2012), street interventions (H.I.J.O.S. *escraches*) or 'occupations' (Colombo and Schindel, 2014).

These insights are not easily applied to the Peruvian case. Writing about/ in Peru takes place from a space declared as post-war/post-exception but where there is no safe distance, because all is still under suspicion and surveillance. Governments continue to declare 'states of emergency' in Peruvian provinces at an increasing rate since the transition in the 2000s.[1] In a country where the victim/perpetrator dichotomy does not neatly fit the Southern Cone focus on 'state terrorism', there is a reluctance to create spaces of/for memory. It involves a necessary scrutiny of the role of state violence, its systematic use and the actors involved, some of whom remained in the political landscape and even in government (such as Alan García who held a second presidency in 2006) and increasingly numbers of (ex-)military men in public office (Granados Moya, 2021). There remains a 'haunting' that needs to be documented, this haunting is the exception to be noted and (re)constructed in opposition to the largely 'normal' safety of the academic space.

In the face of our new challenges in Peru and the need to become more *dialogical* with the methods-in-use, I re-engaged with the testimonial work

---

[1] 'State of emergency' in Peru: legal declaration of exception in territories where specific civil rights are suspended and the area is under military control. Ninety provinces were so declared in the early 1990s with the Fujimori regime, decreasing the next decade with the transition government, only to slowly increase again. Protests in 2014–2015 by several Andean communities against large mining corporations led the government to declare their territories under state of emergency. No public information is available on how long provinces remain under such ruling. In June 2015 newspapers reported that the government lifted it in the Alto Huallaga region after 30 years.

in different ways with each of the HIJXS. In this chapter, I explore the experiences with Rafael and Iris after their return to Peru, in particular how they highlighted the importance of spaces/places in our memory work. This is not to say that spaces/places were not present before, but that our awareness of our relationships with them in doing memory work only became evident back in Peru, revisiting the testimonial work. The experiences with Iris and Rafael show practices of reclaiming and transforming places/spaces in the way de Certeau explored everyday 'spatial practices' as 'a labour that constantly transforms places' (1988: 118). They both used spaces/places as devices to create 'communicating vessels' (Vargas Llosa, 1997) either to anchor their memories of the past or produce new memories, and ultimately glimpses of being transformed by spaces/places.

In the final section I explore the prison and '*carcelería*' as a particular kind of precarious space, the result of the HIJXS' experiences of 'visiting' prison as a common space present in the testimonial narratives. This was at once, paradoxically, an oppressive space and a space of freedom for the HIJXS. It includes my own experience of visiting one prison in an attempt to enter that HIJXS space of shared experiences by being-in-place.

Memory and place in Latin America

The exploration of memory and places in Latin America has taken different directions closely related to national contexts, history and political processes. The focus – both in memory practices and in scholarship – has been on spaces of exception created by state violence. At one end of the spectrum is Argentina's focus on justice in the transition from dictatorship to democracy, which creates a spatiality based on remembering, and at the other is Uruguay's focus on reconciliation, based on forgetting. Argentine scholarship on spaces/ places and memory has focused both on preserving and on representing and transmitting memory. It involves 'recovering'/'transforming' violent spaces of state repression into sites for memory archives, local sites/museums of memory, signposting (plaques) specific places for remembering significant events/people, landmarks and monuments (even street art), among other initiatives (Arfuch, 2013).[2] In the 1990s it went beyond creating static monuments that freeze memory by accompanying them with creative cultural productions. For instance, the ESMA, the largest clandestine detention centre in Buenos Aires, became a cultural space for performative acts, rituals and

---

[2] Arfuch refers to *Memorias en la ciudad. Señales del terrorismo de Estado en Buenos Aires* (2010) accounting for the intense activity of signposting the city with 240 markers of state terrorism in 45 neighbourhoods, including 202 remembrance sites and 38 illegal detention centres transformed into memory sites.

conversations, disrupting the monument concept to constantly recreate its meaning (Saona, 2014).

In contrast, Uruguay saw less state support for preserving the traces of state violence. While many detention centres were transformed into memorials in Argentina, one prison became a shopping mall in Uruguay (Lessa, 2013). It is evident that countries with ongoing transition (and conflicts) like Colombia and countries with (by now) institutionalized memory initiatives like Argentina, produce different efforts to explore the links between memory and places/spaces. In Colombia, the focus is on forced displacement of communities and the resulting experiences of place-making through memory work linked to violence (Riaño-Alcalá, 2002; Sánchez, 2007): how it alters the social fabric as well as cultural identity, how de-territorialization and territorialization practices alter cities, and how violence and terror (including forced disappearance) become a matter of daily life in war-torn places (Taussig, 2005) for which emplaced knowledge-sharing through storytelling is key for survival (Riaño-Alcalá, 2002; Riaño-Alcalá and Baines, 2011).

The research on space and memory in Peru traces fierce struggles over memory that have made the institutionalizing of memory sites both difficult *and* controversial (Hite, 2007; Ulfe, 2009; Feldman, 2012). Although the Truth and Reconciliation Commission (TRC) – the only state-sanctioned initiative to confront the past and account for the violence – issued clear recommendations to the state, successive governments have demonstrated little political will to implement them and, even more, have also opposed new initiatives (Macher, 2007; Ulfe and Milton, 2011).

The TRC explicitly called for the Peruvian state to assume direct responsibility for creating '*recordatorios or lugares de memoria*' as symbolic reparations to victims of violence (Saona, 2014). The *recordatorios* would include installing plaques in public parks, public squares and cemeteries, and dedicating spaces as remembrance for recovered unknown bodies. It also recommended changing symbolic places (that is, military bases) that 'remain associated in the collective memory with the use of violence by State/public servants' in affected territories (TRC, 2003c: 167). In particular, the state is to ensure that a central public space – or a monument in the capital as well as in the regions – would transmit the 'national tragedy' to the new generations.

There is no seeking of a consensus on the narratives of the internal war. Particularly difficult is to discuss the role of the state and military violence, and the lack of sufficient space for discussion on the root causes, or the political aspects of the war.[3] In fact, controversies rather than debate regarding

---

[3] Milton (2014: 9) argues that 'much heated debate is fuelled by competing versions of the text of the conflict (and even of what to call it – conflict/war/political violence)'.

memory spaces have arisen at several moments since the TRC report (2003) and its anniversary commemorations, the photographic exhibition Yuyanapaq on the years of violence (2003) (Poole and Rojas-Perez, 2011), the sculpture as memorial site for the victims called *El Ojo Que Llora*/The Eye That Cries (2007) (Drinot, 2009; Milton, 2011). Even theatre plays, as performing spaces of memory, such as '*La Cautiva*' (2015) have been subjected to surveillance by the national counter-terrorist unit (Townsend, 2015).

In terms of research on memory spaces/places, it is also sparse with exceptions on some locally established memorial sites, the iconic Memory Museum by ANFASEP in Ayacucho.[4] Mostly, discussion is about memory spaces in the capital, in particular the Lugar de la Memoria, LUM (literally Place of Memory). A national museum of memory that has sparked numerous controversies and subsequent changes of direction, between its conception in 2009, its partial opening in 2015 and the forced retirement of its director in 2017, it epitomizes the state's reluctance to be involved in producing spaces for memory on the internal war that it does not control.[5] That reluctance was evident in the governments of García (2006–2011) and Humala (2011–2016), and the subsequent governments where the National Congress was controlled by Fujimorism, as they all had something at stake if state violence were to come under scrutiny.[6] The memory discourse is particularly mobilized during electoral campaigns or times of political turmoil, always effective for galvanizing support/attacking an opponent, or shifting attention to other polemical issues.

While the formally designed sites for remembrance have been the focus of intense controversy, there remain many neglected memory spaces that

---

The memory battles are fuelled during electoral periods, and as Drinot (2009) argues, the fundamental differences in how to talk about the violence and account for the past reflects underlying different ontologies of violence: 'two underlying discourses on the nature or the very essence of violence in Peru'.

[4] The Asociación Nacional de Familiares, Secuestrados, Detenidos y Desaparecidos del Perú (ANFASEP), founded its Memory Museum in 2005. There are other memory sites and commemorative spaces in several provinces of Ayacucho, Junín, Huancavelica and Apurimac (Ulfe, 2009). In 2009 a project mapped diverse forms of memory spaces: proyecto-lugaresdememoria.pucp.edu.pe. Such spaces are the result of long struggles by communities affected by violence. On the contrary, in Lima, most marks on public spaces have few connections with surrounding communities.

[5] 'There is a growing literature on the Lugar de la Memoria (Cánepa 2009, Rodrigo 2010) … [but] Ulfe (2009: 24–25) also notes an evident marginality of existing memory projects in the central Andes within "national" conversations about the museum' (Feldman, 2012: 512).

[6] Several cases under investigation happened during Alan García's first presidential mandate (1985–1990). Ollanta Humala (2011–2016 presidency) had a case against him for human rights violations during his military service in a province under 'state of emergency' in 1992.

'witnessed' traumatic events. These 'haunted places' connect us with violent events in the past, and are in a legal sense 'crime scenes' (Saona, 2014). Perhaps this explains why so few of them are officially recognized as memory spaces: the majority remain clandestine even in the post-war context. Up until today the military and police (including the Ministry of Defence and the Ministry of the Interior) refuse to open their archives to public examination even when judicial procedures demand it; as Burt and Cagley (2013) note, a 'culture of secrecy underlies impunity in Peru'.

Relevant here is that memory spaces in Peru have entered the literature and research agenda as places that highlight the struggles over memory, much of it shaped by the politics-of-memory approach (Jelin, 2003). These spaces have been studied as windows or vehicles that reveal the existent approaches to (meanings of) a violent past and the different/competing narratives of it circulating in society, which can also be seen in Argentinean scholarship (Durán et al, 2014), the opposite ontologies of the violence (Drinot, 2009) and the problematic continuous exclusion of the local, its sociopolitical processes and its citizens (Ulfe, 2009). In addition, there has been explorations of the connection between memory spaces/places and local struggles for 'recognition' (Portugal, 2015), including the initial proposal of the Lugar de la Memoria, as an open 'plural space' that could build bridges between different narratives of the violence, a space of recognition for co-existence, dialogue and learning (del Pino and Agüero, 2014).

The following stories are part of shifting our attention from memorializing sites of terror and creating territorial markers, towards a more complex understanding of space to explore its entanglements with memory (Schindel and Colombo, 2014). These stories bring to the fore spatial entanglements with memory while doing memory work. They are written based on my experiences of a walking itinerary with Rafael, travelling with Iris to her father's grave, and visiting prison. The first two stories explore different uses of the connections between memory and spaces/places: using the latter to provide a much-needed materiality to memories, or to catalyse a creative process for memory-making. The third story adds how being-in-place and the relationships cultivated there can produce a different (at times paradoxical) experience of space, and how 'being-in-place' is used to create a shared-story space.

A walking itinerary with Rafael

Rafael and I decided to walk around Lima and create a *recorrido*; an itinerary of those places he held significant in his life history. He designed this tour through those iconic spaces where his *testimonio* unravelled. I, like a good technologically driven researcher, took my camera and digital voice recorder as memory aids. It was a loose experiment driven by a strong desire to traverse those spaces mentioned in that old conversation recorded in Cuba five years ago. I also had the feeling that it could perhaps provide some materiality effect to those memories he talked about, make them somehow more 'real' by 'being there'; or maybe I could get closer to them. At the same time, it was part of an interest I acquired on my own return: to move around Lima, get to know places, and remember a city where I once lived.

But Lima is a large city, spread around 3,000km^2 it takes four hours to drive a car from north to south. So, Rafael carefully chose some places over others and designed a way to visit them that worked in terms of proximity. We created a trajectory that was more space-led than chronology-led, aware of our time restrictions to move around the city in one day. Every place we stopped, I passed the camera to Rafael and encouraged him to take pictures. I also took some myself. But our main activity was to walk and talk, and observe where we were. We were taking our conversations (the memory work) out for a stroll, and letting them roam 'out-and-about'.

One stop was the house where Rafael saw his father the last time, where his grandmother had lived. It is important to mention that Rafael hadn't been back since he was nine. The task was not easy, not only because Rafael was nervous about it (I was as well), but also because he did not know the address and was relying on his recollections of the place. As we approached the neighbourhood, he told me he would take me first to 'where I've always pictured the house' any time he had passed near or through this neighbourhood. When we arrived, we walked around a bit and Rafael said it might be this or that area. In the end he chose one and we took pictures and got closer, talking about his memories of the place, including of the girl next door he liked but never talked to and the view of the parking lot turned football field by the children at the time. As we started walking away, I felt dissatisfaction in his tone. Something was not making sense: the distance from this house to a nearby block of flats where other relatives lived long ago was further than he remembered. He remarked that distances 'tend to shrink as you grow up, not widen'. Something did not add up. So, we headed towards the flats to get another perspective on the area and on Rafael's sense of space.

Once we got near them Rafael's confusion morphed into a slight anxiety. Suddenly, all the houses in the parallel streets we walked looked the same. We stumbled again and again on the same arrangement of houses with parking lots turned football fields followed by long alleys with two-storey houses. By this time, I had become concerned about walking around like tourists, with a camera and voice recorder on full display in what seemed to me like empty streets.

Maybe it was more a reflection of my own anxieties than an attempt to soothe Rafael's that I told him it didn't really matter, we could just settle for the house we had 'found' and photographed as 'the house'. But such a suggestion irritated him. So, I asked if there was anyone who might remember a more precise location of the house. Rafael found a public payphone in a small shop and called one of his father's relatives for directions. It quickly became evident that he was right to doubt; the house he was looking for was actually just 100 metres down the road we were standing on.

Again, we repeated the ritual, this time with 'the real one': walking closer, taking turns to take pictures, him telling stories. … Except this time it was 'the real one'. And except this time, it had lost a bit of its meaning, or maybe just its excitement. Still, except for that feeling of 'staging a scene for a picture's sake after failing to capture a spontaneous moment', Rafael was happier as we got to the front door and he felt he remembered more things.

When we finally walked away, he looked from across the street with a smile and sighed like confirming that the landscape made sense with his memories. The scene was as beautiful as it was brief because Rafael immediately started to panic, saying 'that's exactly how I felt about the first house'. Then came a flood of questions: What if all the places he always thought were 'his places' were wrong? What if everything he knows as remembered was wrong? What if everything, like his father's house, is misplaced? What if it's our doing, as if we, by this *recorrido*, were displacing the memories? All of a sudden, our *revisiting* became scary; it threatened to destabilize the carefully stitched memories that constituted his knowledge of the past and of his father, which in turn constituted himself in the present.

I kept thinking there was something beautiful about watching a sort of remaking of the memories, and how old places became somehow new ones (or the other way around) in front of us. Strangely I would have thought Rafael would like this sort of confirmation of knowing which house was 'the real house' and not feel the anxiety of not-knowing and of memories getting misplaced. For me the moment was telling of the several opportunities presented to us for remaking memories and enjoying how being in different places springs up different memories. For Rafael it was more about unsettling memories; and the threat of misplacing them made him more aware of how unstable they are.

Rafael later said that what he remembered most about the walk was precisely the feeling of loss over his memories of living in that house that turned out not to be the 'real' one. Was this the awkward feeling of a memory lost when made to fit with 'the real house' or the anxiety produced by the unreliability of our memories and the way we think of memory or remembrance practices and their function in our lives?

Walking alongside others has been part of research since ethnography existed, as part of the idea of immersing into a culture with its varied practices of living alongside others. Later it was explored as part of the participatory research repertoire (for example, transect walks). More recently it has received more attention as a method and received names such as 'walking interview' (Emmel and Clark, 2009) or 'talking-whilst-walking' (Anderson, 2004), with more researchers incorporating space as an analytically important lens for critical research, and more geographers discussing the methodological implications of embodied practices and collaborative methods (including collaboration between places and people) in producing other knowledges.

In this case, walking as a method, with the design of the route and use of the camera, helped put Rafael in control of the activity and hence of his narrative. As the route was not negotiated but completely decided by him, my role was to walk along and listen. This was our variation of the 'walking interview' in the sense that we moved from place to place by bus, but walked around each area (Emmel and Clark, 2009) and were also open to chance encounters. But it went beyond that, as we were drifting from place to place and dwelling in some places, and were talking but also keeping silent, letting some places sink inside us and bring up some memories, and talking a bit more. We talked (and kept quiet), mostly led by Rafael's stories of the places, how he moved to and through them or they called for silence or conversation. As Rebeca Solnit (2001: 5) has explored, the 'art of walking' requires a certain predisposition but also connections between the body, senses, emotions and meanings as we 'wander from plans to recollections to observations'. The group Precarias a la Deriva (2005) and the Counter Cartographies Collective, Dalton and Mason-Deese (2012) call it a 'situated drifting', highlighting its dual characteristic as method of research and of spatial intervention.

The experience of walking with Rafael made me realize first of all that seemingly harmless practices, such as walks in places of remembrance, can become unwelcome threats to remembrance practices. This requires careful consideration of the context, as in Peru, where the HIJXS' places of remembrance have no space in the public eye. Within such limited memory space, the HIJXS find the possibility of territorial markers for their memories in the public space reduced further. Such experience made me wonder about the links between places and being-in-places and memories. Do places suggest or release other memories? Could these disturb the memories we hold so dearly? By walking and being-in-place, memories become more corporeal, they feel closer and with more of our bodies (maybe just different?); they become more embodied, even for those witnessing the doing-memory-in-place.

Walking as reclaiming space was in itself an important albeit ephemeral activity of producing territorial memory markers, making hidden/silenced memories part of the public space even if only between two people. Doing-memory-in-place brought another way of inhabiting those spaces – previously charged with silence and now part of spoken and recorded stories.

It was a way of inserting ourselves into that space in a different position, in turn now producing other stories. At the same time, it is important to consider the problem of unsettling existent remembrance practices that have been carefully constructed as part of survival strategies. For Rafael, 'misplacing memories' becomes ever more problematic in his constant search to reaffirm his story: finding material markers that anchor a story of being the son of a father killed by the police under torture, a story that has been denied as real or rejected as wrong and out of place, becomes an important strategy for himself and his struggle for recognition.

Travelling with Iris to her father's place

And start living with my past as a companion, having it alongside in my present, in my plans for the future, instead of buried deep inside as a weight.

Iris, Havana, Cuba, 2012

The next time I saw Iris was five years after our first encounter, once I returned to Cuba in 2012. I was visiting after my first fieldwork in Peru, and became surprised at how our conversations changed to include more reflections about her father. According to Iris, he had been largely absent in our first conversations, perhaps reflecting his limited presence in her life. Yet place becomes important in the process of connecting with her father's story, making him more present.

In our initial conversations (2007), Iris mentions that not having seen her father's grave, living without knowing the location of his body, made her father more of a disappeared than a deceased. This fed her childhood dreams. 'During that time, I dreamt a lot of my dad. … I imagined he was alive, that he came back for me.' But by 2012, she highlighted how her father's presence in her story had changed. He had become important for her future plans. She made space for him in her life. And somehow his presence was linked to places; the last place he lived and where he was buried.

Iris told me of the several projects she embarked on during her summer breaks to get more involved in her father's story, and involve her father in hers. The first was to interview people who had known her father, as *compañeros de lucha*, and in daily life. She recorded conversations with relatives and *compañeros*. Next, she embarked on a search for his grave. She got from her mother (aunt) Armida the name of the small town in the Cusco region where it was located and an idea of how it might look. Armida, her father's sister, had been the only one present in his quick, quiet burial, and she had blurry memories of an unmarked grave. Iris went nonetheless. Once she returned to Cuba to finish her studies, she had her mind made up on a plan: after becoming a doctor she would move to that same town and do her year of social service there.[7]

The importance she attributed to that specific place, her father's space, for her future plans surprised me. She seemed determined and confident, even I would say slightly stubborn, about being in that place. The way she phrased it made me think she wanted to 'go back' to find a connection with her father, and also be 'of service' to that community. It was not that she was not scared or worried about going to an unknown place, being signalled and stigmatized as '*la hija del tuco*' ('the daughter of a terrorist').[8] It was more that she felt she would have the company of her father (and HIJXS) once she arrived.

This reminded me of another sense of space, 'space to be constantly open to change and becoming, rather than only or mainly as the more settled' (Crouch, 2010: 7). Iris wanted to imagine the possibility of new meanings infused into that place, and experiencing it differently by positioning herself inside those 'social relations [that] constitute a "geometry of power"' (Massey, 1994: 4) ... [in] a dynamic and changing process' (Robertson, 2009: 6) as a practising doctor.

So, I decided to go with her as she followed her father's story the next year during my second phase of fieldwork in Peru (2013). Once there, the first thing she told me was that the place was 'almost magical' for her. Iris felt her father's presence, even his protection, everywhere. She could 'visit' him and easily learnt to talk to him, and imagine him looking at that same sky and *apus*, imagine him walking the same rural roads into the mountains she had to walk, imagine him even tired like her on those long distances to attend to those who had no access to the health centre.

> My main goal, or my only goal, was to be here, close to him. To be where he had been, to walk the ground his feet had walked, and to see the things his eyes had seen. ... I felt closer; somehow, experiencing the same things (like watching the same fireworks against that exact same black pitch sky with no moon) made me part of his life.

For Iris, the awakened magic of the place was also made evident in the amount of people who became drawn to it:

> My dad made me come here and when I finally found him and talked to him in the cemetery, I promised him I would bring my mom Armida

---

[7] Medical students have a mandatory year of social service in public health facilities before becoming fully licensed. The exact location is the result of a lottery, so there was a measure of luck in Iris getting assigned to Cusco.

[8] In Peru the word '*terrorista*' changed in colloquial conversation into '*terruco*', later shortened to '*tuco*' (Aguirre, 2012).

here to visit him, and one day also my mom Lucero. ... And now, so many people have been coming here, my friend, my mom, my sister, my little brother, and now you.

A short story of my time in Cusco with la doctorita

Cusco is a different place from where Iris grew up in the capital's Northern Cone, a dry landscape with bare hills by the coast filled with never-to-be-finished houses too close to the next one. Cusco was a colourful landscape surrounded by lush mountains spotted with coca patches growing in the '*ceja de selva*' (literally, the jungle's eyebrow), which is neither highlands nor jungle but something 'in-between'. This is how Iris felt there, as in a liminal 'borderland' space, where connections were open to be made, charged with 'almost like magic'.

When visiting her father's grave, first she brought plastic flowers, marked the grave with his name, planted some trees (later stolen) and cleaned the area. In following visits, she brought presents, like his favourite cigarettes on his birthday, or a tie on Father's Day. But mostly Iris talked to him 'at length and without interruptions'. She would tell anyone who asked that her father was buried there, that he died in an accident while working there. It didn't feel too far away from reality and that was enough for her.

Soon after her arrival, Iris was called for duty in the middle of the night. She had to go to the police station to inspect and confirm the death of a body that had been found. The situation made her nervous, because it was the same police station in front of which her father had been killed in a clash with the police, and where most likely his body had been taken (for another doctor to inspect and confirm his death). As if history was repeating for her to witness, she felt sick but went on with it, talking to her dad all the way there.

In the search for her father, Iris connects with other stories, but by taking another position. According to her, this time it was not as 'victim' or 'orphan' but as 'doctor'; a figure with granted authority and legitimacy in the community. By becoming the community doctor, she found it possible to position herself differently, which allowed her to reclaim that space as another. In doing so, she could connect a different story to this place/space of loss now, reclaiming it by inhabiting it differently.

Iris found it complicated to explain her experiences in that place. She was attracted to it, but at the same time found it confusing. She wore her white coat and everyone in town called her '*doctorita*', an affective diminutive of doctor used in the Andean communities that I never heard before. This was a place of the elderly and children. The town officials – the doctor, the teachers – were outsiders who struggled to communicate with the Quechua speakers, and translation happened reluctantly – almost as a way to maintain/sustain distance – so she had to learn a few basic words for body parts, pain and numbers. Still, her days were filled with health campaigns in community assemblies, lengthy walks up and down mountains, crossing rivers on rope bridges to reach more remote places, forcing children to stand still to vaccinate them, stopping cars on the few rural dirt roads filled with curves and precipices that made her throw up, on call at night for different emergencies in the communities, including treating a stabbed pig.

These small, seemingly amusing challenges of being a doctor in the mountains became a clearer signal of the structural 'violence' of poverty and exclusion from public health services the day her first patient died. At a meeting between two towns, with no transport or communication (not even mobile phone signal), she attended to a man suffering a stroke. After struggling to resuscitate him there, and finally finding a truck willing to stop in the Quechua-speaking peasant community, she managed to keep him alive until they arrived at the health centre. But the centre had run out of oxygen, and her patient died. Iris was shaken.

As she put it, her year in that small town was not only meant to bring her closer to her father, it had another purpose: 'to see these places, to get to know more of their people'. This in turn contributed to her understanding of a larger reality than her own, '*conocer la gente, el pueblo por los que dio su vida*', to broaden her understanding of the struggle he died for. In a sense, this being-in-place provided her a way to place her story within a larger landscape, and in doing so, it also changed her.

Connecting to other stories, forming a different understanding of her father's life, and of space filled/made with other people's stories, Iris became aware of the multiplicity of stories simultaneously making that space (Massey, 2005), and of how others were affected by the violence. In her year as a doctor, visiting remote communities by foot or motorbike, she would listen to stories about how the war affected people's lives, and how people continued to be afraid of sharing their stories, the problematics of their own actions during the war, and the continuous fear for the effects of a violence that has not passed, that is feared as it might come back, like it had never really left.

The small towns in the Cusco region and its neighbouring peasant communities bear the marks of the internal war. In a conflict whose victims were unequally distributed along geography, class and ethnicity lines, eight out of ten fatalities came from the rural areas (Theidon, 2004). The early literature on the peasants' involvement with political violence portrayed them as passive actors in a political conflict where armed groups[9] strategically exploited the poverty, the divisions within these communities,

---

9   Such studies refer particularly to Sendero Luminoso (Shining Path) whereas the Tupac Amaru Revolutionary Movement (MRTA) is largely absent unless conflated with Shining

and the absence of the state to rally *campesinos* to their cause (Berg, 1994; Degregori, 1994; Isbell, 1994).

Later studies recognized peasants' shifting positions and alliances (González, 2011), including the strategic use of the presence of armed groups to advance their own interests or solve existing conflicts in their favour (Theidon, 2004). Given such complex forms of participation and 'implicated subjects' (Rothberg, 2014), in the aftermath of the conflict peasant (and many other) communities became reluctant to share their memories of the conflict in public spaces or with those considered outsiders. This reluctance also reflected the pain created by remembering, the inability of narrating to be productive and bring justice or resolve inequality, and the disappointments of the TRC's 'failure' to deliver on its promises (Macher, 2007; 2014). It also came from the 'fratricide' nature of the armed conflict, where every community has 'ex-Senderos, sympathisers, widows, *licenciados*, orphans – a volatile social landscape' (Theidon, 2004: 20) where 'there is not too much or too little memory, there are strategies' (EPAF, 2012: 48).

Iris's practice of being-in-place has also opened a space for becoming more connected, and connecting the HIJXS experiences as part of collective ones (beyond hijxs). This in turn changed their story, complicating it and thus complicating their acting in the present with their stories. Places/spaces are changing the way they view their parents' political actions, moving them from an almost celebratory tone to a more nuanced position where the consequences for their families and others become more visible, more relevant, and perhaps more painful.

Iris at 25
Cusco, Peru, 2013

I fantasized with that; perhaps I was a bit too idealistic, but that's what I wanted to be, like my dad and like my mom, you know ... that mix of commitment and adventure. But once I came here, the wound opened. ... I mean, it was always there, but it stayed covered, and for that reason it didn't heal. Now? Now it's an open wound. Since I found him here, the wound opened. And I thought that after all that we lived, after all that suffering, after all that pain ... a pain that didn't happen only to me, or only to us, but a pain that happened to many, many people, many people ... and I think we're still living it even today, because this isn't over, it doesn't end. How it affects us

---

Path, without exploring the MRTA or the differences between the two groups. Mario Meza's doctoral thesis (2012) *El MRTA y las fuentes de la revolución en América Latina* and La Serna's book (2020) *With Masses and Arms: Peru's Tupac Amaru Revolutionary Movement* are notable exceptions.

and those around us, how it goes on, like domino pieces falling one after the other … and that, in many, many lives, is what happened to the country.

Writing with Rafael and Iris

In these specific experiences with Rafael and Iris, memory practices are not just about being-in-place. They are also about allowing ourselves to wander around and dwell on places as memory triggers for our collective memory work, and to occupy space in a different manner with our stories. And, particularly for Iris, with others' stories as well.

As a result of a project to interview those who knew their parents (a joint project between Iris and Rafael), Iris decided not to write her father's life (at least not at the moment). Instead, after moving to that small town in Cusco and entering her father's space, Iris was inspired to write about imagining her father's last minutes of life. Of that, I found the introductory paragraph interesting:

> This is the story I wanted to write; it is not what I THINK/BELIEVE that my father felt in his last minutes of life but instead it is what I WANT him to have thought. I wish these were the thoughts that were in his head when he knew that his death was close. I have pieced together and placed here the information I was able to collect during the interviews I conducted before I met my father's grave. (Iris, 2012; my translation)

Iris and Rafael engaged in particular memory work about the presence/absence of their fathers, places (and being-in-place) are made into devices that create 'communicating vessels'[10] between different stories, between different lives experienced at different times, between that which is considered the real and the imagined.

For Rafael, places are anchors for memory, making possible the fixing of memories in their materiality, removing their instability and thus unreliability. Both elements produce anxiety, alluding to the possibility that his father's memory would vanish (or, as Rafael phrased it, get 'misplaced'). This is an important aspect because it is still difficult to make the state

---

[10] Communicating vessels in literature refers to a writing where story-lines belonging to different time, space or reality levels are/become connected and affect one another, ultimately altering and enriching both (Vargas Llosa, 1997). Used as a metaphor by Breton for how the dreamed/imagined and the real world are both part of a complex system of communicating vessels, it was later painted by Diego Rivera in 1938.

accountable for how his father was killed, and Rafael always faces the urge to fix his memories. For Iris, however, places are devices that produce new memories, or recreate old ones, which infuse her present. She engages in the more creative acts of memory work. By traversing landscapes inhabited by her father she finds connections that allow her to create memories of her own with a father she did not remember before. While new memories are produced by 'visiting' a father's grave, Iris produces a different way of inhabiting space with an awareness of space being populated by a myriad of stories, some still-to-be-told.

The process of 'searching' for remains or traces of their parents has been discussed in the H.I.J.O.S. Argentina literature. Ana Ros describes this process as the necessary mourning of their parents, 'first they have to "know" who they were: they need to "encounter" them only to paradoxically lose them again' (2012: 31). The photographs or others' stories (by relatives or *compañerxs*) are precious objects that the H.I.J.O.S. seek, record and treasure, but 'these are never sufficient, and become another reminder of the impossible encounter' of their loss.

Both Rafael and Iris embark on a search similar to what Ros (2012) described, first by interviewing those who knew their parents, which turned out to be insufficient and pushed them to a second search by being-in-place and moving/traversing through their parents' spaces. More than objects (that is, photographs or others' memories) they look for experiences in particular places, in the form of spatial memory practices that could produce new connections with their parents (or reproduce old ones as for Rafael) as an attempt to engage differently with their loss from the present by doing (walking and telling stories in a city or living as a doctor in a rural community). It is in their different engagements with space that we can glimpse at peculiar connections made between space and memory as well as the ways Rafael and Iris' practices of space may transform them. Iris' transformation is embraced as her search allows her to place her story in a larger/complex space alongside multiple other stories. Rafael is faced with anxiety as his search is for providing a more material effect to his memories instead of their misplacement.

Visiting prison; prisons as precarious spaces

It was Iris who asked me to go to the women's maximum-security prison in Chorrillos, Lima in 2013. She was asking me to 'visit' her mother. It was not the first time it had been suggested, either by one of the HIJXS or by a group of researchers I met in Lima for whom prisons were part of their research projects. Probably my own questions had also led to these suggestions, but despite being curious I had always dismissed them. At the time of my first trip to Peru, I was still trying to maintain a boundary between parents (the previous generation, protagonists during the internal war) and HIJXS (the protagonists in this project).

Such boundary was partly an academic effort to delineate the focus of a project that was already too large and complicated. It also, however, reflected my fears about the potential problems of entering into contact with people formerly linked to the MRTA and consequences for the research and for myself. The possibility of being criminalized under the fuzzy category of 'apologia' of terrorism looms over research projects that inquire into the internal war in Peru. The so-called 'post-conflict' does not share the characteristic of other Latin American countries where former armed groups morphed into political parties participating in electoral politics within the renewed democracies.

In Peru, the armed groups were defeated (exterminated in the case of the MRTA) and remained criminalized even after the war.[11] Living outside Peru and coming from UK academia were positive credentials that contributed to feeling relatively safe, yet at the same time being an outsider (in these same terms), meant that I did not know how researchers navigated this undefined area of research or how to deal with possible surveillance.[12] I had decided to keep a low profile and stay away from spaces such as prisons where my ID would be recorded.

This time it was different, not only because my generation-based border-control efforts had already collapsed, but also because Iris' suggestion was not about visiting prison but about visiting her mother. I felt I had built a support network and with it a slightly better grasp of how to navigate the complicated politics surrounding research projects on the war.[13] Also, Iris' request was hard to refuse as I had already been at everyone else's houses meeting their mothers (and other relatives).

Prison occupies a special 'space' in the HIJXS narratives. Commonly present in their accounts of their lives, it is an oppressive, controlled space, which perhaps paradoxically, also *becomes* their space of freedom, where they no longer have to hide where they come from and their parents' involvement in the MRTA.

---

[11] 'The reconciliation proposal dominant in Peru does not include one of the warring sides, and in opposition to what happened in other countries such as Uruguay and Colombia, here former insurgents are excluded of any dialogue' (Durand, 2015).

[12] See Rojas-Perez (2013) about the continuities of violence in the 'post-conflict' by mobilizing the 'terrorist' figure in political discourse and applying the anti-terrorist legislation, in an expansive manner to criminalize protests.

[13] I thank a collective of women researchers from different nationalities and research affiliations, which started during my brief stay in Lima. We discussed our experiences researching the Peruvian internal war and provided support to each other. Despite the group's brief life, friendships remained and it was key to learning to 'navigate' the politics of research in such context while keeping myself relatively safe.

The prison is a space seemingly devoid of ambiguity. The coercion, the consequences are all too apparent, blame is assigned and repercussions delivered. All is on the table. Outside the prison walls, and before prison, there was/is always the lurking possibility of being punished; the over-presence of a threat. Once inside (almost) everything that could go wrong has already done so. You have already lost control of your agency, your story. It is not that the struggle disappears, just that its actors are out in the open, with its winners and losers.

Since Foucault (1977), prisons cannot be conceived simply as spaces of top-down oppression. He invites us to think of power as a complex network and also as productive. Rather than totalizing spaces, prisons are a terrain of ongoing negotiations of subjectivity and rules. Ugelvik (2014) shows that prisoners reclaim spaces of freedom and (re)construct themselves through a complex array of resistance practices such as spatial transformations, food and self-repositioning. Similar practices emerge in the prison spaces that HIJXS experienced, whereby repressive institutions could become spaces of freedom.

The story of prisons in Peru is one of overpopulated places and limited access to food and health. But it is also one of organized struggle and resistance, often broken violently by the state (in the form of *requisas*, massacres and transfers, even bombing, as in El Fronton in 1986, with approximately 300 killed by the army). According to Rénique (2003), Shining Path sought during the 1980s to transform prisons into 'shining trenches of combat' where prisoners organized their daily lives and conquered the space from within, approximating a military camp where they trained militarily and ideologically for the return to the outside. Their strategy was to subvert the prison's imposed order.

Local authorities eased up the rules the longer they shared daily life in the prison space and co-produced complex networks of exchange and corruption (Valenzuela, 2012), but the central state's response was violent, bombing Sendero-controlled prisons. During Fujimori's time, the approach was to regain control over prisons, and create spaces with limited communication between prisoners, making group activity impossible: a military prison for the leaders (the naval base) and the Yanamayo prison using the 'altiplano as a territory of exile' where new prisons were created (Rénique, 2003: 94). Yanamayo itself locked its prisoners in windowless cells at below freezing temperatures for 23 hours each day. The Peruvian Ombudsman's Office described Yanamayo's regime as 'at odds with our constitutional requirements, international standards and human dignity'. It called for the state to review its practices of 'long confinement in cells, the visit systems with *locutorio*, and the illegal practice that forbids access to any information'. It was Yanamayo's '*carcelería*' that HIJXS experienced and recalled in their early *testimonios* in Cuba.

The *carcelería* isn't just the time in prison. It's mainly the conditions in which people lived there. I'm unsure where the word comes from, I guess from the relatives in *la visita*. It's our word for all things lived because of those prisons, including what we, as relatives, had to put up with. Even now it isn't over, the *carcelería* continues. True, it's now less complicated than at first, now he's in Lima. ... *Carcelería* is what you directly lived, but also knowing all the stories from other *compañeros* ... what their families endured, or so often how their families abandoned them, or how they couldn't see their children, and how you explain to little kids that their dad or mom is in prison condemned for 'terrorism'. (Adelín, Havana, Cuba, 2007)

Prison produced its own language and space, a culture shared between those inside and outside the prisons. The HIJXS' use of '*Carcelería*' seeks to capture how the prisons affect both the people inside and the children and relatives in general outside. It is used also to designate the time served, as in '*el tiempo de carcelería*', which is a particularly interesting broader meaning that includes how 'the visits' are experienced.

In order to confront my problems with belonging (or not) to the HIJXS, I pushed myself to enter such space, to become a 'visitor' and enter a 'shared space' with its own language. When I finally visited, I had all their stories resounding in my head. I asked them what to expect but they had no advice for me, as for them it was the 'normalcy' of prison they grew up with where unpredictable change is a constant. It made me even more aware that I would only be able to retell this time (June 2013) in this particular prison.

At the entrance I gave my ID, which was checked and recorded. This seemingly simple transaction made me uneasy because only a month earlier I obtained my first Peruvian-issued ID. Immediately, you must also say who you are visiting; you evidently get a particular nod when the person is one of the three women formerly involved in the MRTA. It is all very mechanical, slow but with little time to think, just wait attentively for the next procedure: your arm gets stamped three times (no time to mention my chronic pain and the need for gentle handling), three times with different stamps, one saying the prison you are in, the second saying you are a 'visitor' and the last a big letter determining the pavilion you visit. Also, a large number written with thick blue marker: I'm number 129.

Entering has many rules, from the stuff you can bring the prisoners to the things you can have on yourself, plus a dress code. For example, certain fruits that can be fermented are forbidden, although I was told stories of the (in)famous alcohol made out of rice; it seems grapes and pineapple are the targets of this rule. No one knows more about those rules and the changing details than the small shops around the prison where mostly women provide space for storing non-allowed objects (in a regular plastic bag sealed with a regular knot and numbered especially for you). They share their knowledge of the things you should bring to people inside and those you should not. Most valuable of all, they will rent you the appropriate outfit, because women visiting prison must wear a skirt or dress; trousers are not allowed. This bizarre rule is enacted in the most bizarre place, right outside prison, where women change trousers for long skirts in makeshift changing rooms divided by curtains inside small dark shops. The women running the shop will even advise which skirts suit you and, when you are wearing inappropriate shoes (shoelaces are not allowed), recommend renting matching flip-flops.

I can hear the HIJXS' voices in my head. It must be understood that conditions nowadays are nothing like the 1990s under the Fujimori regime with its faceless judges in military courts. There are no traces now of the *locutorios* and no comparison between the Chorrillos prison today and the naval base prison where Iris' mother was kept for five years and Miguel's father remains, or Yanamayo where Abel and Adelín visited their father. I remember Abel's words that the history of imprisonment was 'a history of struggle … prisoners were not just sitting locked up in there; they were in constant daily struggles to improve conditions, for access to basic rights, and territorial struggles' (Abel, Havana, Cuba, 2007).

Even in those harsher times, HIJXS wrestle the prison space from its oppressiveness. In some cases, it was the only space in which they got to know their parents. Thus, they not only remember the control and humiliations as they crossed from outside to inside the prisons, but also remember it as a space of socialization and learning, a space of joy shared with their loved ones. I remember Miguel (Havana, Cuba, 2007) mentioning how the visits were joyful for his sister as a little child, a space for sharing with her father and others, mostly painting and being the only child entering the naval base. And Abel's memories:

> Every time I saw my dad, it was a happy time; the long trips didn't matter, nor the *soroche* [altitude sickness], the freezing cold, the cheap hostels, the bad food, the army soldiers, the waiting, the mistreatment at the gates, all their arbitrary rules, walk over here and not there, all the hushing, all the stripping for the check-ups feeling their hands everywhere. … I saw him … well, through the *locutorio* [tight metal grid separating visitors from interns], but we talked and he was surviving … and it made me happy. (Abel, Havana, Cuba, 2017)

Again and again the HIJXS' *testimonios* remind me of what their relatives made of the prison space, and how they learnt about resistance and creating their own space even inside places such as prisons, designed to control all aspects of their lives. And how painting, chess games or meals became activities for sharing and learning in that 'visiting' space. References to the worst conditions of incarceration or the hard-fought improvements in such conditions were retold with humour. A lesson on how laughter and joy could pierce the confinement, the sadness and the rage, and transform the 'visiting' space into a space of hope.

There was also the parents' simultaneous struggle to resist and transform the prison space into one where it was safer for the HIJXS to be; safer than the outside as grown-up children of '*terrorista* X', as the hegemonic post-war discourse continues to construct their parents. Once they crossed the entrance, inside, their parents become '*políticos*' (Valenzuela, 2012), political prisoners. In some cases they have also gained certain respect after more than two decades living alongside other prisoners and authorities.

If Yanamayo was built to break their will (Rénique, 2003), those imprisoned aimed to slowly break the authorities' domain. From small acts of disobedience and defiance to hunger strikes and mutiny, prisoners had small (temporary) victories that created spaces (albeit limited) of freedom within the prison walls. Early on, the HIJXS remembered proudly how their parents' spirits could not be broken or how only inside the prison walls could they take part in commemorative activities, where the collective spirit was felt as a strength rather than defeat. But those are stories from another time when they were children and their parents were younger, much different to the current picture where the prison population has reduced and also grown old and ill after close to 30 years of imprisonment.[14]

Strangely, the prison was also conceived as a space – unwittingly – co-constructed by the prisoners and the authorities that became 'freer' for the HIJXS. In it, the HIJXS are temporarily freed from the burden of having to manage the legacy of their parents and navigate the complicated life 'outside' with the stigma of 'children of terrorists'. Prison is a safe space for their stories; although it retains the oppressive quality present in their *testimonios*, it also gives respite from the daily conflicting problematics of not knowing what to say or how to say it.

Still, such spaces of freedom are precarious spaces. Things change from one day to another. New rules are created, old customs altered. A change in local authorities can alter years of co-existence. A change in government even worse. A review of a book by a former MRTA prisoner described it like this:

> [E]very so often, when a politician hungry for popularity revives the ghost of terrorism, the former [and current] prisoners see their daily lives and their processes of reintegration affected, their benefits annulled

---

[14] Of the former prisoners that ended their 20+-year-sentences a few died of cancer within a couple of years of their release, including Abel and Adelin's father, and Willy's aunt.

[parole or regime change over the years], their assets seized, their possibilities of teaching forbidden, or when they are foreigners they are expelled from the country with no possibility of return, disregarding that they have families in Peru. (Durand, 2015)

Once I am inside the Chorrillos prison, it does feel like a space of small freedoms; we can talk, we can laugh ... sometimes lowering our voices, but still conversations flow. So much so that I almost forget I am inside a prison, little details remind me where I am and what this place means: incarceration, confinement, the opposite of freedom ... and I feel embarrassed, slightly ashamed of feeling good here. ... This is not gratuitous ... there has been and continuous to be hard work to make it a 'safe' space. Even the TRC acknowledged the problems of Fujimori's prison regime:

> The penitentiary policy designed by the previous regime was aimed at exercising a double penalty on those convicted of terrorism. This was not only in the execution of the sentence, but in a series of spatial, temporal and physical restrictions, not only for inmates but also for the family and even state personnel in charge (INPE or PNP). As the purpose is rehabilitation of inmates, certain prisons should not continue in operation and inmates should be taken to other prisons. (TRC, 2003c: 167–168)

'In' prison, HIJXS then occupy a sort of 'borderland' space. They are not prisoners themselves, yet they must enter prisons to see their relatives (in some cases more than one). The 'visits', the 'transit' through the prison space, the temporary spatial inhabiting stays with them; it lingers and it colours the way they understand the outside, or better said blurring the distinction between outside and inside, since *carcelería* does not have a clear spatial fix, it does not only apply to the prisoners inside, or even the visitors inside, but extends its reach beyond. *Carcelería* further colours the way the HIJXS construct and understand the political, the forms and (im)possibilities of doing politics and their activism; an activism that lives with the spectre of imprisonment (and its companion, torture).

In Argentina the clandestine detention centres had 'porous borders' with society so that the effects of terror would spread through society (Schindel and Colombo, 2014). Peru's maximum-security prisons are not clandestine, but the 'rule of law' for prisoners and relatives alike seem capricious, constantly changing, producing a precarious space. The borders are at the same time fixed and porous, and sometimes the prison's fear effects can be felt more strongly at the entrance, or even outside, than inside.

When I am about to leave, it feels like going back to reality as if only now I am recovering my senses, and my heart sinks as I queue at the exit and a little more when those gates close behind me. The border between inside and outside is not fuzzy or blurry, but neat and large, made of heavy hard metal, topped with barbed wire, and guarded by armed people in uniform. Only outside though, I look over my shoulder, and have the strange feeling that someone might have seen me, and could follow me. Yes, I am slightly paranoid. My impulse is to keep moving, and return to my low-profile strategy. ... Am I under surveillance? Am I surveilling myself? Is this the self-disciplining thing Foucault taught us about?

I promise to return but I do not. I learn two years later that the rules have changed once again and if anyone wants to visit, they must be registered on a list submitted by each prisoner and approved by the prison authorities. I ask if such a list can be amended and names added later; no one knows.

Memory practices and the testimonial spaces/places

Testimonial work typically conceives of testimonial spaces as produced through the act of telling-and-listening. When, back in Peru, we experienced difficulties in recreating those safe spaces through the formal acts of recording conversations, we ventured out, into a 'doing and being-in-place'. This changed my writing by becoming aware of the entanglements between memory and spaces/places. I no longer wrote the prison as a memory space to be glimpsed, with its terrors, from the recorded testimonials, but as an embodied experience. No longer shielded by the safe distance of the recordings, I could inhabit the porous/fixed borderlands that the prison produces. Perhaps, in that second phase of fieldwork, I was trying to run away from writing as academic practice, from constantly connecting the theoretical and the lived. Instead of creating the secluded spaces where memories could be recorded and then written down, I wandered around, moved through spaces, and got lost, activities that became in themselves a method. In doing so, we occupied spaces differently with our stories, we made room for our stories but also allowed space to transform us. Particularly with Iris, an 'almost' magical, productive power of space became visible.

Testimonio in itself has also been seen as challenging the spaces/places of knowledge. Haig-Brown (2003) even discussed it as 'impossible knowledge', a type of knowledge that lives 'outside the walls of academe' and can be encountered in 'unaccustomed places'. Testimonial practices then are seen as creating spaces for other knowledges possible, and still the place of *testimonio* within academic research remains a precarious space. Furthermore, back in Peru, I felt there was neither material nor discursive space available for them/ us and their/our stories, and this fuelled my/our impulse to co-construct and co-embody new testimonial places/spaces for placing their/my stories within the larger landscape of memories in the country.

The space-aware memory practices of Rafael and Iris remind me of different practices of doing *testimonio* that co-exist in the HIJXS space. There is a search for realist accounts that can provide a much-needed fixture, turning fleeting unstable memories into fixed materialities to relate to. And at the same time, a search for practices that release memory from its realist account to provide space for creative writing which may open up to the possibility of a life with new memories. Both ways of doing *testimonio* appear at different moments in the conversations with the HIJXS, and in the practices we engaged during my visits to Peru. If moving through spaces/ places produced renewed practices of memory work, it also made us more aware of the changing character of silences and secrecy.

10

Silences, Secrets and Clandestine Lives

This chapter explores the presence of the absence; the silences and secrets in the HIJXS' testimonial narratives and the lives that follow. Here, I present a possible account (among many) of the ways in which (writing) the HIJXS *testimonios* negotiated silences and the use of secrecy. My emphasis is not on revealing the content of such silences and secrets (González, 2011), a departure from 'interpretation' well-established in the *testimonio* scholarship (Sommer, 1994), but on the changing relationships with silences in each *testimonio*. In acknowledging the presence/absence of certain silences and hushed voices, I explore what silences were doing, and the excuses they provided for other conversations.

Testimonio has an uneasy relationship with silence and secrets. At first sight, its very existence relies on a refusal to keep silent about (the state's) 'secret' practices of oppression. *Testimonio* practice itself is considered a move against lives (and stories) that are repressed and silenced. It embodies a promise to 'testify', to break silence and 'seems to offer itself transparently' (Sommer, 1991: 51). Yet, Sommer (1994) argues, holding *testimonio* accountable for transparency misreads its complexity. In *Rigoberta's Secrets*, Sommer examines the famous closing lines of Menchú's *testimonio*: 'I'm still keeping secret what I think no-one should know. Not even anthropologists or intellectuals, no matter how many books they have, can find out all our secrets' (Menchú quoted in Sommer, 1991: 33). That Menchú protects communal secrets can be read as a strategic narrative move, almost cautionary, remarking the distance between her community and the reader. Such strategic silences also contain the seeds of another resistance to the particular 'violence of the ethnographic encounter' (Salazar, 2013: 102) and the general expectation of a confessional narrative that is often placed on *testimonio* (Sommer, 1994; Nance, 2006).

Testimonio scholarship has thus travelled from 'surveillant readings of unreliable texts to incompetent readers of resistant texts' (Sommer, 1994).

Such a journey echoes broader epistemological reflections on silence. Mazzei's (2007) concept of 'inhabited silences' urges researchers to give up finding the truth of the silences. She warns that there is no methodology that can make all intelligible the 'written or unwritten, silent or spoken' (Mazzei, 2007: 26). Lather (2000a) also draws important 'lessons of undecidability and language', pointing out that the narrators are paradoxically both unreliable and bearers of knowledge, navigating their (narrative) way through discontinuities, ruptures and contingencies that traditional research downplays in 'data' (Lather, 2000a: 158–159).

Accompanied by these ideas, the *postalitas* can be thought of as re-presentational devices that allow further inquiry into the negotiations of narrating speech and silences. The following *postalita* accounts for my first encounter with Miguel, who at first was reluctant to talk, and resistant to recording.

Miguel at 20
Havana, Cuba, 2007

I'm going to tell you my story, but some things I cannot talk about, because it's not my story, you know ... it's my parents', and many more. I can talk about my dad; he's public ... imprisoned ... but not Elena. You learn these things but now it's weird, because WE want to tell our stories but we can't tell everything. It's not safe ... and it's not about me. I don't know.

It's hard ... if you want to hear about me, still I won't tell you the bad parts. I mean not how it has affected me personally. I don't want to talk about that; I don't want to give them something so they can say I am damaged because my parents were in the MRTA [Tupac Amaru Revolutionary Movement].

This *postalita* accounts for some instances during my first recorded encounter with Miguel, and to think with that conversation about specific narrative moves. I looked into writing about how the boundaries of our testimonial work were delineated during the testimonial encounter. The specific narrative moves establish what can be said and what cannot; what Miguel at that moment was unwilling to say because of the way it might be used or interpreted against him or those he cares about.

As a narrative form that bears witness to people's lives at the margins (Beverley, 2005) *testimonio* is made public as part of their survival strategies (Yúdice, 1996). The body of literature discussing Latin American *testimonio*[1]

---

[1]   Despite its circulation since the 1960s, it only entered academia in the mid 1980s, and became relevant in education through the 1990s. Translated at its best as testimonial 'literature' or 'narrative' it remained known in the original word, *testimonio* (Gugelberger, 1996).

is riddled with the controversies it triggered on entering academia. Its 'authenticity' was challenged, fuelling debates on issues of representation and the politics of *testimonio*. Post-colonial and postmodern scholars (Yúdice, 1996; Denegri, 2003; Nance, 2006) problematized *testimonio*'s reification within academia, portraying the institutionalization of *testimonio* as an act of appropriation that took away its transgressiveness.[2]

The acts by the narrators/protagonists of retaining control over their own narrative and 'keeping secrets' have also been part of the academic conversation. The latter is in line with some understandings of *testimonio* that were elaborated in response to the controversies over Menchú's *testimonio*. If *testimonios* are 'punctuated by silences' (Salazar, 2013), it is important to ask what is it that they do during the ethnographic encounters (González, 2011). Our testimonial encounters, as glimpsed in Miguel's *postalita*, point to three cross-cutting issues: concerns over ownership of the story; the safety/ risks for those involved; and political intentionality. Their weight is uneven across the *testimonio*, and so is my attention to them.

Rather, I explore the stories that 'struck a chord' in me (Speedy, 2008: 110), or the one whose 'reverberations' could be felt in following conversations (Clandinin et al, 2012). In so doing, I highlight the shape silences took given certain conditions (that is, legal/judicial issues or party politics); particular moments in the HIJXS' lives (that is, death or new romantic relationships), or the peculiar negotiations between speech and silence that took place at the moment of our individual or collective conversations, negotiations reflecting my direct questions, plain boredom, the presence of someone else, or suspicions over the presence of the recording device. The reasons do not matter as much as the way silences and secrecy worked in the testimonial practice and how they became excuses for continuing the conversations about their/our changes, as absences that became present or presences that became absent in the continuing negotiations between speech and silence.

Whose story is it?

Miguel's *postalita* exposes an internal contradiction regarding ownership of the story: does the story of the HIJXS' past belong to them or their parents, the ones involved in the internal war? It touches an issue that remains unresolved in narrative and life history research, and the ethics of narrating one's life,

---

[2]   Lather proposes going 'against Western tendencies to explore, interpret, understand, empathize, assimilate. The problems raised by presumptive, masterful understanding are both epistemological and ethical ... an ethical reminder of difference that locates meaning elsewhere, beyond translation' (Lather, 2000a: 156).

one that necessarily involves interactions with others, often in intimate spaces: do we need our relatives' 'consent' for the narration of our lives?

The issue goes beyond this narrative ethical concern, and moves into the territory of second-generation memories, in what Hirsch (2008) called 'post-memory' in working with children of Holocaust survivors. Are these memories theirs, or do they belong to the first generation? In our case the question is, are HIJXS the protagonists of the *testimonio*?

The question is important because *testimonio* is commonly described as a first-person account by a witness/protagonist of the events narrated (Beverley, 2004). Similarly, oral history research (based on/led by testimonial narratives) is conducted with the protagonists. Susana Kaiser's (2005) oral history research with young Argentineans' memories of state terror, for instance, offers a disclaimer about including her book within an oral history collection, because it does not resort to 'first-hand memory' about the events. Kaiser instead employs 'postmemories', changing the focus to how younger people make sense of such past events (a parent's traumatic experiences) in the present (2005: ix). In contrast, Mariana Eva Perez challenges the distinction underpinning 'postmemory' to search for 'new categories that can account for what this group of former child victims has lived *first-hand*' (Perez, 2013: 6; emphasis in original). She questions the idea that the 'so-called second generation' speaks of traumatic events of others instead of its own.[3]

For me, the HIJXS testimonial narratives, my writings, Miguel's *postalita*, are their/our stutterings to establish precisely that: What story we are referring to? Is it about Miguel's parents or is it about Miguel himself growing up with a father in the MRTA during Peru's internal war? Is it even possible to make such a distinction? What is the story and what is the HIJXS' place in it?

The HIJXS' *testimonios* constitute a (re)working through these questions, a back-and-forth movement from a *testimonio* about their parents' political life and state repression to figuring out the relationships between their own life experiences and those of their relatives. This movement includes reworking questions such as how the HIJXS lived state repression as children (and continue to do so), and the effects of torture and imprisonment on their parents, but also on themselves. But this is not solely about childhood stories. Revisiting the *testimonios* during my fieldwork in Peru, I heard more stories about the HIJXS' political lives, how living with state repression, carrying a stigma, and the clandestine lives of their parents continue to be

---

[3]   Perez proposes the categories of 'former child victims' and 'transgenerational transmission of trauma' in Argentina to reflect 'the particular experience of being raised by grandparents or other relatives also affected by the disappearance of the parents' (Perez, 2013: 14).

felt within their activism and even shape it; first-hand experiences not only of the past (Perez, 2013) but also of the present. Silences and secrecy are a big and lingering part of those effects.

HIJXS' changing stories highlight the shortcomings of the term 'postmemory' as a useful analytical category that promises closure. While everything eventually goes back to the parents, the HIJXS stubbornly refuse to settle all questions, precisely because they cannot be settled – as if embracing the category of 'child victims' and fleshing out the traumas of 'first-hand' experiences would do away with the worries over what and whose story it is, as if the HIJXS could neatly separate our experiences from our parents'.

Such stories of state repression are much more generationally entangled than that. Our testimonial process bears witness to the difficulties of fitting into neat categories that define whose experiences and whose memories matter (or which are the 'real' ones – connected to the experience – and which the 'post' memories – farther removed from the experience). For the HIJXS, the testimonial process does not mean they had already figured out whose story it was and therefore what can be said. In their multiple instances and conversations over time and space, it became instead a figuring out of what the story was about, where (if at all) the victim discourse fitted in it, as well as which silences/secrets could be broken or discussed and which ones remained silent.

Here it becomes important to note that Miguel's *postalita* also contains the refusal to speak of how he has been affected personally, seemingly against Perez's suggestion of a category of 'former child victims'. By sustaining silences, Miguel's *postalita* is perhaps performing a refusal to identify himself as victim.

Adelín's *testimonio* never mentions the idea of victimhood but instead explores at length the impact on her family life, her brother, mother, aunt and uncle, cousins and (half-)sister. Listening to her for the first time, I felt the texture of a strong denouncing voice, proudly claiming her father's legacy by first and foremost defining herself as 'the daughter of a political prisoner', from an entire family of 'political prisoners' at some point or another. Her *testimonio* echoes what Fiona Ross (2001) observed in the South African Truth and Reconciliation Commission (TRC) testimonies. Women's narratives, she argued, demanded different hearings; an ear for how silences shape the narratives:

[S]he did not identify herself as a victim but as someone imparting expert knowledge. Her credibility as a witness was predicated on her knowledge and the way she was able to present it. ... The information was stark, presented linearly, and with emotion held in check. ... Testimony of this kind located the speaker as someone who 'knows' and who has valuable information to impart. ... Their testimonies do not directly impute victimhood to self. (Ross, 2001: 259)

Listening to Adelín involved witnessing a delicate redrawing of her (and her family's) private space; a careful guarding of her stories that I brought up in subsequent revisiting encounters. There, Adelín laughed at the ways she pushed aside questions she considered irrelevant for the *testimonio* at first. One of them was related to her father's 'other daughter'. A first easy reading was that she did not want to 'stain' her father's public image. But the conversation moved towards Adelín's concern for how the boundaries of her private life were blown apart during the most repressive times when her father was arrested. The strain that the father's affair and revelation of a half-sister brought to the family life were enormous, but became worse because there was no respect for their private life. The police and prison officers both exposed and used their family life against them. This was a double betrayal that left Adelín with no possibility of dealing with her feelings or talking about it with her father. There was neither time nor place to process: 'it was stolen from us', said Adelín.

In our conversations over the years, I learnt to set aside my initial frustration at Adelín's safeguarding of her stories. Instead I saw the importance of performing certain silences as seeking to re-establish dignity and deal with shame (Jelin, 2012); an attempt to redraw and mark spaces of intimacy not to be exposed to others. Adelín's 'secrets' can also be seen as a way to sustain social distance with the imagined audience, to rebuild fences that will keep others out. This is a common trait after state repression (torture in particular) and how it becomes inscribed on bodies, breaking the private/ public cultural divide, leaving survivors with a paradox of rebuilding intimacy through silences and at the same time the need for a public narrative to be shared with an 'other'. 'Silences in personal narratives are, at this point, fundamental' (Jelin, 2012: 141). Some experiences of horror and pain cannot be articulated in language, but this does not always mean they are unrepresentable. Sometimes people 'create silence' in agentic ways, in acts of 'refusal to give experience words, in the ability to do something with the experience (i.e. to hold it inside, silent)' (Ross, 2001: 272).[4]

Adelín at 26
Havana, Cuba, 2007

My dad has been a political prisoner for 14 years. Four of my relatives have been or still are in prison: my dad, my uncle, my aunt and a cousin

---

[4] Ross went beyond writers of the Holocaust who consider experiences of mass violence unrepresentable, and followed Veena Das' argument of silence as an expression of women's agency. Thus, producing silence should be accounted as representation.

... and Carlos, who was killed. My parents never told me anything about this, I just grew up in it and you just know.

You know what? I don't know ... not talking. The only talk I remember was with my mom when my dad was caught but I was already 13. I was scared when my mom went asking for him. The rule was that they could tell you they had them but won't let you see them for seven days ... everyone knew that was the torturing period. The police also told us he had his wife with him ... and that's how we found out he had another family ... all along. ... I hated him, but I couldn't hate him, I couldn't even tell him. ... It's OK now.

Adelín became more open to sharing those stories once her father finished his prison sentence and returned to their house, and once Adelín had built a relationship with her (half-)sister. Then that story became part of her narrative and talking became possible again, as did (re)constructing relationships outside prison. Silences that built fences were less needed. Perhaps pain was dislocated elsewhere, and these conversations gained more space. Perhaps the story of her father's secret child became non-exceptional as other HIJXS discovered stories of secret half-siblings as well. When I asked Adelín, she laughed and said with a recriminating tone, 'They were all terrible husbands ... all of them.' And right there I saw another line redrawn between the politics of social justice and equality outside and inside the homes, as if Adelín had expected them to fit and now acknowledged (albeit less painfully) that it was not the case, at least not for the previous generation.

Willy's silences cut even deeper inside the home. In his *testimonio*, I wrote a detailed account about sustained silences; about a family dedicated to preserving secrets, even from each other. My writing of Willy's *testimonio* reflected what I imagined as the result of all sides of the war co-existing in one family. Sometimes secrets are held as a generational divide with certain transgressions allowed over time. When your family contains all the main characters in the war at different moments – a father in the Navy, an aunt in the MRTA, and another relative in Shining Path – then silences are not worked through but instead there is a muteness that leads to isolation.

This way of sustaining silences might be an allegory of the country's way of dealing with the internal war through stillness; a reticent voice that is produced only under pressure, when unavoidable, and only to return to silence immediately after. Willy's experience is hardly exceptional. Uccelli et al (2013) documented how new generations that did not live the internal war learn about it by 'contagion' and not open conversation.

Gradually, especially after his return to Peru, Willy was allowed 'entrance' into additional family secrets. Different relatives shared stories in one-to-one talks at unexpected times. Still, Willy could not have open conversations with them about the internal war or other sensitive matters. In line with Taussig's idea of 'public secrets' which are made of stuff that is privately known but collectively denied and where the most important thing is 'knowing what not to know' (1999: 51), Willy learnt what he was not supposed to talk about.

The question of what and whose story it is had no easy answer for Willy. Which side of the multiple stories uneasily co-habiting in his family was he to tell? Which secrets to keep? Was the story of his uncle dying of AIDS relevant to the *testimonio*? It was, after all, another display of the way his family kept secrets as well as an example of the 'secretly familiar' (Taussig, 1999) they all knew but no one talked about. It was for Willy as frustrating as the other secrets; those closer to the internal war. The testimonial process provided him the possibility of opening up and sustaining conversations outside his family; of constructing a story of his own. Still, he was constantly careful when shifting from one-to-one conversations to the collective memory work, where he retained certain silences about his father. Thus, the testimonial process could be seen as Willy's testing ground, a way of experiencing and experimenting with a story. *Testimonio como una experiencia.*

Eventually, Willy distanced himself from the group. This seemed to be temporary, as it had happened with many others at different moments of their lives. But Willy's unfinished studies and his ongoing economic survival efforts that moved him to the provinces weighed heavily. Perhaps, for some in the group, the memory work with the testimonials was exhausted, and like Willy, they recreated their lives the way they could at the moments we worked on it, and then moved on. The group can also be seen then as a temporary stage in the HIJXS' lives, something they would also grow out of. Although the group remains an important affective reference, being actively involved is no longer crucial. Other concerns such as employment, economic struggles and starting a new family gained priority. After voicing and narrating, there is a renewed space to live with silences in a different way, perhaps less oppressively and more comfortably seated next to us.

Traversing Willy's *testimonio*, as much as with the others, there remains the question of persistent silences that reflect 'clandestine' childhoods. We absorbed secrecy from childhood in the clandestine or semi-clandestine lives of our parents (or other close relatives). In the *testimonio* work, this legacy produced not only particular silences but also particular modes of living with silences. At first, HIJXS shared mostly what could be made public. In the recorded 'testimonial space' we did not touch on stories that could not leave the HIJXS circle. Years later, while revisiting, more stories were shared and even recorded, with some 'corrections' or 'context' stories added. These 'new' or 'corrected' stories provided more nuance, with fuller roles for some actors, more complex twists, and even contradictory understandings of the HIJXS. But not all silences were broken. There is also that which is not silenced but hushed, in low voice, what is half heard, what is half seen, behind doors, adult conversations that leak to the children's world.

It's like you know, but you don't know, know … until you find out, and you realize you always knew or kind of knew, you know? (Miguel, Lima, Peru, 2012)

Martín Kohan (2014) referred to something similar as the *'entrever'* (something like a glimpse, literally 'seeing in-between') which is present in the new documentaries being produced by hijxs in Argentina such as *Infancias Clandestinas* ([*Clandestine Childhood*], 2012). Here the hijxs are no longer those who did not know or see anything, but those who caught a glimpse and built their knowledge on those glimpses, and thus also experienced the clandestine or semi-clandestine lives of their parents or other relatives.

[T]hat's what I remember, but I don't know if I remember very well. It sounds too horrible, so it's hard to believe that's how it happened, but I have it as a vivid memory, so, I don't know if it can be included or not. (Rafael, Lima, Peru, 2012)

Referring to the creative ways in which a new generation approaches memory work in the Southern Cone, Gatti (2011) wrote of 'loud silences and serious parodies' to reflect on the necessary language innovations to confront the 'catastrophe' (referring specifically to forced disappearance), characterized by breaking the bonds between sign and object, and where meaning no longer makes sense. Similarly, Mariana Eva Perez (2012) proposes a more playful take on language in the face of extreme violence. Both are 'children of the disappeared' from Argentina and Uruguay, although both position their writings outside HIJXS organizations. Both have particular writing styles that break traditional assumptions about the relationship between language and the world. They have a keen sense for the use of irreverent forms and humour. However, incorporating humour has proven challenging for me, as it often loses its nuance in translation – from Spanish to English, across cultures in general, and especially from HIJXS contexts to the wider world.

What knowledge is then possible in the middle of uncertainty? Taussig (1993) suggested the idea of an 'epistemic murk' by reflecting on the famously Colombian phrase *'in Colombia nunca se sabe'*. The phrase reflects a double meaning; one as 'you never know' that which is impossible to grasp in a place of terror, and another 'you can never be sure', that which keeps moving and changing. Both are useful ways to think about the knowledge possible from clandestine childhoods. There is a peculiar role of the 'affective' and inheritance of emotions in the HIJXS production of another knowledge. We grew up with José Martí's quote, 'It had to be done in silence',[5] in our

---

[5] 'It had to be done in silence, and indirectly, because to achieve certain things, they must be kept under cover; to proclaim them for what they are would raise such great difficulties

homes. Maybe not all knew of it, but we somehow had a grasp of it; that silence was necessary and was there to stay.

Nevertheless, respecting some silences creates a space of 'unchecked assumptions'; the things we do not talk about become largely unchecked and 'murkier'. These are things we do not even discuss among ourselves; things that have to do with our parents' actions during the internal war, the uses and consequences of violence, and also our emotions around loss in the present (that is, those who died, those who remain in prison, those who shared a generation's mindset). These, scholarship on Argentina's H.I.J.O.S. has approached as the 'taboo of the war' (da Silva Catela, 2009; Ros, 2012; Sosa, 2012; Tello, 2012). As the HIJXS positions changed with time, the taboo, if not as strong, remains. It is this part of the inherited silences that I consider problematic. It renders it difficult to identify and even discuss, for example, the effects that silence had (and continues to have) as political practice in the concentration and abuse of power, and in the production of vertical and hierarchical political practices.

Such clandestine practices were not learnt in adulthood, as they were for the previous generation, but instead by living alongside it or sometimes inside it since early childhood. Inherited silences reduce our possibilities of learning from those histories, from where we come from. Many of those things are difficult to discuss openly, emotionally painful, and hard to explain or even to find a vocabulary that could make fitting them into words possible. Those things clash with what is possible to enunciate in the present political landscape, and with the affective links to that history. Moreover, they complicate lives, and how the HIJXS positions towards past actions of the parents that they disagree with or even condemn. How do we separate the affective side that links them to that history? Is it necessary? Is it even possible, given the enduring concerns over safety? Why would they have to give explanations for something they were not really part of, anyway?

Breaking silence, loosening safety measures

For the HIJXS, testimonial work guided by the explicit purpose of making the stories publicly available raises complex questions over safety. There is a constant awareness of state repression and of the clandestine mode in which the previous generation lived its politics. The post-war context did little to change this anxiety. The fact that the armed groups and those who participated in them continue to be criminalized and stripped of basic rights, creates a problematic context that the HIJXS have difficulties navigating in the present.

---

that the objectives could not be attained' is a phrase extracted from a letter by José Martí from 1895, which was turned into a slogan during the Cuban revolution and later formed the basis for a television series and graphic novel.

The testimonial project and the writing of this book have not escaped such a problematic (but dwelled on it and at times have even been paralysed by it). The problem has been how to contribute to the HIJXS testimonial project and also to my own inquiries without compromising their safety. Gready (2008) reflects on the South African TRC's public archives to draw attention to the disempowering effects for the protagonists of testimonies turned objects of research. I have considered his suggestions by sustaining a relationship with those involved in this testimonial project. I also attempt to sidestep the ethical-political dilemmas by working with the testimonials and their protagonists, and the reflections our encounters produced instead of analysing them. Still, I remain anxious and worried about the impossibility of controlling the uses and abuses that might occur once the testimonial narratives are publicly available.

I found some comfort in Josselson's (1996) idea that 'being worried' is a vital characteristic of an ethical relationship in narrative research; a necessary part of a 'reflexive relational ethics' (Etherington, 2007) and commitment to those participating in the research to be explored in dialogue with them and exposed in the written text. Such 'ethics of care' developed by feminist researchers as a framework for working with violence against women. Worrying makes researchers careful about going too far, a necessity when *testimonio* is conceived as 'an act, a tactic by means of which people engage in the process of self-constitution and survival' (Yúdice, 1996: 46).

A series of stories around the HIJXS experiences and what is deemed legal could not be written in their original form. Yet, these were crucial to our discussions and understanding of silences. Faced with the impossible task of breaking the silence while safeguarding it, of revealing my reflections without compromising the safety of those involved, I opted for creativity. I anonymized and fictionalized details in specific stories, weaving them together to create a composite character named Lat. In crafting Lat's story, I selected stories where my listening was attuned to how silences are mobilized as survival strategies: stories and details that must remain hidden, especially in lives marked by dealings with the judicial system.

The Peruvian judicial system leaves little room for blurry lines or challenges to the mainstream narrative. In it you are either innocent or not. The case of the La Cantuta massacre illustrates this starkly. Under the Fujimori regime in July 1992, the military death squad Grupo Colina disappeared then killed nine students and a professor of La Cantuta public university. Found guilty in 1993–1994, Grupo Colina was pardoned by military court under Fujimori's 1995 Amnesty Law. After the fall of the regime, Fujimori's own trial (2007–2009) then decreed La Cantuta as crimes against humanity. During the long legal battle, the media and defence attorneys cast doubt over the 'innocence' of the students, raising suspicions of 'terrorism'. The final sentence (2009) stated 'categorically' the 'innocence' of the victims, establishing that they 'were not linked to terrorist activities of PCP-SL

[Shining Path], nor were members of that criminal organisation' (Sullivan, 2010: 837). Their relatives and human rights organizations applauded the sentence, seeing the reclaiming of the victims' 'innocence' as a reparative measure to remove stigma and intimidation that weighed heavily on their families (Burt, 2009). Others questioned the necessity of declaring their 'innocence', as if this were a precondition to access justice.

Such a stark distinction, even in the prosecution of state crimes, leaves no space for justice for those who do not fit the 'innocent' category. It denies rights or recognition as political subjects by turning them into 'terrorists' who can be killed (Rafael's father) or illegally detained and imprisoned for years with no evidence (Lat's family). Although the judicial system has been changing over the years, the HIJXS still perceive it as a very limited space. And the Peruvian TRC failed to open up that space. It elicited testimonies without considering that these are 'partial and subjective accounts of people's experiences, based on personal memories and interpretations' (Coxshall, 2005: 209). Without ethnographic work, it is not possible to understand the processes that constituted such narratives – from where they are enunciated, their entanglements of kinship and conflict, their necessary silences (Theidon, 2010) – and thus the complexities of the political violence.

Rather, the TRC created a dilemma as its public hearings assumed truth-telling in a 'model of speech acts that cannot incorporate silence' (Coxshall, 2005: 212). It did not consider that people refuse to provide their testimonials in public hearings in order to protect themselves (safety concerns like in the making of Lat's stories) and their sense of dignity, or to reduce their already exposed personal vulnerability (redrawing their private lives like Adelín's). The public hearings made it hard to consider silence as an aspect of testimonial narratives. In part, the TRC brushed over silences and 'ambiguous truths' because of the contested context in which it worked (Theidon, 2010). Under attack from the very start, it produced testimonies that continue to be questioned for their 'credibility'. That suspicion has also entered the recent trials against the military in the Accomarca case where testimonies of relatives are dismissed as evidence because they are considered biased (Burt and Rodríguez, 2015).

In contexts where persecution and prosecution, as well as social stigma, are not matters of the past, silences must also be considered as carefully devised strategies, delineating the limits of 'breaking the silence'. This, scholars have shown, has often been the case with women involved in TRC processes. In South Africa, Ross (2003) argues, women often employed silences as 'survival strategies' and these silences should be respected rather than probed. In Peru, Theidon (2003) notes that Andean women, faced with TRC teams that insisted 'talking is good', felt the opposite, that talking was dangerous, that words could become weapons against them, whereas silence was powerful and protective.

Such intuitions about the elusive character of what Olga González (2011) has named 'dangerous truths' – the knowledge in 'post-conflict' situations that poses an ethical and political challenge to both protagonists and researchers – have proved justified. During the time of my inquiry, the controversies around the Boston College Belfast Project oral history archives provided a warning that confidentiality is impossible to guarantee. States can 'legally' obtain and use oral history archives against the protagonists or their communities.[6]

Perhaps it was a similar intuition that guided Lat's stories. I wrote a *postalita* about a name out of the several name-stories in the group, and remembering stories about my own name. Only after writing the *postalita*, I realized the additional complications that arise when your name carries a secret. What's in a name? For Lat, that which cannot be told, learning secrecy, but also certain complicity with the parents' lives, a special feeling of taking part in a shared secret. Once I was brought into the secrets, I also developed a constant carefulness around distinguishing the sharing within the group and the outside. I repeatedly heard the HIJXS saying: 'It's not over, it never is.' It (re)sounded in my head as a warning.

Lat at 20
Havana, Cuba, 2007

You see, my name is Lat ... and for me it's about my name, it's a weird name, people ask about it. Like, when the boys ask me, I make up stories. Here, is the first time I can talk about it. My name is an acronym for the name of an armed action by MRTA, where my dad was a *militante*, and where my uncle died. My dad told me that ... and my mom told me not to tell. That was before he was disappeared. ... When I was little, I was proud of my name, like a secret. Growing up I've been embarrassed by it. I've also been scared about it, and I thought it was a very silly name too. Now I like it, it means something in the group, of course they tease me about it, still ... it's not like I can talk about it.

Lat's *postalita* expresses the (in)ability to talk about who you are and where you come from, learning silence. One of the questions that arise if we have an understanding that we are constituted through language (Belsey, 2002) is what happens when it is impossible to talk about ourselves or to name who we are outside the available language of the war. Her name directly

---

[6] In the Boston College case, the confidential interviews with former Irish Republican Army members in Northern Ireland were subpoenaed and turned over to the police. It's one of the most controversial cases in oral history (McMurtrie, 2014). Using the legal framework to define what can be recorded or not assumes that what is 'legal' is fixed instead of a political category that changes over time. Legally, in Peru, armed groups such as the MRTA are terrorist groups, and there are ever expansive anti-terrorist laws that include persecution of ideas under the umbrella term of 'apologia'.

enacted the taboo over people's participation in the internal war (Coxshall, 2005; Durand, 2005; Theidon, 2010) that HIJXS in Peru and elsewhere have been confronted with.

With each conversation over the years, the HIJXS shared new stories and expanded on old ones. At each turn, with each opening, there also came a closing; a warning not to share such stories. It was confusing at the time (and slightly frustrating). I was left not knowing what to do with stories told in secret, with 'public secrets' (Taussig, 1992) where researchers become enmeshed in that delicate negotiation between speech and silence (González, 2011). In that delicate negotiation, I was allowed passage inside the circle of shared secrets; secrecy as a bind and a bond. It was as if I had become more trustworthy with the development of our relationship, and at the same time as if I was being patiently instructed, a teaching of secrecy. Memory work, Kuhn (2002: 6) remarked, is 'potentially interminable'; it never offers closure, resolutions or (happy?) endings; all the stories 'could be pursued further'.

The negotiation of silences does not stop with names in the HIJXS group. The legal process involving a father's extrajudicial killing that was supposed to bring everything out in the open instead yielded new silencing practices and (unresolvable) questions. For example, a case that was included in the TRC cases for judicial investigation in 2003 and ever so slowly followed its course inside the legal system. During my second trip to Peru in 2013, the investigation was part of the prosecution case against the paramilitary group Comando Rodrigo Franco, sponsored by the Alan García government and his Interior Minister Agustín Mantilla in the 1980s. The judicial route posed more questions about what can be said and what not in certain spaces. As González puts it, the 'public secret' also involves 'knowing what not to say and what not to ask' (González, 2011: 148). The questions at those moments went like this: 'Should my parents' militancy be part of the trial against the paramilitary group that killed them?' 'Maybe it should, but can it be?' 'Will that contribute to obtaining justice, to an investigation regarding *paramilitarismo* sponsored by a party in government? Or will it be a distraction that will only "justify" the crime? Will that bring additional effects into our lives, again?' 'Is that really up to me/us [HIJXS group]? Or beyond me/us?' 'Does it matter?'

While some have remained at the margins of trials and official investigations against those who either tortured, killed or disappeared their relatives, Iris was publicly involved in the new trial against the leaders of the MRTA after the transition government. I wondered with Iris about her presence during the civilian trial of her mother Lucero, *el megajuicio*, and her brief (but terrible memory of) exposure in the media. What happens when your story is already out, made public by others and you are exposed as the *hija* (daughter of)?

Iris at 18
Havana, Cuba, 2007

I've only known my mom in prison. She was pregnant with me when they caught her. I remember visiting her in the naval base; you go through so many gates. ... I remember her in the news ... they called her terrorist. ... I've had my doubts but to me she is the best person in the world. Everybody says I look exactly like her. True, we have the same laughter, but she is a really strong woman. At her trial, '*el megajuicio*', she was so strong ... but when she saw me, she cried. I made her weak. And after the trial with all the press around me, I couldn't be like her ... I cried ... only said: 'She is not a terrorist, she's my mom, the MRTA was only responsible for 1.5 per cent of the victims' ... blah, blah, blah ... you know, that speech. Every time I remember this, I was terrible. ... I could have done something, and I just cried ... so unlike her ... she is an amazing woman.

The public exposure came with a permanent suspicion of being recognized by others, bearing a stigma for being Lucero's daughter, the woman presented in the newspapers in full uniform with an assault rifle. The stigma carried the double transgression of being a woman in arms. It was not easy for Iris to escape the comparison with her mother:

My life story is not my mother's story but at the same time it will always have my mother's story, even if only as a reference, it marked me. (Iris, Havana, Cuba, 2012)

Back in Peru, Iris produced new silences. As detailed earlier, she took a one-year assignment as a doctor in the place where her father was buried. There she kept her story to herself without feeling repressed (although still complicated). She lived her silence as a necessary 'interruption', telling half-truths without fully revealing. In our conversations, Iris elaborated on her decision to withhold in order to explore and reconstruct another story – that of her father. Creating silences became important for Iris in order to set boundaries and produce new stories to fill in the gaps and silences; the enigmas of her father's life and death in that small town in Cusco.

Rafael's silences evolved differently. His first return to Lima did not go according to the 'desire to tell' that emerged in Cuba. Renewed safety concerns resulted in an unexpected dilemma:

Rafael at 24
Havana, Cuba, 2008

After the first year in Cuba, we went to Lima during the break and had planned to do some public stuff ... appear with pictures of our parents on our shirts, things like that. When I told my mom, she went mad. She said that she sent me away to stay out of trouble; that she wasn't going to visit another person in prison. ... 'Do you want all your friends to know about your dad?' she asked. If I was ready for that. And you know ... I didn't go to any activity; I didn't even return the HIJXS phone calls while in Lima. When we got back [to Cuba], they weren't even speaking to me. And they are important to me, because they understand my father's death, and that part of my life. But I think it's going to be very hard to do all this in Lima. ... I don't want to lose my friends, you know ... and my mom, but my father... .

I wrote this *postalita* to connect several conversations with Rafael and the HIJXS about that episode. I wanted to bring out how living under the burden of the 'children of terrorists' stigma in Peru was very much alive in the present to the point of countering their collective impulse to 'break the silence'. The stigma had effects not only on how they lived (imposed) silences and secrecy but also gave rise to (self-)censoring because of the impossibility of clear-cut delineations between 'imagined' and 'real' risks. People who live in such contexts for long(er) deploy careful strategies to navigate the risks (Theidon, 2014) and represent 'dangerous truths' (González, 2011), in turn allowing their circulation as 'subterraneous truths' (da Silva Catela, 2009).[7]

The memories in their families of a 'problematic past' that felt recent and even present, as well as fears in the present given that the surveillance mechanisms are still in place (Isbell, 2009), posed an additional issue to be negotiated for the HIJXS. For Rafael's mother, establishing connections to his father in public lacked the subtlety demanded by dangerous truths.

For HIJXS, Rafael's decision was lived as a 'betrayal' and it took time to rebuild trust as a group. He was strongly criticized and questioned, and back in Cuba it became a difficult experience to overcome for the collective. With the years, I witnessed change. Probably because the return to Peru was challenging for each of the HIJXS, the collective became open to different individual processes. '*Cada quien tiene su proceso*' is now a common saying among HIJXS and it refers to each one's way of dealing with their memories in their present lives: have them 'in front', keep them 'on the side', or leave them 'behind'? As such, they have each developed their own way of dealing with their stories and negotiating which part(s) is out and which is not, and in which spaces. This is the result of a mix of individual and collective processes, which I could call individual decisions, but it refers to the sort of individuality that comes from collective life where they are influenced by one another and the collective.

---

[7]   Da Silva Catela developed this from Pollak's *memorias subterráneas* (Pollak, 2006).

Thinking about the strategies around silences and truth-telling fuels the importance I place on problematizing *testimonio* as a particular form of memory narratives, not as revealing evidence of a silenced past but as tools of memory work in recreating a past for political purposes. This view is aligned with the more complex and nuanced views from the politics of memory developed in Latin America by Jelin and Stern, where *testimonios* contain a multiplicity of voices, the circulation of multiple 'truths' and also of several silences and things unsaid (Jelin, 2012: 124).[8]

Reclaiming the transgressive potential of *testimonio* requires understanding it as 'both an art and a strategy of subaltern memory' (Beverley, 2005: 561), based more on what it does than the form it takes, as an act to 'engage in the process of self-constitution and survival' (Yúdice, 1996: 46). This has implications for *testimonios* use in educational settings, and in the ways in which *testimonios* are pedagogical. I will return to elaborating on this in the epilogue while calling for an understanding of *testimonio* as pedagogy within the Latin American critical (and creative) pedagogy tradition.

What I want to do with my story

The political intentionality of the testimonial narrative plays an important role in shaping the limits of the account and what remains silenced. Here the question that prevails is the imagined audience. Throughout our conversations, I heard recurring discussions and distinctive narrative moves as attempts to retain control over their narratives and the possible (mis)uses by an imagined audience; the awareness that *testimonios* can be used for completely different purposes than our own and even against our own.

The political purposes of testimonial narratives have been part of the scholarly conversation on *testimonio*. This includes debates over its definition and place within academia. Is it literature or 'against' literature (Beverley, 2004)? Can it be evidence, for historical research (Calveiro, 2006), for truth and reconciliation commissions (Coxshall, 2005) or for judicial procedures?

Creating a 'conversation', as it were, between Abel and Rafael's *testimonios* offers a useful point of entry for reflecting on silences and political intentionality. Both have reflected (and argued with each other) on how to negotiate silences in

---

[8] In the Southern Cone, Jelin (2003) depicts memory as a battlefield focusing on the construction of hegemonic memory, which is the result of complex mechanisms at play. 'Layered memories' competing for framing and providing meaning to narratives of the past use language and social institutions to acquire materiality in 'vehicles of memory' that make it appear as natural mirrors of the past. Stern (2000) doesn't see a hegemonic memory made of forgetting/erasing the real memory, and instead proposes that there is no one single more truthful or real memory but pluralities of memories which are the result of a dialectical relationship between remembering and forgetting, social products that require interpretive frames from the collective to read and retell the past.

the public sphere regarding their involvement in party politics or with collectives that engage with political parties at national level. During our first encounter Abel and Rafael seemed to share views on how outspoken they should[9] be about their parents' involvement in the MRTA and the consequences they lived in terms of state repression, social stigma and breakage of family bonds. Their involvement in politics back in Peru changed that.

For Abel, some silences are a necessary condition for reform and acceptance of the other. His rethinking of silence reflects Jelin's (2012; 2014) suggestion of shifting the question from what protagonists do not say towards what audiences cannot listen to. *Testimonio*'s silences in this sense are an anticipated response to what others are prepared to listen to. *Testimonio* invites us to think of how the capacity to listen is created.[10] Inside the same group, it can be a ritualized repetition rather than a creative act of dialogue; but beyond, there is a relationship with an 'other' which from its alterity contributes to constructing a social narrative with meaning. *Testimonio* as sense-making endeavour wants another to listen and enter into dialogue.

In Abel's story, silence as that which is produced by what others cannot listen to becomes evident in the political arenas he joins. Some silences were necessary for him to enter broader party politics, an entrance complicated by his family history. Most people that know him, already know that history, so more than silence it's about that which is known but not allowed a voice. The strategic negotiation of his identity led Abel to speak of living with a sense of 'split identities'; of being one person in one space and another elsewhere. Still, and as troubled as Abel was during our conversations in Lima, I had a sense that he has been stubbornly making his life a political one; a life dedicated to *la Política*, Politics with a capital P. Abel was slowly creating a space for what he wanted for himself. This required careful learning of new languages and new modes of politics for new places, from an inherited language of revolutionary struggle in his childhood to a language of reformism as a possible politics in his adult life.

Nance (2001: 578) cites several examples in *testimonio* (from Rigoberta Menchú to Domitila Barrios and Poniatowska's Jesusa) where speakers 'demonstrate a keen understanding of the various forms of appropriation and resistance through their anticipatory countermoves aimed at disarming these defences'. The protagonists constantly 'inscribe and reinstate' the

---

[9] Upon relistening to the recorded conversations, I notice that while others in HIJXS speak of what they 'want to do' with their stories, Abel and Rafael referred to what they 'should do'. As if it was more of a duty than a desire.

[10] The Zapatistas' writings on how silence can take control of the word-space (*el espacio de la palabra*) and be powerful when words fail to communicate with an unwilling audience: 'in silence we spoke ... without speaking our words spoke'; 'against our silence crashed again and again their sharp lies' (Reforma, 10 de febrero de 1997, in Rajchenberg and Héau-Lambert, 2004).

places/positions of readers and texts according to desired reader responses 'by reminding them of their privileged difference' and their 'responsibility to act'. 'Disarming readings have the paradoxical effect of placing at once too many and too few people on the speakers' side' (Nance, 2001: 581).

Back in Peru, Abel, on the one hand, learnt to deal with, and work together with, people from different corners of life and with different perspectives on the internal war, including the terrorist discourse. I remember him summarizing his view of the past as 'a tragedy that should not be repeated'. This was an all-encompassing remark that stresses the 'not to repeat' motto of the TRCs around the world. He has become more aware of the need for the HIJXS to enter into dialogue with other memories of the internal war, and of the importance of working with others and not only among themselves; a way of moving beyond a potentially problematic '*nosotros*'.

Rafael, on the other hand, returned to Peru determined to be 'completely out'. After his first 'failed' attempt early on, his form of political activism would be a journey of public disclosure. In our conversations, Rafael dismissed the idea of 'negotiating a testimonial narrative' since, in his view, 'nobody even listens to us'. Yet his journey has been marked by detours and bypasses over the years. At times, being singled out as 'red' or 'terrorist' on social media brought back fears and worries, making Rafael rethink his silences. So have the recriminations of 'hiding his past' made by those who knew his father. But he also carried the feeling of being at a crossroad, wondering how not to carry his story as a burden and live it instead in more productive ways in relation with others.[11]

The HIJXS have become increasingly uncomfortable with public spaces that recognize their presence but keep it subtly quiet. Abel and Rafael, for example, have felt uneasy with the fact that their stories are known but not voiced; an acknowledgement of their presence but also of how inconvenient it is that they are publicly out. There is a tacit agreement that their stories should not be at the forefront of activism that reminds me of Taussig's 'public secret'. As long as where they come from and what they lived/think of the internal war is not part of the collective activism, they are accepted. Yet there comes a point where the collective 'silent knowing' also becomes challenged; when the public secret is eager to be broken.

> I had to force myself to speak in this 'other' space [outside our space or friendly spaces]. I was nervous, even trembling, but I started reaffirming myself in our truths, our reflexions and our proposals. I presented myself as a victim, as the son of a person who took up arms during the

---

[11] This took a different turn once Rafael had children, left the country and decided to write his *memorias* of violence in a book (Salgado, 2022) partly as a way to process and imagine future conversations with them.

conflict. In Peru, dividing us between innocents and non-innocents has caused much harm and worked against a united struggle against the impunity of state crimes. (Rafael, Lima, Peru, 2015)

We have been condemned to silence, pushed outside of the discourse. Our battle is for recognition. What are we? That's a key question, Are we victims? No. Are we guilty? No. We simply are not. Nobodies. We want to be one of the actors within *familiares*, the relatives' movement, demanding justice as well. We are struggling for recognition, for a place at the table, a space to talk about what WE lived as well, and to be part of reconstructing a better present, a different way of doing politics engaged with the people. For us it is not reform or revolution like the older generation, one or the other, but reform *and* revolution, or maybe not those exactly, but our generation is one of always adding, always 'and'. (Abel, Lima, Peru, 2015)

Rafael and Abel have slightly different emphases when it comes to their actions on the matter and how to be 'out'. Whereas Rafael relies more on the subjective side of things, that is on the struggles over memory within himself and in interacting with his surroundings, exploring the feelings and impacts on the 'personal' life, Abel looks for a 'Political' mode more related to the broader society. Such struggles over memory at a broader discursive level do not necessarily start from the personal but instead place more emphasis on the search for recognition as a political subject.

Both their journeys continue, coming closer and getting more distant every now and then. And they both remain in the HIJXS group initiatives as the group becomes increasingly aware of the importance of and complications in entering into dialogue with others outside their community, and of the demands to recognize and respect others' sensibilities for their losses during the war. How do we move away from upfront rejection and learn to listen? Their journeys and that feeling of being uncomfortable with their 'conditioned' presence in the public sphere go hand in hand with the latest voices from their generation in Peru, speaking out and constructing their memories for a wider audience. It is no coincidence that in the years in which I have been writing our memory work, a few young adults (not in HIJXS) who were 'children of ...' during the war, have published their stories in books and theatre plays.[12]

---

[12] Some examples of productions by a second generation marked by their parents' involvement in the internal war are *Los Rendidos* by José Carlos Agüero, whose parents were in the Shining Path; *La distancia que nos separa* by Renato Cisneros, whose father was in the army; *Proyecto 1980/2000*, a theatre play by Sebastian Rubio, which portrays stories of people

The story of Lucho's *testimonio* suggests a careful reading of the growing openness for HIJXS and others to engage publicly. Lucho's *testimonio* did not make it into the testimonial narratives in the first movement, as I could never decide how to write it without 'outing' people who are not publicly recognized as being part of the MRTA (or linked to it in the past). At different moments, I asked Lucho if it would be possible to include certain figures that are important to his narrative without causing harm, or how we could (re)write his *testimonio* with that in mind. Lucho replied every time, 'that is precisely the problem', followed by 'that's something you have to figure out', meaning *how* to write it. Part of me feels as if I let him down by not finding a way to write his stories. But there is also another part that considers it worse to think I had found a way and then be wrong about it, thus reproducing harm. As an alternative, I turned to write some lessons on the difficulties that imposed silences face in retelling our lives.

Another HIJXS participant withdrew from the project in the revisiting stage because his family situation had changed. Opening his story to public scrutiny could have harmed his father's life in a way it did not in the first stage of the testimonial project. I offered him the possibility of anonymizing or fictionalizing his story, but he rejected both. For him, it was important that the story come out publicly, maybe later on, but under his name and with all their names in it. He would rather keep it temporarily silenced than change it.

When your parents remain at risk because they were not prosecuted, at least not in the 1990s, then being part of HIJXS and telling stories about how it was to live state violence, basically incriminates your parents for links to an illegal organization and activities described by the state as 'terrorism'. This framing erases the political aspect of the violence by turning them into criminals, even monsters with no rights, the abject subject expelled from society. Still, with Lucho, I learnt about another hurtful side of keeping silent for those who were not prosecuted. The remnants of the internal war never vanish; rather there is a continuation of a learnt surveillance attitude and a general distrust of vertical organizing structures as well as political parties. For Lucho, this led to a community-based activism inspired in popular education movements based on learning alongside people from their struggles and possibilities for small-scale change. Over the years, Lucho also changed regarding the stories he 'remembered' and we recorded. Much later his father's union life became part of a documentary film. As more people joined the HIJXS, new stories were included in Lucho's recordings. Still, none of them made it into this book.

---

reflecting on their condition as 'the children of …'; and Isaac Ernesto Ruiz Velasco's short film, *No, no me acuerdo* (2018).

> I asked my parents how to write about myself within this testimonial project without affecting them. Their replies were strikingly similar to Lucho: that's something I have to figure out. I'm still struggling to do so. Some families were not prosecuted or incriminated in the publicly available legal records. Since I left Peru I have led different lives in different countries with different relationships to violence and politics, and ultimately with different categories to narrate them.

I also learnt from him that we could not discuss certain things in depth: those 'taboos' that were troublesome even for us. Things that led him to believe that the so-called post-conflict never arrived because otherwise we could have talked about these issues openly. As absurd as it was, I asked Lucho: 'Like what…?' After the necessary outburst of laughter from both of us, Lucho offered the example of how the limited spaces for conversation in his prison visits created for him an idealized image of the previous generation's struggles: *los compañeros*. This image changed slowly, becoming a different story after meeting them outside prison and learning of the internal struggles and divisions that linger into the present, and all the instances in which they were/ are wrong. And yet, even now, open conversation about these is not possible.

There is in Lucho a respect for his previous generation's politics, their lives led by convictions. Yet he made an important remark about a necessary distancing, for example, regarding methods and the importance placed on the processes of organizing and learning alongside people, and of community-based activism and small-scale changes. I found it important to learn from Lucho (and others) about those moments when 'the image fell and broke into pieces', and also that crucial moment when you can respect their history but challenge their present; when respect (admiration even) for them becomes different from requiring their approval. The moment when you feel you can be different and create your own politics without denying their histories.

Playing with silences: reflections on writing with silences

The testimonial project with HIJXS, their desire to share their stories, is part of an effort to break imposed silences in a context of heavy state and societal repression by intervening in the political realm and its available narratives of the internal war. Their experiences of repression were, and yet were not, direct (in the way it was for their parents). They were also lived through silences and secrecy. Long established practices of silencing rooted censoring and self-censoring practices in people's lives.

There is an inherent (or apparent?) contradiction between *testimonios* as 'breaking the silence' and the sustaining of silences enacted in the testimonial space when *testimonios* are thought of as entering into public memory struggles. The desire to 'tell' confronts the paradox of retaining silences as an important testimonial feature. Theidon (2014) writes that conducting research in post-war contexts carries an additional concern that is not so much a privacy issue but a matter of safety, of life and death (or imprisonment). But raising the 'possibility of ambiguity' (Lather, 2000a) around secrets and silences, or political intentionality in testimonial narratives, does not seem like a good idea if one is claiming a 'truth-finding' mission. According to Coxshall (2005: 210), TRCs 'cannot afford to openly problematize narrative testimonies because they are the principal data and method of research that defines and legitimates them as a particular kind of institution'. This leaves out lessons from South African testimonies by women where 'silence too is a legitimate discourse of pain if it is acknowledged' especially considering 'the validity of silence as means of communicating particular kinds of experience' (Ross, 2001: 272).

In our testimonial project, silence appeared and disappeared; it was there in the presence of gaps, holes and contradictions. As González (2011: 90) noted, testimonial representations expose those 'dangerous truths' in the aftermath of war as absences, affirming the 'secrecy around traumatic memories of war'. By reflecting on silence and secrecy, I considered the glimpses into that borderland space of direct and indirect experience inhabited by the HIJXS *testimonio*. The group carefully negotiated the intergenerational transmission of silences and secrets. The inquiry process became a space for them/me/us to test the limits of their/our silences, identifying the ones they/we are comfortable with, pondering which ones can be reworked or abandoned, and even which ones must be defended. The testimonial process became a testing ground over space and time for 'coming out' and for retreating, confronting these silences with the broader public as an imagined audience, to enter into conversation with the less sympathetic 'other'.

Such a testing ground provided an awareness of testimonial work as work-in-progress, ongoing and open-ended. Silences and secrets are recognized as multiple, and also continuously changing but not in a linear fashion where more silences are broken or more secrets unveiled. The changes are more about awareness of the presence of silences and constant renegotiation of their place in different spaces and at different times: playing with the way they themselves learnt about their own history. '[T]he intergenerational transmission does not transit through explicit verbal channels and tracks but also through silences, gaps and fears' (Jelin, 2012: 144).

Revisiting the *testimonios* with the HIJXS five years later and back in Peru opened a space for some silences to become words. New conversations with the previous generation (usually provoked as an after-effect of the testimonial work) either produced new stories or challenged old ones. Also, the HIJXS were more willing to share with me certain stories that were previously silenced, but they were less willing to make them public. I was let inside to share the secrets, but told not to reveal them. Sometimes, when certain silences are more comfortably present, it is possible to become playful with silences, to allude to them.

Silences have been explored in narrative inquiry, foregrounding the idea that there are only fragments, and that the seemingly continuous narrative is a product of our writing, a meaning-making endeavour. For us in the HIJXS, the silences are very much linked to our experiences with our parents' clandestine or semi-clandestine lives. They are also linked to the secrecy in which we learnt to live, something absorbed from childhood, not learnt as adults. This produced particular silences and also particular ways of living with silences. In a context of continuous state repression and widespread use of narratives of 'terrorism', that which was clandestine remains silenced in the present.

The more we know each other and the deeper the relationship we have outside the boundaries of 'research', the more previously undisclosed stories the HIJXS and their relatives tell me. At the same time, the boundaries of what can be publicly shared and used in these pages are delineated, reinforced even, to cover some of the things we are now sharing. I interpret such change as a sign of my acceptance as belonging to the HIJXS group, and also them getting used to the recorder, and lowering their guard. It may also respond to the broader context of a wave of second-generation narratives becoming available. Even though more/new/corrected stories were added to my collection of recordings, I could not use them. This can be seen at the same time as building that 'ethnographic refusal' (Tuck and Yang, 2014) given my researcher role, and a 'gift exchange' (González, 2011) in the teaching of secrecy.

My position became ever more problematic as I wrote the dissertation back in 2016 and later revised those pages as part of a book in 2024. It adds even further weight to the multiple ethical complications. Do I write as a member of HIJXS? As an activist committed/implicated in a cause? As a collector of stories? As a sociologist/education researcher? As 'child of' (myself as *hija*)? As an exile? Most academic ethical guidelines assume we parachute into a place with non-existent ethical frameworks. Instead, I think that we should be open to learn from the ethics of their relationships, and that meant respecting silences. Luttrell (2003: 273) said there are 'epistemological tensions in ethnographic knowing' due to the presence of 'the unsayable'. But the HIJXS conversations make me wonder about the knowledges that have been produced outside of the voiced, instead more affectively and instinctively. As Ross writes, one of the lessons from women's enactment of silences is that words and speech are not the only means of knowledge.

This can be used in this context of inheritance of silences, clandestine childhoods and the production of 'murky' knowledge. The concept of multiple ontologies by anthropologist Holbraad (2012) may also be useful here for the recognition that people are living or being positioned in spaces with multiple ontologies. For our memory work it means writing from a stance that sees memories as containing an entanglement of 'real facts' and creative aspects for other possibilities of living. This is a turn towards thinking of lives in the borderlands between speech and silence, between the real and the imagined, not as opposites but as creating a messy in-between-ness, thus producing another knowledge. But I still wonder how then to write about that?

PART III

The Third Movement:
Poetics of Memory

The third movement engages with ideas and theories to revisit the problems of/with the process of writing memory, and particularly *testimonio* (and its politics) in its realist and its fictionalized attempts. It includes a further troubling of the fact/fiction binary particularly for the making of *testimonio* (the writing and reading of it) but moreover for qualitative inquiry and memory work.

The poetics of memory explores the 'troubling' strategy deployed in the second movement and the troubles it produced as well as its productivity resulting in diverse writing practices for a more creative understanding of the process of doing memory work, and of memory as artful.

Overall, it reflects on writing (about) violence and the crisis of representation in the aftermath of war and the persistence of state violence.

11

Troubles with Fiction,
Writing and Memory

But we don't want fiction … we want the *testimonio* to tell
the truth.

HIJXS collective conversation, Lima, Peru, 2013

In this quote, the HIJXS react to my proposal to use fictionalization as
testimonio during my fieldwork in Peru. It also illustrates complex questions
over truth, voice and representation running through this book.

Voice has a strong, albeit complicated, presence in qualitative research.
Jackson and Mazzei's (2009) reflection on the 'limits of voice' suggests there
has been either too much or too little voice, leaving unfulfilled promises that
hint at its 'insufficiency'. In *testimonio*, this insufficiency, intimately linked to
ideas of truth, was recast as a movement between ' "the subaltern can speak"
and "the subaltern cannot speak" ' (Detwiler and Breckenridge, 2012: 1).

Echoes of this debate can be traced to the struggle over the meaning of
doing *testimonio* in this book. Well aware of the ongoing controversies over
testimonio, including its potential 'death' (Beverley, 2004), and the possible
stigmatization that *testimonios*, in their truth-mode, could bring to their
protagonists, I imagined fictionalizations as a way of *trans-genreing testimonio*, of
exposing *testimonio*'s production, its limits in communicating experiences of
repression (and their protagonists) as changing. The use of the term 'fictions'
here does not refer to the opposite of 'the real' which I consider is always some
sort of fictionalization (Freeman, 2007), but to that which is not claimed
to be retold 'as it was' but rather 'as if it were' (Reed, 2011). Reclaiming
its transgressive potential means understanding the art of *testimonio* (and its
artfulness) based on what it does rather than the form it takes.

In my desire to engage with the HIJXS, I initiated a journey of exploring
how and under what conditions I could reappropriate the term *testimonio*
to reflect our meaning-making over what counts as political and doing
politics, our struggles over my role and theirs, our different views on

the conflict and post-conflict, and our shifting positionings in relation to the previous generation. These dilemmas are not mine alone but part of a broader field of reflections on memory work in post-conflict societies, and particularly on forms of representing such work (Lazzara, 2006; Strejilevich, 2006; Lindbladh, 2008). As Nouzeilles (2005: 270) writes, representation after collective trauma 'can also be objectionable or undesirable ... it also increases vulnerability by exposing oneself to the look and judgement of others'. My intention was to shift from the accuracy of voice and its companion concern over what is lost from the oral sources and experiential encounters, to what was being produced instead. With creative writing, we could explore our role (mine and theirs) in producing our own accounts, re-storying in a way, and bringing myself into the testimonial narratives.

For this, *testimonio* has to be de-linked from its 'truth-revealing' anchor, and move the inquiry into what the production of *testimonio* can tell us. This approach requires unpacking testimonial production based on the ethics of its relationships, and problematizing its 'voicing' aspect that carries from its critical theory upbringing (where the researcher role is a mere medium for 'giving voice' to excluded/marginal subjects).

This chapter explores the challenges raised by an approach that 'troubles' (Lather, 1997) *testimonio* from the 'borderlands' (Anzaldúa, 1987), those in-between spaces/categories. It considers such 'troubling' both necessary and problematic.

Testimonio, organizing a clash of fictions

In Chapter 2, I recount a discussion over using 'life histories' to refer to HIJXS *testimonios* which was not about word choice. Our conflict contained a struggle to establish the boundaries of how I and others were to engage with their lives, the urgency for intervening in the present with the resistant texture of their narratives, and a desire to open an intergenerational dialogue. However, I accepted to work with *testimonio* by troubling it (Lather and Smithies, 1997), that mode of problematizing a category as a possibility to stubbornly continue using it.

My position was not solely about reclaiming the importance of one's story in larger narratives of conflict. A life-histories approach could also solve broader questions of meaning and representation that *testimonio* raised. Post-colonial authors considered *testimonio* problematic in its construction and reification within academia; an appropriation act that took away its transgressiveness by institutionalizing it (Denegri, 2003; Nance, 2006). While the 'expressed desire of their narrators to construct their own history' (Denegri, 2003: 229) remained very much alive, it had become clear that *testimonio*'s politics and disruption of conventions (that is, who has the authority over truth?) had not only created solidarity but also fervent opposition, mobilized around an unproblematized idea of truth (Beverley, 2004). Having transgressed multiple artificial divides – public/private; oral/ written; inside/against literature; academia/political activism; researcher/ participant; individual/collective; mediator/protagonist – *testimonio*'s last battleground was truth/fiction.

Similar concerns with ethics underpin *testimonio* work. For example, oral history sources have been described not as discovered but as created, and as 'always the result of a relationship' (Portelli, 1981: 103). I am not claiming to conduct oral history because I do not compare the HIJXS narratives with (or check against) other 'historical' sources (that is, archives) of the retold events, but the fact that my project is based on relationships for constructing narratives as a meaning-making endeavour shares what Portelli has argued about oral history 'as a work of relationships'. The ethics of our testimonial project is based in our relationship; beyond confidentiality, it is connected to relationships, re-presentation acts, authorship, truth-claims and the contingency of knowledge production. As a result, I see creative writings embodying the co-constructive character of research.

More recently, trauma *testimonio* and its multiple representations have (re)appeared as a form of cultural politics in post-dictatorial Argentina and Chile (Lazzara, 2006; Strejilevich, 2006) and post-totalitarian Eastern Europe (Lindbladh, 2008). These authors discuss the difficulties in representing trauma and the emergence of a 'poetics of memory' embracing memory as messy, fragmented, enigmatic and affective. Drawing lessons from Holocaust testimony, Lazzara (2006) elaborates on the impossible narration of traumatic experiences which are unsayable, and the impossible witness for lack of survivors. Similarly, Strejilevich (2006) considers *testimonio* as containing 'other truths', not factual but affective and emotional truths, producing therefore different types of knowledge. They both embrace emergent forms of re-presentation within *testimonio* that put together a political, ethical and aesthetical project in a desire to challenge hegemonic narratives of state violence. I embraced fictionalizations as a way of trans-genreing *testimonio*, as part of its politics by exposing *testimonio*'s production and its limits in communicating violence and for providing space to consider its protagonists as multiple and changing.

Reclaiming *testimonio*'s transgressive potential thus means understanding the 'art of *testimonio*' based more on what it does than the form it takes. Contrary to traditional *testimonio* work, I consider fictions and creative writings can be *testimonios* as well. Focusing on *testimonio*'s doings (its function and effects on those involved) would allow a space for fictions as they 'stand for testimony to … [an event] for the characters whose voices mainly tell the events' (Reed, 2011: 14).

Drawing on Anzaldúa's idea of borderlands and Speedy's liminal narrative spaces (2008), I see *testimonio* and fiction as artificially separated by imaginary lines that construct divisions with material consequences. Exploring the spaces in-between offers an alternative space from which to challenge hegemonic narratives of the Peruvian post-war, guided by the following recurrent themes that in turn offers.

Moving beyond the binary logic means challenging the definition of *testimonio* by blurring its division with fiction, and bringing to the surface *testimonio*'s undecidability, 'its inextricable connection with fiction' (Blanchot and Derrida, 2000: 27),[1] considering it as haunted and occupied by fiction or as containing only traces of the real. Fiction, then, is not the problem of *testimonio* but its 'condition of possibility' (Cubilie and Good, 2003) especially in experiences of trauma and state repression.[2]

There is a transgressive impulse in creating fiction as *testimonio*, or better for considering *testimonio* as a site of messy togetherness, which also comes from seeing experiences as fictions to begin with. This is not because they did not happen, but because they are experienced by people and therefore mediated by their subjectivities, available language and discourses, the spaces of (re)telling (and listening), memories, meaning and constant reinterpretation. In this light, what stories tell us might not be so much the experiences themselves, but the social relations where such experiences were lived and ultimately told.

The traditional testimonial impulse went hand in hand with the idea of 'giving voice' as part of its 'empowering' narrative. These were entrenched in a critical theory tradition and second-wave feminism with their epistemological standpoint and drive to uncover knowledge produced at the margins. However, ethnographers, narrative inquirers and new generations of feminists insisted on the need to reflexively pick on the researchers' role as part of the multiple mediations and translation acts in the production of social research. Within this, privileging first-person verbatim quotations (instead of fictions) provided that 'giving voice' illusion while at the same time working 'to mask inequalities rather than redress them' (Andrews, 2007: 41). Researchers' embedded interpretations went undercover in the previous 'giving voice' desire, as if they were mediums.

Alternatives to such processes involve fragmenting voice by paying attention to the multiplicity of voices and troubling its reification (Jackson and

---

[1]   'As a promise to make truth … testimony always goes hand in hand with at least the possibility of fiction, perjury and lie … testimony will always suffer both, having, undecidably a connection with fiction' (Blanchot and Derrida, 2000: 27).

[2]   'In order to remain testimony, it must therefore allow itself to be haunted. It must allow itself to be parasitized by precisely what it excludes from its inner depths, the possibility, at least, of literature' (Blanchot and Derrida, 2000: 29–30).

Mazzei, 2009), the many multiple stories that produce that voice including the unsaid (Lather, 2007; 2009), and the silences as inhabited considering them not as absence but a 'vital aspect of the fabric of discourse' (Mazzei, 2007). Seeing silences as constitutive of *testimonios*, as political acts, that may only become shareable in the fictionalized, opened more inquiring spaces to work in conversation with them.

In addition, *testimonio* from a Foucauldian perspective also produce *testimonio*-subjects (Tamboukou, 2008), disciplined by their own desire to produce *testimonios*. *Testimonios* can be oppressive, generating anxiety around producing 'true' accounts of experience; as such, testimonial work brings with it mechanisms for narrators policing themselves and each other (as it is a collective impulse) on what can be said, what is unsayable, and how it is to be said. As a result, the testimonial process may become an additional repressive technology almost as the violence of imposed silences and social stigma.

In response, feminist poststructuralists offer a way of understanding the subject under erasure. Davies and Gannon (2006) explored the multiple selves in 'discontinuous fragments informed by memory, the body, photographs, other texts, and, most importantly, other people' (Gannon, 2006: 491), the impossible out-of-language which constitutes us as subjects but also contains the conditions of possibilities for resistance by its transgressive use (Belsey, 2002).

Using writing for transgressing required understanding testimonial work as something that continues to involve the 'tellers' in the writing, in discussions over re-presentation processes and the uses of *testimonio*. It also required considering writing and creative representations as possibilities for exploring their *testimonios* as sites of reproduction and resistance to larger narratives of the war and post-war. This can be seen as part of 'writing as performative methodology' (Speedy et al, 2005) just as in performative documentary filmmaking (that is, *Los Rubios* [2003]) where what was previously known as the product is in itself the inquiring process. Within this, getting over the artificial division between form and content is implied, with intertwined aesthetics and ethics as political projects for transgressing embedded power relations. As Richardson said, '*How* we are expected to write affects *what* we can write, the form in which we write shapes the content' (Richardson, 2003: 187; emphasis in original).

These theoretical reflections were the ones I travelled with in my inquiry journey. They provided the grounding for approaching *testimonio* from a *troubling epistemology* (as an approach to knowledge(s) being produced in the doing), *methodology* (as a way into an inquiry with *testimonio* by 'poking holes' in it), and *method* by revisiting and using creative writing as a tool to spark new conversations and interrogating the narratives we were producing. And yet, during the course of this work and in constant dialogue with the HIJXS, I encountered that in the process of *troubling* I produced even more troubles.

The trouble with troubling

In making this inquiry into cycles of action and reflection with the HIJXS, the process continued its path and became a never-ending conversation over its problematics. Some of the conversations around the conditions of producing *testimonio* that I wrote in the second movement as the politics of memory make explicit the tensions that run through this project, including aspects that remain unresolved. The issues I address in this third movement reflect on the writing process as a poetics of memory, inspired by Jackson and Mazzei's proposition 'to exploit what is produced by the trouble of (or with) voice' (2009: 3).

Similar strategies of troubling have been explored in and through filmmaking documentaries that have tested the boundaries of their genre by using animation. Documentary films connect questions of data, interpretation and representation; their images reflect the interlinked nature of the medium of collecting and the medium of representing. Viewed as attempts to 'organize a clash of fictions', documentaries can create spaces for reflecting on how *testimonio*, memory and fiction can come together. '[Y]ou have your stories, people have theirs and there is a confrontation between yours and theirs that produces a third way' (Gheerbrant, 2008).

Two such documentary films produced by the second generation (now adults) of the disappeared/imprisoned in South America can illuminate a renewed poetics of memory work. *Alias Alejandro* (2005) by Alejandro Cardenas (Germany/Peru) and *Los Rubios* (2003) by Albertina Carri (Argentina) deal with memory and representation by challenging them, and use animation to bear witness to 'a reality'.

Alias Alejandro shows the filmmaker's search for his father, a leader in the Tupac Amaru Revolutionary Movement (MRTA) imprisoned since 1992 in the Peruvian naval base.[3] Documenting the first encounter with his father clashes with the prohibition of filming inside a military prison. Here animation appears to re-present their encounter. The animation (black-and-white hand-drawings with no dialogue), far from trying to be 'realistic', is quite symbolic, bringing forward the feelings and the setting. In addition, the film contains fragments of unresolved conversations with his mother, contrasting getting closer with an impossibility of understanding.

Los Rubios, made by Albertina Carri whose parents were disappeared by Argentina's dictatorship in the 1970s, takes a step further. Its tagline reads: '*Los*

---

[3] Peter Cárdenas Schultz finished his 25-year prison sentence and was released from the naval base prison on 18 October 2015. He now lives abroad.

Rubios focuses on the director's search for her disappeared parents. Is it possible to get to the truth or they are only fictions, imaginary characters from everyone who remembers them?'

Here, the animation (Playmobil figures with stop-motion technique) shows the parents being taken by aliens (a controversial scene accused of portraying the kidnappings as fictional). The director also uses other unconventional resources: adopting a 'making of' style with an actress playing her role (both appear at several moments), showing fragments of herself TV-watching her own interviews with her parents' *compañeros*, all mixed showing the impossibilities of memory as truth: 'And this remembrance, how much truth does it contain, anyway, and how much whim? … All I have are vague memories contaminated by so many versions. However I try to get closer to the truth, it only takes me farther away from it' (*Los Rubios*, 2003).

Both documentaries are tales from another generation, focused on their parents' forced absence (imprisoned and disappeared, respectively) and the politics surrounding such absences. They connect their personal and national histories and provide no answers, but rather counterpoints to hegemonic stories. They also play with re-presentation while facing the impossibility of their stories being portrayed on film: the impossibility of entering spaces (filming inside a military prison) and the impossibility of memory (as fragmented and mixed with others). *Los Rubios* fictionalizes memory sustained by its impossibility as representation; it creatively constructs memories by dismantling the concept itself, exploring absence, fragments, contradictions, and imaginations: '[an] attempt to *fictionalize memory*, by stating that the construction of the past includes always a novelistic plot, spectralized' (Kletnicki, 2010: 22; emphasis in original).

These documentaries also illustrate the difficulties that troubling processes face. Critics described their use of animation as 'paradoxical' and questioned their 'true' genre. *Los Rubios* was called a pseudo-documentary, a hybrid, and even fictional documentary, as it blurs the fiction/non-fiction categories 'to the point of their dissolution' (Gandsman, 2006: 253). From an alternative perspective Biehl (2013) suggests that ethnographic writing similar to literature and documentary films can push its limits 'as it seeks to bear witness to living in a manner that does not bound, reduce, or make caricatures of people but liberates, if always only partially, some of the epistemological force and authority of their travails and stories that might break open alternative styles of reasoning' (Biehl, 2013: 587).

This, in turn, brings me back to thinking about genre definitions and categorical divides, about Anzaldúa's borderlands together with Lather's ethics against slicing people up into categories. Both stances made me aware that people's lives bring an increased complexity to the academic exercise, defying its attempts to impose categories onto realities. The previous generation's *testimonio* needs to be changed, since the current generation faces a different politics of memory. Different boundaries need to be broken in order to irrupt the political space.

I have called these complications *the troubles of troubling* and went on exploring them as the productive outcomes of such a *troubling* stance at three levels.

The first level refers to the troubles with the HIJXS over what we refer to as 'the real story' or 'the facts', and therefore to what the work of *testimonio* is for:

If *testimonio* is about memories that are already fictionalized versions, then is what happened to us not real?

Then they won't see it as legitimate … and what is the point of de-legitimizing ourselves.

If memories keep changing, how are we to do activism on such moving ground?

The HIJXS questioned my abstract meanderings over the idea of fictionalization for *testimonio*-making, and I understood what Lather referred to as 'getting drunk' on theory. I was disappointed as I thought the *postalitas* were not only interesting but also aesthetically attractive. Still, I respected HIJXS' position because that was my decision with this work to make it into activist research produced with the protagonists for their purposes of acting in their world. Yet, the group also began to use creative writing, the deliberate use of imagination, for their memory work. I was taken by surprise that over the years I re-evaluated the necessary presence of 'the realist' tales for HIJXS and that they also reconsidered the potential of creative writing for themselves. And yet we both continue considering them (the realist tales and the creative writings) problematic.

Collective *postalita*
(multivoiced)
Lima, Peru, 2013

There is nothing fictional about it, nothing to be creative at all. This is what you and all of you don't understand. That when it comes to us, none of what you discuss really matters. His father was killed by the police at the detention centre, hers by the paramilitary, our relatives tortured and isolated in prison. We've been marked. That is not a representation; it is a fact. If you try to say it otherwise, then you are no better than those who deny it all. That is MY fact. One I have kept hidden for too long. And now that I want to shout it to everyone, you come and tell me about creative memory, no facts, no single truths. ... What am I supposed to do with that?

Don't get me wrong I enjoy the conversations; I liked this fictionalizing you brought, I can write my stories. ... Now, I can tell the story of the first time I visited the prison in the way I want to remember it. ... Now, I can tell the story of my father's last day as I imagine it, and that created that memory for me. And it has the meaning I wanted it to have. It does feel great and makes living possible.

But then you are messing with what happened and nothing good can come out of that ... then you are no better than those who deny that what happened was systematic state repression to destroy opposition, to eliminate resistance, to crush the defeated ... and to make all that a lasting legacy. Then, you are no better than THEM.

We can't deny that after we recorded the testimonios, there were things that we did end up remaking in stories for ourselves. And it gives us the feeling like we don't have to apologize for how we tell our stories. It's like no one can tell us, how we are meant to remember or not. Well, in any case they don't believe in us to begin with. So, why not?

The testimonial project with and without its use of creative writing, in all its cycles and movements, always produced strong reactions and intense conversations with the HIJXS. At one point my inquiry was even challenged for being methodological and 'not political enough'. I still find it puzzling that 'methodological' discussions are considered outside 'the political'. It seemed that the idea of an 'academic' text granting legitimacy to the *testimonios* was not possible if I was challenging such authority to begin with, and rejecting a position where I would be the producer of an 'analysis' of the *testimonio* revealing or interpreting its 'true' meaning.

As a result, the book includes in its first movements the realist tales, a more traditional *testimonio* text from the first recorded conversations with additional editorial work, inevitably influenced by the unrecorded conversations, some archival references and the following encounters over the years. This means that some changes we explored with the HIJXS during the revisiting affected my writing of *testimonio*. For example, some harsh statements about family members who were not supportive (to say the least) during their worst experiences of the repressive Fujimori regime were watered down as these relationships are on the mend and the HIJXS have a more understanding view on the problematic positions people take during war/under violence, and all that they may do (or not do) due to fear. Another example was the HIJXS' encounters with other stories of people affected by the violence. Such encounters allowed them to enter into dialogue with those stories and place their own back into the landscape of memories in Peru, which also made them revise their views and particularly their former certainties. Such was the case in the following *postalita* based on a conversation with Miguel after his return to Lima.

Miguel at 25
Lima, Peru, 2012

When I listened to myself, I found a voice with huge confidence. This certainty ... I don't think I understood the dimension of what happened here. I didn't understand the dimension of what this place was. I didn't know how things were here. I hadn't appreciated, everything that people lived here, the relatives, my grandmother, the hijxs. Only recently, only after being here, have I started to learn everything that people suffered. And the hijxs who did live here, the youngest ones, were just little kids, and many didn't even meet their parents. I didn't understand how it was ... the dimension of what happened. Of the politics here. Of how huge this country is. Of its complexity. ... Before, things were much simpler. Before, what our parents did, I saw it as something heroic, very heroic. ... Everything they did. Being here, now, I see a lot of suffering that has been caused as a consequence of the violence, of the repression unleashed. ... Before, I couldn't grasp the consequences of all that. All that the relatives have suffered, all that they themselves suffered. That's what has changed, that's what I've changed.

Since the time we met in Peru, the HIJXS have continued their own projects. They have become a small but somehow known group in some spaces, a group whose existence questions the single story of the internal war, joining other memory initiatives and forms of activism, volunteering in marginalized communities without access to health services, and even taking part in electoral politics (and dealing with hostilities and direct attacks by social and traditional media alike). They are part of those 'memory militants' (Gatti, 2014), putting forward their memories in the 'battlefield' of the current 'struggles over memory' (Jelin, 2012). They continue moving and changing, making daily decisions to live and act in their worlds. The space of what is untellable continues shifting, not slightly but with sudden waves, 'irruptions of memory' wrote Wilde (1999) referring to Chile's transition; those events that feel like a 'sudden intrusion' to the seemingly stable (albeit conflictive) memory landscape, making available connections with the past more explicit than usual.[4]

---

[4] 'These charged events are woven into the very fabric of its politics today – symbolic issues, beyond the institutional arrangements well analyzed by political scientists' (Wilde, 1999: 475).

The second level refers to the troubles with myself, because in the process of troubling *testimonio* I also troubled myself.

I wandered and got lost wondering: how much were the stories about me versus them, or both? I started acknowledging that 'the HIJXS' stories were my way back to Peru, a country I left 22 years ago' (fieldwork notes, Lima, Peru, 2013). I had a constant concern about what to say and what not due to its risks, but mostly I was troubled when faced with my own story; the more I learned about my own history, the more complicated it became to decide on privacy, safety and the other people involved in my life (relatives and friends). I envisioned a more collective/collaborative writing but the HIJXS were simply not up for that; for them that was my task. But how was I to select what to write about? At every editorial step of the writing of *testimonio*, I have felt as if I were cutting them (the stories and the people) to pieces … exercising an additional violence to their lives … censoring their voices, for them but more because of what writing their stories might mean/bring for me.

This led to uncertain feelings and acute bodily pain when talking/writing about others' painful stories while I was finding it emotionally exhausting to even process my own … which went at a much slower pace than theirs … they lived in Peru most their lives, while I was going back for three-month-only fieldwork after 22 years … and I felt like I still needed time to make something out of it, which was awfully inadequate according to my doctoral student plans at the time. I used more creative writings when it came to my story, such as the following piece produced in the 'writing as inquiry' mode.

'No, not her' one shouted. 'The muki … enraged will bring down the mine' they said.

She will never come as close to a mine as that day. Her eyes were robbed of its adoration of a father who did not argue her case. She promised herself not to be stopped from entering any spaces, not on the basis of being a woman at least.

Fixed on this thought, she discovered how to enter people's minds and invite them to walk her through their tunnels of secret memories. Armed with this power, she called herself a researcher. No 'muki' would ever get in my way. Until secrets started chasing her and memories changing … some stories refused to be told and others wildly mixed up with one another. She felt useless as stories seem to have lost their minds. … Inexplicably, one day she got caught up inside this one:

Princess entered a world that expected and assumed her to be male. Along the years we moved to four different houses and she always came with us. After settling in our last house, we discovered Princess had been carrying a secret pregnancy. One night she dug a tunnel in the backyard and deposited ten little ones, only five will live.

She was part of all their movings but not this time. 'She is too many'/'They will never allow her in' said the parents. This time her family broke up into small pieces and came out in separate locations. Princess was left to the house and its unknown future inhabitants.

One year later, when the newspapers displayed pictures of that house being raided, they showed the tunnel in the backyard as their most compelling evidence. Princess was charged. She was prosecuted in absence by 'faceless judges' who decided she was guilty of treason and terrorism. No one saw or heard of Princess ever again, no pictures were kept, no stories were shared, and her name, unvoiced, left nothing but fear ... or was it guilt?

Nothing would be the same after that. *When was it, anyway?* Once a story was done with her, it unceremoniously spat her out like used chewing gum. She wandered around drunk, rambling to herself and furiously writing encrypted notes in countless tiny paper scraps that she stuffed inside her pillow in an attempt to dream with them. Until it happened again when she may have absent-mindedly fallen underground this or that time, getting caught up into another story ...

My own stories were only written in fragments and surreptitiously inserted in the *postalitas*. My own stories were not the planned material of this research, and at the same time my stories run throughout the whole process. I was constantly (re)writing myself, but I did not want to steal the spotlight from the HIJXS collective. This was the limit I imposed on the inclusion of my reflexive accounts of this journey. Still, there were leakages. At times it became necessary to include myself because otherwise I would be writing myself off, and that was never my intention. Neither was it possible.

The third level refers to the troubles with academia, because in the process of troubling *testimonio*, I also had troubles with academia.

A series of questions came up: what makes a valid doctoral dissertation? Countless times I was told 'storytelling does not make a dissertation' and that it requires 'the construction of an argument anchored in theory and data analysis' (as if that was not a story as well).[5] The problem is that I refused to consider people's stories and the HIJXS testimonial narratives as objects, as 'data', and I rejected the idea of 'analysing' their *testimonio*. I shared Behar's

---

[5] I was inspired to do otherwise by ethnography as genre explained by Biehl (2013: 591): 'Philosophers tell stories with concepts. Filmmakers tell stories with blocks of movements and duration. Anthropologists ... tell stories with instances of human becomings: people learning to live, living on, not learning to accept death, resisting death in all possible forms. Our characters are those who might otherwise remain forgotten, and they want to be represented, as Catarina did: to be part of a matrix in which there is someone else to listen and to think with and through their travails.' See also Van Maanen (2011) where he presents three genres of cultural representation for research writing: realist

fears. 'It worries me that one does violence to the life history of the story by turning it into the disposable commodity of information ... with its echoes of surveillance and disclosures of truth' (Behar, 2003: 13).

This stance pushed me to change the focus; the object of my research moved from *testimonio* to the process of constructing testimonial narratives. I was then left wondering how a process is studied. (Slippery!) My decision was to reflect in the final writing the 'cycling' of this inquiry as a way to theorize memory work in three movements, mimicking the process we journeyed through. Each cycle produced a different mode of writing, and different knowledges were made available.

More challenging was the question of how to include the testimonial narratives inside the corpus of the book, since they are the purpose of this project. The HIJXS entrusted me with their *testimonio* to intervene in the publicly available narratives of the Peruvian war. We engaged in a process of revisiting and sustaining conversations over producing the stories they wanted to tell. So, are the testimonial narratives their words (our conversations provided the raw material) or mine (I rewrote and edited them), are they data or analysis? The *testimonios* are evidently a co-production, and still their place at the centre of what was initially a doctoral dissertation (not as an appendix) required a constant struggle and difficult negotiation of academic rules and arguments. And the *postalitas*? Are those data or analysis, or what exactly?

The *postalitas* became even more complicated as deliberate creative writings based on our encounters. Some are easily recognizable from their specific *testimonios*, others not at all. They became objects to inquire into, we used them to engage in group conversations over fictionalizing and revisiting the testimonial, and ultimately from the second movement, to explore the politics of memory, in conversations about the collective, spaces/places and silences. The *postalitas* are not quotes, they are made up. And yet, they are 'real' in the sense that they are significant and re-represent knots and threads in the stories we produced during our encounters about our lives. They contain stories that can be shared, stories we live by. They are close to what Isbell (2005), writing an ethnographic novel and performances about the Peruvian war, considered the reality of 'the really made up' that Taussig (1984) was referring to.

'The stories possible thus far ...'

Over the years I realized the existence of other stories, and that the places in which they were enacted (told) mattered. Spaces and places heavily marked the stories possible, as it happened to us, while travelling from

---

tales (matter of fact, assumption of legitimacy), confessional tales (acknowledging the personal journey of the researcher increases results legitimacy) and impressionist tales (dramatic storytelling tone of crucial event, affective legitimacy).

Peru (where they were experienced albeit individually), to Cuba (where they were recorded and became collective), and back to Peru (where they were revisited and continued living), and even to the UK (where they were mostly written).

I was driven to further inquire into the story-making process, convinced that there are more 'stories possible'. I was moved by the idea that our stories could not be contained in any of the available narratives of the Peruvian internal war but that they are at the same time constrained by that which was available, by that which framed the possibilities of the listening. So, actually, what I felt is an urge, a craving, a need to create a different space for other possible stories. Creative writing and the poetics of memory, then, were about opening ourselves to imagination. Those might just be the ways I could think of to create another space for other stories to be made possible.

And also, I thought that if you can enter into the task of rewriting your story it would mean you own it. In her auto-ethnographic novel Winterson describes the writing of her stories as a peculiar form of exercising control: 'in such a way as to leave a gap, an opening. It is a version, but never the final one. And perhaps we hope that the silences will be heard by someone else, and the story can continue, can be retold' (Winterson, 2011: 8). I did have that impulse for making these stories matter to us, for reclaiming them as our stories. So much has happened in our lives by others' decisions that I felt I owe it to ourselves to make it possible to own our stories and the ways we tell them, and to make it at the same time an offer; an opening to encounter (and even clash against) other stories.

12

Writing (about) Violence

I always thought *silence* was the most difficult part of the whole thing. Thus, I imagined starting my writing by saying how hard it was to keep silent and how safeguarding the silenced for all these years has also been harmful. I pictured a starting line saying 'All in all silence has been the worst' (which would have neatly fit as a prelude to the subsequent telling of the stories).

My own journey demonstrates how powerful silences are. I lived in Peru as a child during the internal war, left in 1991 and returned only in 2012, over 20 years later. Yet every time I listen to the Cuba recordings, I can feel at work mechanisms of censoring and self-censoring cemented by a widely used politics of fear (Burt, 2006; 2008) through the decades that have left effects on me (and others). On my return to Peru, I found the mix of silence and speech to be more complicated than before, different than how I lived it abroad. And still, I could feel it.

But after listening and relistening to all those stories recorded first in Cuba (2007) and then in Lima (2012, 2013), and keeping them in encrypted electronic files with more than one back-up, and in yellow paper notes with blue ink and graphite, which I have fearfully taken with me on every trip around four different countries ... I no longer think silence was the most difficult part.

Long kept silences are not simple, especially when they are not in a vacuum ... when silences are hushed, only their corners mentioned by cryptic words, when they are replaced by other made-up stories ... cover-up stories ... those stories that sustain the silences. Altering one story, exposing one silence will make everything crumble. Such silences are not easily broken, because the grid of stories sustaining them makes it impossible to figure out the tellable from untellable ... to foresee what might happen if or when silences are exposed.

I relisten to the recordings and hear myself repetitively trying to find out how they learned to live with the clandestine lives of their parents. My question is received

> as absurd, rather irrelevant to them. I hear a feeling of disbelief in my silence ... as if they just lived it.

Telling or talking about our stories has been much harder ... and ultimately *writing* proved to be even more complicated. Probably because the outcomes of the process would not stay between us, in the group, but shared with others. Sharing requires creating a way to make sense of our experiences, and for that to find a language to narrate, another language because the available one is not suitable for our stories (Gatti, 2011; 2014).[1] Even more, it requires an audience willing to listen to certain war and post-war stories, which is particularly hard in a polarized society where stories that do not conform to the neat terrorism–victims narrative are suffocated. These are 'dangerous truths' in the post-war memory landscape (but who or what is in danger?). Yet, in the process of making *testimonio* a written object, I am also afraid of losing what makes such stories unique, and somehow ourselves as well, and the bond we have built based on that, and ... Sometimes, it felt as if I was going through a sort of mourning. It got even more complicated as I thought about the content of the stories. What is to be told and what can be told about them, about me, about us? What can and will be heard/read from such writings?

Silvio Rodríguez (1975), the trova singer of the Cuban revolution, once evoked the difficulties of writing – writing war, writing revolutions, writing violence – in his song 'Playa Girón'. His song was a close companion since the beginning of writing. With urgency, it asks other *compañeros* – poets, musicians and historians – how to represent the Playa Girón stories.[2] To each, he communicates the urgency of his quest as well as the complexities gripping each form of re-presentation.

---

1   Gatti (2014) argues that forced disappearance produces also a catastrophe of language. Language (as we know it) shatters in the face of catastrophe. A new language must be created from those who inhabit the world leftover by such devastating force. Gatti explains, '[catastrophe] is the disarticulation of words from things, of meanings from facts, a disarticulation turned into structure. It is distinguishable from trauma in that it is impossible to fix; it is different from an event in its duration. And like trauma, even if it seems impossible, it is characterized because in it life and meaning are created and contained' (2014: 15–16).

2   Playa Girón refers both to the name of a Cuban fishing boat where Rodriguez was forced to live for several months as punishment, and of the bay where the Cubans defeated the Central Intelligence Agency-sponsored invasion. The song is about sung and unsung heroes, alluding to the difficulty of writing the stories of those who are never considered in the narratives of the revolution.

To poets, he asks what sorts of adjectives could be used to write a poem that is neither over-sentimental nor just a propaganda pamphlet, or not revolutionary enough. To musicians, he asks what sort of harmonies could be used to write a song about men who barely had a childhood, 'black, and red, and blue men' that inhabit the Playa Girón. And lastly, to historians:

> [C]onsidering how implacable the truth must be/ ... what should I say?/ what borders should I respect?/ if someone steals food and later sacrifices his life/ what do you do?/ how far can we follow these truths/ how much do we really know?/ So, let them write the history, their own history, the men of Playa Girón.

It is in this last dialogue that the song touches on the ideas of borderlands used here as 'a vague and undetermined place created by the emotional residue of an unnatural boundary ... in a constant state of transition. The prohibited and the forbidden are its inhabitants' (Anzaldúa, 1987: 3). The act of writing armed revolutions, Rodríguez implies, is a borderland activity that organizes (clashing) fictions and delineates temporary truths precisely because its protagonists inhabit borderlands, from thieves (terrorists?) to revolutionary martyrs (or the other way around). Writing (violent) defeats, as this project is doing, drives one deeper into borderlands because the pain and anguish of 'otherness' is the pain and anguish of the 'defeated': the 'terrorists', whose children, now adults, caught in the victims/perpetrators dichotomy, seek to negotiate resistance through *testimonio*. Writing with the protagonists of these stories, it turns out, is not without ambiguity and contradiction, neither here nor there: using realist tales and creative writing; challenging one discourse of re-presentation and at the same time using it to gain legitimacy, and in the process producing new problems, creating a constant movement, a crossing between one side of the border to the other, restlessly.

Writing in the borderlands often requires writing (about) violence. Indeed, borderlands are highly repressive spaces of the prohibited and the forbidden. Writing *testimonios* draws attention to the specific challenges that confront researchers who work on violence when making decisions about how to write violence. While *testimonio* debates have provided thoughtful and critical insights regarding the challenges of re-presentation (Gugelberger, 1996; Arias, 2001), such discussions barely touch on the practical as well as ethical and methodological dilemmas researchers face when writing (about) violence and in particular the effects such writings have on producing and reproducing particular discursive and material realities, more violence.

How do we write about acts of violence, such as torture, without creating what Taussig (1992) termed 'the pornography of terror' that makes a spectacle of violence for our readers yet without also rendering our work a trivial account devoid of meaning? There are recurrent questions that violence forces us to confront when making decisions over writing encounters with violence that may be (re)told in past tense but resonate in the present and continue to be lived in the present tense.

> I notice some silences of the too horrible to voice … (I worry about that thin divide from voyeurism) and there's a lowering of voices that reminds me we should not be recording these … the *testimonios* themselves then as sites of struggles over memory. And yes, what about my own silences? Have I not also learnt by now that some things should not/cannot be talked about, to be 'careful'?

The fact that I cannot answer such questions has troubled me throughout this testimonial work. It weighs so strongly that it even stops me from writing altogether. A substantive body of scholarship has examined representations of violence and their effects in our discursive and material realities (Nordstrom and Robben, 1995; Feitlowitz, 1999; Lorey and Beezley, 2002; Crandall, 2004; Sontag, 2004; Carpenter, 2007; Esparza et al, 2009). This literature however pays less attention to the question of how we re-present violence in our research given such awareness. How do we write about violence in a meaningful way, knowing that the stories we were told in the field matter, when we are haunted by how violence is presented in our writing and when we try to bring about some form of change?

Geertz (1973) introduced the term 'thick description' to encourage ethnographic accounts that embrace a fully fleshed, interpretive and contextualized writing style. But how was I to write a thick description of *experiencias límite*, at those borders where meaning escapes and interpretations feel so insufficient that they become more of a guessing game? Moreover, how to use it for testimonial writing in a context of continuing repression? *Testimonio*, with the HIJXS, became our effort to bear witness to that which is beyond representation by stubbornly re-presenting it nonetheless (or around it as in the case of silences), only to later challenge it. Still, the group required producing first the testimonial object in its realist form to later question and challenge it from their changing lives over time and the spaces we traversed.

I have a difficult relationship with my writing, but never have I been more troubled than when I faced the problems of writing about experiences of torture by the second generation (the children of, the hijxs). Their accounts in some cases included detailed descriptions about torture. How am I to re-present this in my writing?

For instance, in our first recorded conversations, Willy gave me a detailed account of his aunt Gladys' torture, not once but twice (about a week in between). I wrote several versions, and at each decision, I was confronted with another question, another concern. I ended up settling for a much shorter (sanitized?) version in the *testimonio* presented in the first movement. I also included a footnote with statements made before the Inter-American Court of Human Rights about the brutal and systematic use of torture, including sexual violence, by the state security forces against Willy's aunt, as well as how the different state institutions in Peru all the way up to the judicial system have neglected any investigation, justice or reparations because within the legal system she is considered a 'terrorist'.

Having the different cycles of inquiry contributed to sustaining the questions that the writing brought upon; questions that remained in the back of my mind and reinforced the need for further inquiry into this 'writing dilemma', to leave some space to write the 'writing stories'. After all, the movement to a poetics of memory became necessary precisely to make space for exploring the problems encountered in, and produced by, the writing of *testimonio* as process. Broadly speaking, it has been inspired by Richardson's writing as a method of inquiry, and her suggestion of 'writing writing-stories' (2002).

In what follows I reproduce the two different transcripts from my conversations with Willy that touched explicitly on his aunt's torture.

Transcript 1

And from Gladys' own mouth I heard it when I visited in Chorrillos that she was tortured. They were caught and separated, Rafael's dad and Gladys; they started torturing them separately, telling them to talk about their things, sing! sing! ... *habla! canta!* They didn't say anything and worse and worse, they broke their nails, they would take her nail off, they put cables on her body, they electrocute her, they burn her, they beat her, they tried to rape her, and to Rafael's old man as well, they beat him, *les dieron de alma*, and they never revealed anything. But the worst was that they would bring Rafael's dad in front of Gladys, she would be hooded and they beat her and beat her, and they would do that to force him to speak. And that was every day, every day. And that lasted several days. And they would move them to different locations, constantly. Because my uncle Manuel and my grandma together with the International Red Cross were looking for Gladys everywhere, but they would transfer her to different locations so they could never find her. So, one of those times, Aunt Gladys was beaten so much that she lost consciousness and she couldn't see anymore. Even now she can't see well, and her left ear is ... she can hear but only with her right ear. ... *En ese maltrato fue donde fallece el papá de Rafael, mi tía también ya se daba por muerta.* Rafael's dad died as a result of the torture, my aunt herself thought she was dead.

Transcript 2

> She was tortured in so many different ways, at many different moments. Let's start with the psychological. They isolated her in a dark cell when she was incarcerated. And then it was physical torture, like burning the tip of her fingers, extracting each of her fingernails slowly, burning her with a soldering tool. They also electrocuted her, they beat her, they kicked her, they punched her. She was probably raped as well, it wouldn't surprise me, it's what I understood from what she told me, it was implicit in what she said, *la ultrajaban*, she was embarrassed to tell her nephew that she was raped. She said it in a way that might be understood. Also, the psychological torture of making Rafael's father watch how she was tortured, and the other way around. She was left unconscious and woken up with a load of cold water, then again and again, every day. She didn't even know where she was, or recognize any of her torturers, many times she couldn't even see due to the bruises, nor even hear because they ruptured her ear *de un golpe*. She couldn't stand up; she was sleeping on her side because of the bodily pain. It was constant, to force her to speak … and she never said anything.

On the one hand, my concern is about erasing the details as a form of sanitizing the account so as to make readers (and myself as writer/reader) less uncomfortable, and in doing so, taking out something he was explicitly denouncing. Would I not be imposing a further violence to Willy's attempt to break imposed silences by silencing his 'detailed' account? When the whole testimonial process was based on the idea of challenging the several forms of silencing experiences they have lived, it is hard to again reproduce such silencing upon their stories. On the other hand, including all those details might also become that sort of 'pornography of terror', or produce a sort of voyeuristic reader (and writer). Would I simply end up producing a text that provided space for getting off on the spectacle of violence or me as the writer exploiting this to attract readers' attention (or feel better about myself)?

There is also a concern that the effect of 'listing' torture methods makes them banal and that I would end up trivializing a traumatic experience with a text devoid of meaning, or at least not as meaningful/powerful as it was felt in our conversations. Or even worse, that a description of torture also contributes to reproducing torture's intended 'fear' effects ('*meter miedo*'), and as a result I would become an accomplice of torture, warning people of what happens with opposition and resistance against the government.

I find all alternatives scary, even as I write them. I had to write both versions from transcripts of our conversation, and then write also how problematic I found each: how do we talk about terror without it haunting us, without us becoming it … to acknowledge how ungraspable it is? How it escapes our (writing) control, no matter what we intend or what we decide? '[H]olding it at arm's length', Taussig recommended, because 'terror's talk always talks back' (1992: 11).

This exposes the difficulties of writing torture, as it is an extreme experience. In trauma and Holocaust literature it is considered one of those un-narratable experiences beyond representation. The question, then, is: how do we communicate such extreme experiences (that is, state perpetration of torture) for the purpose of denouncing without reproducing their effects as well? I say this because, all along, I was also thinking of Clifford and Marcus' *Writing Culture* (1986) where it was no longer a matter of writing about culture, but writing with the awareness of the problematic relationship between text and experience (once there is no transparent relationship between the word and the world [Lather, 2007: 83]). Writing here is not a means to describe culture but a way of inscribing it.

It caught my attention that there was a strong presence of torture in the HIJXS *imaginario* and our testimonial conversations. It is telling of how they experienced torture, although it was not what is called direct experience. This brings me back once again to the problematics of the direct/indirect experience distinction for memory purposes (and the concept of post-memory) and with that the granting of greater legitimacy to the 'direct' experience testimony for memory work or oral history.

> 1, 2, 3 ... 10, 11, 12 ... 20, 21 ... hold it ... and just when you think you can't hold it any longer, wait a little bit more ... sometimes your ears pop, or you may just hear a low-key buzzing ... must hold it ... just a bit longer.
>
> Years later, my brother and I realized that every time we go swimming, we test ourselves to see how far we can swim without taking a breath. I can do 25 metres easily; my record is 30 strokes. Cannot remember how I learnt that ... but it had everything to do with the presence of torture and the idea of waterboarding as a plausible experience, something around the corner ... something that in our child's mind we could be prepared for ... we had no idea.

It might be that it caught my attention because I, as well, grew up surrounded by the presence of a torture *imaginario* as part of the larger context of repression, which also fed on stories heard and news and films watched like *Jacobo Timerman: Prisoner Without a Name, Cell Without a Number* (1983) based on Timerman's writings on his detention under the Argentine dictatorship. Torture was always there.

In the end, as with many problematic writings, and the knots encountered, I wrote 'my way in' (Speedy, 2014) in two forms: as in the earlier discussion of possible ways to understand an issue (mixed with ramblings), and as in the extract in the previous text box about my own life, digging into it and how I feel part of such issue. I also wrote 'my way out' of it, as usual throughout this inquiry, with a *postalita*. I wrote the following *postalita* taking our conversations with Willy about torture, fragments from conversations with hijxs, and my own impressions.

Willy at 23
Havana, Cuba, 2007

Torture has a way of getting hold of you, *te llega hasta dentro … se te mete* under your skin. Once you know it has happened close to you … you can feel … there is fear and there is anger, even hate. And these weird fantasies … nightmares I should say. I once used a soldering tool on myself just to imagine how she'd felt, and it made me sick … it made me question how it is possible that someone uses that on another person. … Normal things are not seen in the same way, like objects, films, or the news … or military and police officers … not even your own family.

Writing in the in-between spaces, the borderlands of not-knowing that appear in the doing of research, as Speedy (2014) said about collaborative inquiry (dig in deeper, explore the stuck or the unknown places by writing from/ within them). What does this mean for writing violence? I opted to operate with the cycles of inquiry as they unfolded over time and space. First, to write the *testimonios* as realist tales; second, to engage critically with their politics and what can be said and what not, for what purposes, contributing to or opposing which narratives of the internal war; and then, third, to connect with the multiple possibilities of re-presenting violence, a poetics of memory to ponder on how each writing attempt brought up another problematic.

There is another question that I notice burning at the back of my mind after writing this problem with writing torture … why did those who were tortured by the state communicate their experiences to their own children (the young adults I worked with) … why would a father write his son a letter (also read by his nephew and niece) describing the ways he was tortured by the army? Why would an aunt hold a conversation with her nephew detailing the police torture she endured?

Silencing, Taussig (1992) explains, is not the same as 'silence' or 'oblivion'. It is not about erasing what happened, but keeping it alive although confined to the private sphere. It is not about 'forgetting' memories but systematic acts of *silencing* memories. Maybe it is possible to see that communicating torture to their next generation is a countermove to such silencing; sharing such extreme experience with those who would believe it (their children), with those who should be warned (repression threatened their families). Maybe it was an attempt to pass on knowledge of the brutalities of state repression so they too know how the system works and do not believe the available mainstream knowledge; the image so carefully drawn by the media. And maybe it is about constructing and passing on the heroic tale, of how they did not speak under torture, as the stories of torture are always told by the ones who did not speak (as da Silva Catela [2009] discussed in Argentina). Or maybe it was a story about demonstrating the strength of their convictions, how much they were willing to take for what they believed in, the so-called 'revolutionary mystique'. Maybe it was a warning tale for them to be careful or be safe ... or maybe even a story about clandestine lives and safety, about lives lived on the edge, where what you know about others becomes a matter of life and death, and thus be mindful of the things they knew, the things they should forget, and the things they should not know ... and of course the things the HIJXS cannot talk about. And maybe, just maybe, it was all those many reasons jumbled up together. Now, all that wondering forces me to ask myself, why is it I find such communication of torture experiences within the family disturbing?

On one hand, I am still unreconciled with the idea of growing up in such an environment; I think children should be spared that pain. Sometimes I find myself very critical of parents who hide their political lives and keep their children in the dark, leaving their children to live in this world with only half-heard explanations (*entre el ver y no-ver, entreviendo*), only to be suddenly taken by surprise later with unexplainable losses and fear. Other times, I find myself critical of the stories told to children, painful, disturbing stories about extreme injustices and the horrors of repression and war, or how in some cases they became implicated in their parents' political lives. Sometimes in the abstract it sounds wrong to get children involved (that is, bring them to certain activities, trips or 'safe' houses) and yet, in that reality it sounds like their only way to be close to the children; it was either that or exclude them. Keeping them 'safe' was equivalent to not being with them. And for many that was the way (I do not want to say option, because it seems that, during war, those were not lived as options). There is no easy answer, and I find myself at odds in this idea of judging the parents' decisions in the now, from another time with hindsight, another place and another context, without being fully able to understand the reality they were living and how they lived it. It reminds me that I write from that space of not-knowing, and yet a space in which my own life unfolded, a space of working for other forms of writing these tentative forms of knowing; my effort to make my own borderlands a productive space.

Writing practices (I)

Several forms of writing were produced in the process that this cycling for inquiry opened. Indeed, with all its repressiveness, the borderlands are at the same time a productive space. Referring to forced disappearance as a catastrophe that collapsed identity and meaning (and thus language) Gatti argues that, and contrary to expectations, '[e]xistence is possible there, and meaning is constructed' (2014: 12).

Without claiming that the experiences of state repression for the HIJXS in Peru are the same as of those lived around the detained-disappeared in the Southern Cone, there are connections evident in the use of the H.I.J.O.S. acronym and strong differences such as the prevalence of a widespread 'children of the terrorist' stigma in Peru. At the same time, the Peruvian internal war also brought catastrophic consequences for language and meaning-making practices. Hence the importance of memory work and the 'labours of memory' (Jelin, 2003), that praxis of working through.

During my second stay in Peru in 2013, we travelled with a few of the HIJXS to Huancayo in the central highlands, to connect with other stories we had heard plenty about, and look for other 'children of'. Near Huancayo lies Molinos, where in April 1989 there was an armed confrontation between the army and a Tupac Amaru Revolutionary Movement (MRTA) column, according to some, or an ambush by the army, according to others. Almost all the MRTA militants there were killed. In the aftermath an unknown number of people from the surrounding communities of Huertas and Molinos were taken by the army in a sweep that left no witnesses, *un rastrillaje*; the Truth and Reconciliation Commission (TRC) registers 22 (TRC, 2003a), seven of whom remain disappeared. Thirty-four years later a judicial investigation into these forced disappearances is still open but never seems to progress. But those were not the only disappeared. The army also took the bodies of the MRTA militants, making it impossible to investigate how they died (in combat or extrajudicial killings?). Fifty-five bodies were said to be buried in a mass grave without markers, as N.N., cement and a steamroller were used on top ... when the relatives built a memory stone to mark the mass grave, it was blown up. Visiting their dead became dangerous for the relatives. For the children of MRTA militants the absence of the bodies and of reliable information about what happened or their identity and the lack of personal grave markers deny them the certainty of death. They still retain a stubborn hope that their parents might have escaped, remain hidden and eventually might return. *Será que vuelven?*[3]

---

[3] The phrase *será que vuelven?* comes from a conversation with someone whose father disappeared in Molinos and which I incorporated in a text while researching the case. In 2019, a collaboration with Isaac Ernesto Ruiz resulted in a video with the same title: www.isaacernesto.com/video/seraquevuelven

In 1995, all the bodies were exhumed from the mass grave by the forensic team as part of the legal investigations into the whereabouts of the missing community members. In order to identify them, it was necessary to establish which bodies were in the mass grave. The relatives of the MRTA militants provided DNA samples in order to identify their own and receive their bodies for burial, or have some ritual. But 28 years later no one provides an explanation, as if no one could be held accountable for that process. Every now and then, the relatives receive notice that the bodies will be returned, but nothing happens. People say the bones are in boxes in the local Public Prosecutor's Office in Jauja (near Molinos), no one knows in what condition.

Once, I accompanied the wife of a MRTA militant killed in Molinos to the Public Prosecutor's Office to inquire about the investigations and the news of a possible trial. Upon our arrival, the first question was if her relative was a 'victim' or a 'terrorist'. The distinction was key to the Prosecutor, pigeonholing this woman in such categories was a necessary first step. And yet, once that was established, it did not grant access to information, or maybe precisely because of that.

Right there is another reminder of how they do not fit into the categories of mainstreamed narratives of the Peruvian war, narratives reinforced and acted upon by local public officers and determining the acceptance or denial of elementary human rights. Another reminder of how impossible it feels/is to sustain a conversation when the terms of such conversation are pre-established, at odds with the language available to narrate our experiences in general and in particular the experiences of state repression.

> The thing is that the MRTA militants in Molinos are not disappeared because it is known where and when they were killed, and who they were. Yet they become disappeared because their bodies, taken by the army to a detention centre, were never returned but buried in a mass grave without identification, later to be exhumed and deposited without a name in boxes in an old office of the local public prosecutor. And because of the context in which they died, the search for information as well as their remains was difficult, endless and posed a risk to their relatives' lives. Their children still waiting ... for something.

The people killed at Molinos, be it in combat, ambush and/or extrajudicial killings, and how their absence affected their relatives and particularly their children, do not necessarily fit the detained-disappeared category used in Argentina, Uruguay and Chile. They most certainly do not fit the category of 'disappeared' in Peru, and even less the 'victim' category created in the post-war context and legally established to exclude those who were members of the armed groups.[4] And still, the ripples of the stories from the Southern Cone can be felt in the Molinos case, with the difficulties of openly discussing it (what happened to the community members?) as the complicated positions in which it puts the relatives and 'the children of'.

What is important for me with this story in this section was the complex situation people at the edges of the main narratives of the Peruvian war find themselves in; struggling with language to narrate a shareable story, struggling with language to interact with public institutions and the legal field, struggling with language to be recognized. Similarly, I have then been struggling to write all the stories shared with me by the group and their relatives. Gatti wrote that between believing that language can handle representation, that data, truth and objectivity can continue to be used in spite of catastrophe, and the opposite belief that representation is impossible because language becomes powerless in the face of extreme violence, and there is nothing that can be said, there is another option: 'If the facts went *beyond,* then language must venture out and explore new territories ... language *can always go beyond*' (Gatti, 2014: 118; emphasis in original).

When we started the testimonial recordings, all I was looking for was these sorts of victim stories, yet all I heard then were extraordinary stories about suffering, hardship and surviving the state repression the HIJXS had lived, what they had to face without having had any decision in their involvement. They/we were born into these lives, unlike the parents, who went through a process of deciding to get involved in armed struggle and particularly to be part of the MRTA. Unlike them, the HIJXS stories were about living the consequences of state and societal repression, the clandestine lives of their/our parents, the detention, torture and consequent 'visits' to prison. But that is what I call my flawed listening. ... I do not think they were telling me victim stories, at least not necessarily, but later on I became certain that my listening was focused on exactly that.

Later on, I got to know them, and by this, I mean engaged with them in their lives, hanging out with them in collective meetings, parties and short trips, celebrating birthdays or whatever other things celebrated their collective life, its existence. After all the time waiting for buses (which you do a lot in Cuba) and hanging out (which I later read could be translated into academic language as ethnographic method, as 'deep hanging out') ... they

---

[4] According to the Regulations of Law No. 28592, the law creating the Comprehensive Reparations Plan (PIR) and Article 54 of the Central Victims Registry (RUV) members of subversive organizations are excluded. Supreme Decree No.015-2006-JUS, approved 6 July 2006 (see Macher, 2009). Also Marie Manrique (2014: 70): 'La ley de reparaciones específicamente señala en su artículo 4 que "no son consideradas víctimas y por ende no son beneficiarios de los programas a que se refiere la presente Ley, los miembros de organizaciones subversivas' (Ley 28592, 29 de julio de 2005).

started to become fuller people, more complicated than mere victims, more full of life and contradictions… the more we got drunk, the more I could see their use of humour, even to refer to their lives, their past, their parents' lives … and how full of laughter and caring, solidarity and camaraderie their lives were as well (how they felt very loved and had an emotional/affective relationship with the lives of their parents and their *compañerxs*). Their parents' *compañerxs* (or *tíos*) were perceived to be a large family made out of an intricate mix of blood, ideals and hardship. This was an important change; it changed me and how I saw them. And this in turn made me realize the flawed process of testimonial making we had so far. The more time I spent with them not recording our conversations but doing things and having informal conversations, the more peopled our stories became, the less we reified the victim stories that I first so attentively and exclusively listened to.

And much later on, five years later … our conversations changed tone completely. They became more intimate, more nuanced, less structured … and longer and broader. At some point I thought their stories had changed and become more intimate because time had passed and they were in another place (in their lives and geographically). And maybe this is so, but also maybe it is because our relationship had changed, and the first denouncing testimonial narrative has already been told, leaving or creating more space for other stories, for life to leak into the testimonial. Maybe because we had become more intimate, more vulnerable, more friends, there was also the possibility for other stories to populate the testimonial.

> I felt as if I had more space in my head for other memories, more space to remember other things, and even to forget. (Iris, Cusco, Peru, 2013)

Iris put words to that feeling I was having. Relistening to her own recorded stories five years later surprised Iris for how articulate they were, and how full of little details of those times, details she claims to have now forgotten. Somehow talking for the very first time, at length, in a trusting environment, meant summoning their remembrances, giving shape to memories, creating links between experiences and words to tell them, making a story. And after doing that it felt as if they/we had more space in their/our heads for other memories, more space even to forget.

I only understood that feeling after I finally sat down and wrote the stories; for all the tension and crying, the care and difficulty of finding the words, putting them down on paper also brought relief. Finally, they were leaving my head, finally the voices stopped roaming around aimlessly … they were out there; they had acquired materiality, that I could even touch, revisit, relate to, strikeout or highlight, and even interrogate and problematize.

And I wanted to account for that as well. I no longer wanted anymore the victim stories I was after at the beginning (not those at least). I wanted to celebrate life as well, our lives, as individuals and of course also as a collective. There is a slogan that has stayed with me from other HIJXS groups: '*y finalmente, nuestra máxima venganza será ser felices*' ('and at the end, our ultimate revenge will be, to be happy'). The thing is, I'm not sure I like it or not; it has this good side, but also somehow a certain sadness as well … I guess it depends on what makes us happy … but, I can't help feeling it has some individualistic neoliberal tone to it. Yet, it was so deliberately made for our lives to be bad, full of sorrow and in fear, demoralized to never recover any impulse for political activism of any sort, almost destroyed, but only almost, that somehow to be joyful seems like quite a struggle in light of all that.

Testimonio *reading as victim stories*

The 'innocent' victim narrative as pervasive in the Peruvian context is problematic, and more than that. As Jelin notes, it is 'not only problematic but dangerous' (Jelin, 2013). Such a qualifier of 'innocence' to grant victimhood creates two distinguishable categories of people, whereas those who are considered non-innocent are stripped of their rights, thus legitimizing the human rights violations during the internal war. Several of the trials at the Inter-American Court of Human Rights against the Peruvian state have highlighted a similar issue; those under the 'terrorist' category lose any human rights. In fact, after the TRC the creation of the Central Victims Register includes a clause whereby relatives of 'terrorists' cannot be registered as 'victims'.[5]

The HIJXS *testimonio* collection aimed at intervening in the main narratives of the internal war, including a challenge to the victim narrative. Nevertheless, the stories presented in the first movement can also be read as victim narratives (albeit adding 'victims' from another side previously excluded from the category). Their previous generation's struggles almost fade into the background with a stronger focus on how it affected them and the consequences of state repression. The HIJXS in their rejection of the

---

[5] The issue has been challenged on several occasions, including the case of [Gladys] Espinoza González versus Peru at the Inter-American Court of Human Rights. An extract from the latest statement during the trial in April 2014 follows: 'This case is brought to court because the Peruvian state has not responded to the pressing need to provide reparations and justice to a victim that nowadays is devastated physically and psychologically due to the *ensañamiento* and extreme violence perpetrated against her. The persistence of cases of the same nature presented to the Inter-American System is an indicator that the Peruvian state has not taken effective measures to respond comprehensively in terms of reparations and in terms of justice towards a particular group of victims of the armed conflict, towards the people who had a real or perceived link with terrorism' (my translation from a video extract on the IACHR website, www.youtube.com/watch?v=E0et6XKI9NI).

over-simplistic characters (be it terrorist, victim or hero) resulting from the available narratives fall into difficult territories to narrate. In which landscape should their stories be situated?

Still, this loses sight of the context in which the *testimonios* are produced, a context in which their parents (and relatives) cannot be considered victims in the internal war narrative and not even in the TRC report, because in such a neat perpetrator–victim dichotomy, the HIJXS relatives belong to the perpetrator side. The HIJXS thus have a complicated relationship with the victim category, sometimes rejecting it, other times using it. For example, by simply positioning themselves as victims, they are already problematizing the victim-centred narrative, and more specifically the 'innocent victim' category created in the transition period that remains institutionalized and reproduced in the media and academic research.[6]

Some possible reasons for why these *testimonios* may sound like victim narratives include the presence of silences. First, it is important to consider that the HIJXS continue to be extremely cautious about stating what they think about armed struggle. This is evident in how they very seldom mention the MRTA with its full letters. Also, there are very few references in which they discuss what their parents did as acts of violence, and how they feel about that.

Second, I was also their most immediate audience. They were talking directly to me, someone they assumed was already 'on their side'. Thus, no explanations were required, as we shared a discourse about it. Assumed common/shared knowledge and discourse/position also creates unspoken topics as 'we all know that', things that remain un-enunciated and unproblematized.

In addition, it is clear to me that one does not always construct the story one wants to do, or was aiming for, the story in mind at the outset. Plenty of times, as the writing of this book has made me more aware, you are taken by the stories, taken by the writing. This also means that plenty of times those stories draw from the available language, how to denounce state repression without positioning as victim?

I wrote a *postalita* with a brief dialogue between Abel and Rafael in which they argue about this.

Abel at 26 and Rafael at 24
Havana, Cuba, 2008

Abel: The problem with the TRC is that it doesn't say what happened to us, those on the other side. The defeated. For

---

[6] Before the transition period, during the internal war, even the idea of victim did not exist, any victim was suspicious of having done something '*por algo será*', which gave rise to the 'innocent victim' category and somehow its necessity given the previous context and the environment of suspicion surrounding 'victims' in the aftermath of war.

them we weren't victims. Even afterwards they passed a law saying sons and other relatives of 'terrorists' cannot claim reparations. They don't want to acknowledge us as victims.

Rafael: Victims? I'm not a victim.

Abel: We were all affected by state repression.

Rafael: I know. Yes, there's that ... but still, I don't consider myself a victim. I'm no victim.

Agüero (2015) in *Los Rendidos*, his personal essay about growing up as 'the children of', with both parents Shining Path militants and both killed by state security forces (extrajudicial killings), discusses the complications of the victim position. He reminds us, for example, that the women from Ayacucho, associated in the Asociación Nacional de Familiares, Secuestrados, Detenidos y Desaparecidos del Perú (ANFASEP), used to refer to themselves as 'affected' instead of 'victims', and later incorporated the 'victim' category into their discourse during the TRC context, the *audiencias* and reparations, the consequent Central Victim Registry and the trials against the military.[7] More interesting from Agüero is his own changing position; his unresolved dilemmas of not fitting in, which exposes the absurdity and violence of such neat categories. At some point he writes that he could not consider himself a victim because his mother had 'not raised him to be a victim'.

'Victim' talk produces a dilemma for claiming reparations and rights. This position creates a difficulty, even discomfort, for the HIJXS: are they relating to the victim category as a political claim to denounce the long-held silence of state repression? Are they landing in the disempowering effect of the term, where victims are seen as passive? Would they have to act the 'victim' role? Within the 'democratic transition' and the post-conflict scenario, how do they consider themselves: as rights holders, victims, entitled to justice or reparations, or as accomplices (guilt) with the burden of providing explanations and reparations? The HIJXS find themselves in a borderlands space: somewhere in-between, but more beyond those categories (victim–perpetrator) that were reified in the TRC.

Agüero (2015) sharply challenges the academic discourse (with its almost pendulum movement for and against) that is countering the victim narrative because it reduces actors to passive beings with no agency. It is not that Agüero disagrees completely, at least not in theory, but that in a country like post-war Peru, where positioning as victim might be the only way to

---

[7]   It would be interesting to trace the changes in the category used for self-identity purposes by the communities of relatives demanding a response by the state, that is, how the different contexts also imposed the adoption of different categories as needed in their struggles for recognition.

attain recognition and ultimately citizenship, performing such a category becomes an important one. Regardless of the academic debate, in practice denying the use of the category is equivalent to dismissing the struggles for recognition of those neglected for long enough.

Years after the dialogue between Abel and Rafael, Rafael started a process of his own once back in Peru. He inquired into the possibility of registering his father's killing in the Central Victim Registry. He found that, according to the regulations, because his father's case was one of the 47 emblematic cases the TRC investigated and sent to the Prosecutor's Office (as evidence of the use of torture by the police) his father must have been automatically registered (together with all the TRC investigated cases). That fact rushed his decision to go to the national registry office and 'register' himself. It was not an easy decision, but rather one full of anxiety: what if they question him (interrogate even?) regarding his father's *militancia*? He worried that registering would mean being vulnerable to the accusation of 'terrorism', because according to the law those who were members of armed groups cannot be considered victims. Still, Rafael's father was not charged with terrorism because he was killed at the police station before any trial was possible. Could Rafael register himself as a victim? What effects could that bring? Was it necessary to register, important even? He was extremely anxious before and on the day we went together with his mom to the national office. Once we were there, the whole registration act was nothing more than another bureaucratic procedure, a check in the database, a check of IDs, all very technical resulting in the printing of an official document establishing that indeed Rafael's father was a victim of the 'Internal Armed Conflict' and the state apologized for it. Rafael said the bureaucracy of 'obtaining a diploma' for his father's death was a bizarre experience ('First they killed him, then they give me a diploma, in-between they called him terrorist'). His mom, on the contrary, was very proud of the same document; for her it was evidence of a fact, an official recognition that Rafael's dad was killed; that it was no accident. After so much work denouncing, there it was; proof that it was true, that she was not a crazy woman with made-up claims. There it was, finally, recognition. She was also proud of herself for denouncing and not keeping quiet in spite of the widespread warnings and fear of those times.

Later that day we got together with the HIJXS, just to catch up with each other's lives. Rafael retold his 'registering' story and the 'diploma'. The group, as usual, made jokes about 'Rafael's graduation as a victim' (*el graduado*), and they added another joke about that being the beginning of divisions at the core of the collective; the children of victims on one side and of the imprisoned (guilty?) ones on the other. It was one joke among many, but I wondered: Is it only orphans who can be victims? If Rafael became (bureaucratically sanctioned) a victim, what then were the others in HIJXS? Perpetrators?

More recently Abel framed the HIJXS' work as struggle for recognition; not that they were in-between the categories, but were actually outside them. Being outsiders was not an easy position. If they did not fit into the available categories of victim–perpetrator narratives, who were they? They refused the victim category because, more than 'not raised to be victims' they were raised by those who fought back, took up arms against a system, against the positioning of passive victims, against the state. Denouncing the legacies of state repression, what they inherited as HIJXS was important for all of us. Such denouncing required the 'victim' narrative, reclaiming its possibility even if they rejected victimization. Reclaiming recognition even in 'victim' terms was still important, otherwise what was left would be silence. And accepting *silencing* was not in the HIJXS' collective plans.

> We have been condemned to silence, pushed outside of the discourse. Our battle is for recognition. What are we? That's a key question: Are we victims? No. Are we guilty? No. We simply are not. Nobodies. We want to be one of the actors within *familiares*, the relatives' movement, demanding justice as well. We are struggling for recognition, for a place at the table, a space to talk about what we lived as well, and to be part of reconstructing a better present, a different way of doing politics engaged with the people. ... Nobody wants a war. Least of all us, who have also lived its direct consequences. (Abel, Lima, Peru, 2015)

The HIJXS perform a series of movements in relation to the victim category (as if refusing to stay still), making it difficult to settle for interpretation or analysis.[8] The HIJXS are contesting the available victim category but at the same time acknowledging its necessity and using it (uneasily) in a struggle for recognition. The initial movement of testimonial narratives, then, must be read with the subsequent movements that provide a more nuanced window into problematic and even contradictory practices.

Writing practices (II)

Through the cycling of this inquiry I have presented three movements of writing, theorizing them as constitutive of memory work about/with violence. In the face of the 'stuck places' encountered I deployed several

---

[8]   This may well be another example of Taussig's (1992) 'nervous system'. Practices ready (jittery?) to shake off the categories we ascribe to them with our academic writing exercise.

writing practices. These practices do not solve the problems but allowed me to move out of the 'stuckness', to create some movement to keep going, to produce *testimonio* narratives while at the same time creating a space for troubling such production, and the troubles such methodology created; an attempt to 'go about *representing this impossibility of representing*' (Gatti, 2014: 119; emphasis in original).

> In the testimonial work I used 'you' but sometimes it became 'us'. I can see an un-choreographed dance of pronouns in my writing, sometimes it's 'us', sometimes it's 'they'. Are the stories mine, ours or theirs? Isn't the 'we' playing a smoothing-out-differences act? Isn't the 'they' creating the illusion of objective safe distance? I find the pronouns limiting, static, unable to follow the steps taken, always lagging behind.

In trying to hold myself accountable through reflexivity I find its limits in the necessary silences that run through my research. At the same time, growing up with silences is one of the connections the HIJXS and me have in our conversations. The desire to tell meets the impossibility of openly discussing certain parts of our lives. Still, I do not belong to the HIJXS group in the way they do. A whole complication of the pronouns I use in this writing can be spotted throughout. Sometimes I wrote 'they', when I was also part of it but in a complicated way, sometimes I wrote 'I' when it is actually the result of a mix between them and me to a point that I cannot be sure where the idea came from, and sometimes I wrote 'they/us' to signal the changing sense of belonging/acceptance I had with the HIJXS.

The problem is that the outsider/insider categories became unhelpful, as if I could take one of the labels to understand my position, as if I could remain in one position after all. When I started, I liked the idea of stressing the distinction with other research that is made 'from outside', and thought it was important to highlight how involved I am with the protagonists of this project. There was a reason I called it a project and not research. During my time as a doctoral student working on this I regarded myself as an insider type of researcher. And it was useful during my first writings, particularly for explaining my project.

Later, when I was doing fieldwork, I felt more evidently an outsider, although in the face of other outsiders researching memory in Peru, I felt an insider. So it became a question of insider/outsider in relation to what and where. During my time in Peru, I was an insider in relation to the HIJXS and an outsider in relation to the Peruvian intellectual community working on memory. Although I was born in Peru, I did not grow up there, and was foreign to Peruvian academia: this included their memory debates and their ways of dealing with the language of the internal war, the ethical dilemmas and the surveillance.

The HIJXS considered me part of the group but I had trouble accepting that I belonged to it. This was not only a personal issue I was dealing with. I also felt the group drew me close and pushed me away, depending on the conversations, and the (un)shared experiences. Or they (dis)regarded my opinions as a member of the group or as an ally or guest (but not one of them). There was a curious dance between 'you don't understand' and 'you know, you understand'.

And yet, memory scholars considered me an academic, a group I struggled to identify myself with. It was the doctoral researcher cape that for them signalled my belonging. Only with time were my academic credentials seen as suspicious. I was not considered as knowledgeable and my theoretical background did not match theirs (or I did not care to have more theoretical discussions, which was met with suspicion). While I was not considered the exploitative type of academic that the decolonizing literature warns us of (Tuhiwai Smith, 2012) I was rather seen as the 'confused' one, the one who cared too much and was too troubled by the people she worked with.

Still, my access to academic circles enabled me to have a foot outside the HIJXS. Even more, the fact that I did not live in the country definitely made a difference with the group and what was at stake for us. I had a safety cover with the academic badge I was wearing and with the fact that I was only temporarily living in Peru and will not endure the after-effects of the collective actions. I was, after all, researching for a dissertation about our testimonial project, and not only did not live in Peru during the times the HIJXS recount in their *testimonio* (the 1990s onwards), I was not currently living in Peru. That made me an outsider. Even more, it was this 'outsiderness' that made the testimonial project possible.

Still, for many other (Peruvian or otherwise) scholars paying attention to the political violence in Peru, I was an insider. I was involved and part of the hijxs before I was an academic (even before I started my doctoral studies in the UK). That made me an insider. Even more, it was this 'insiderness' that made my research interesting enough to enter the narrative doctoral programme.

This goes in line with the idea of shifting positionings discussed in feminist research (Osgood, 2010) but also beyond it. In a sense it also reflected the problems I had with belonging. Being the daughter of exiles (notice the 'exile' label is not written upon myself) makes belonging a difficult, unresolved issue; having lived in different countries due first to my parents' exile and later to my own journeys.

During my last stage of writing, the controversy over Alice Goffman's book (2014) broke out, bringing to light references to the 'suspicious' character of ethnography, discussions over getting too close and the veracity of the stories

(Lewis-Kraus, 2016). These resonate with some of the comments I received in earlier presentations of this research: issues of bias, of misconstructions, of a not-so-true account, of not fact-checking, were among the comments I received. My use of scare quotes to refer to terrorism, history or truth had already gained me additional distrust.

Testimonio *writing as productive of other processes*

It haunts me, though, that my rewriting of the testimonial narratives would feel like a disappointment to their protagonists, the HIJXS, like writing that almost touches you but ends up missing the point. I found some consolation in Rafael and Abel's words when I shared my fears of 'getting it wrong'. According to Rafael I should have more faith in the richness of our shared experiences, which means that it would be hard to get it wrong and, even if I do, the shared experiences and the process of writing should matter more than the final written piece. By way of contrast, Abel said it does not matter that much if I get it wrong, at least they would have something to go against, and, who knows, maybe that would inspire them to do their own writings. There is some wisdom and patience in both that I did not expect. Perhaps because for them the experience of working on the testimonial had already happened, whereas for me the writing in the book form, was still pending, still a struggle. And maybe because we have all become used to failures, to the defeat, so we can focus more on the process and the long-term effects or uses that testimonial work as practice has. It makes me ask the question as to the role of writing the process of inquiry. It might be to instigate more projects, to enter another cycle of memory work, to push us even further.

The process of *testimonio*-making incited several other projects, like Rafael and Iris interviewing people who knew their respective fathers to rebuild their history, Abel who collected his father's letters from prison to write around them and with him after his death, my own brother who started filming and interviewing people to reconstruct our family history, or like the digital database with archival research to construct other memories we were developing when the COVID-19 pandemic interrupted us. The resulting text out of the HIJXS *testimonio* project became merely an invitation to open a conversation, for more stories to emerge from the margins, for more protagonists to represent their own stories, and even challenge the ones presented here.

Writing myself into the text

Among the different writing practices, we also wrote 'with four hands' to explore our histories. The following text was written around the memory commemorations of the HIJXS, by writing individually but in response to one another. The purpose was to bring our stories to the public as a form of invitation for other marginal histories to come out and weave themselves into each other. For this, not only the content but also the form of writing in response to one another was important. It was also important for me because it opened the possibility for writing about myself. Here I present only a fragment about myself, and other texts that came after, as if in response to the first one.

> Mine is another story I never felt that great a desire to tell. My parents left Peru in the 1990s, right before those stories they are talking about their parents. And living abroad what I learned from an early age was not to talk about 'that'. In a way I was certain that 'all that story' had stayed behind in a country I no longer felt mine, as if it got buried under so many badly kept secrets and made-up stories that were becoming real. Then ten years later, my parents had to move again to a new country. For me, that was a first sign, like in a ghost-story of 'aparecidos' and soon after I received a second sign, which was the TRC report. Both signs pushed me to get interested in other stories, stories absent in any report. It was then that I started noticing that that story from before will not disappear on its own, and that it was not only my parents' story but also my own. It was in that context, near the year 2005, that I arrived to Cuba where I lived a couple of years and where I met the others.

So, maybe I should start again. This time, by saying I have lied countless times, or let's be less dramatic and say that I have continuously made up stories about where I come from, since I was little. And the story-making which was partly for safety, partly a necessity, and partly a habit, has continued in my adult life. My doctoral research also required some made-up stories. Once someone asked me about the effects of my parents' clandestine lives on my life, and without thinking I said, 'I learnt to make up stories, and to believe in them, and sometimes it's hard to tell them apart from the real ones … and sometimes it's hard to just give up the habit, because it comes so easily to me.' And so, maybe, that explains what drew me into exploring memories and furthermore *testimonio* as living in the ungraspable borderlands of real and fictional. Maybe that gave me the impulse to go on fictionalizing the stories, starting from an understanding that memories are always already fictionalized in the process of narrating.

My research proposal was written as driven by an academic interest in this group and their stories within the Peruvian post-conflict. I never made clear that my story was also one of them, I navigated around this by saying the HIJXS stories were close to mine but different. One of the problems of being part of the HIJXS is that your parents must have been publicly denounced as members of the MRTA for you to be able to publicly belong to the group, otherwise it is like incriminating your family with an organization that in spite of being inexistent today (as it was defeated in the 1990s during what is now called the Internal Armed Conflict) is still criminalized and its former members prosecuted as terrorists. So, if you ask me what's my story? I will take a few minutes to ponder which one to tell you this time.

Nothing seems simple about violence now. Not even how to name it, which words to use: the conflict, the war, the times of fear, or the CAI (acronym of 'internal armed conflict', the TRC word of choice and popular among young academics in the memory field)? Or even the aftermath, post-what? If we can feel and hear the remains as an unfinished past with the persistent use of the 'terrorist' category to organize the Peruvian political landscape (Burt, 2006; Rojas-Perez, 2013; Robin Azevedo, 2021). Perhaps it was much more simple back then in that country and for that generation, where violence was also thought of as revolutionary to bring about change. But I do not really know that. How can I know from the now and from here? How can I say that about violence after all that unravelled? How to dismiss the horror that came with it?

> There is so much death surrounding me in this country. So many dead around me, and not one is mine. Then, why do they touch me like this? Why, then, do I feel them with such intensity? Where do these waves of sharp pain come from? Why do they create this emptiness, if I never met their faces? Am I trying too hard to load/carry their bodies on my shoulders as a form of penitence? '*Andar cargando muerto ajeno*' ('To go on carrying a foreign corpse') they say in my other country, when you take on someone else's responsibilities. But this particular death is no stranger, *no me es ajena*, the body it left is not one of mine but neither is alien. … So many dead bodies, who do they belong to? Whose shoulders carry them? Where do I put them now?

I try to make sense of the violence when it does not make sense. I go against the perspective that violence is just violence, and I return to the political in it. I am concerned with the de-politicization of those who took up arms against the state. At the same time, I worry about justifying violence. But how could I, after living so many of the effects directly in our lives (and continue to do so), after listening to how it affected those I care about and so many more people in ways we have not yet listened to. I cannot. And still, I feel like I understand, although maybe I don't.

More importantly, I think I will have missed the point if I do not attempt to understand their perspectives and their views on violence as politics and of politics as always already violent (Calveiro, 2008); if I do not read closely those who see violence and politics as always interlinked and if I fall in the trap of de-politicizing the violence during the internal war. That would be the best way to miss the lessons we could make out of the war, and the importance of other politics not only by non-state actors but also by the state. This demands challenging the impunity of state violence and of the violence of those in powerful positions, those who benefited (and continue to do so) from that war.

One thing I am sure of, and that is that 'I take sides' in this project. I do not think it is possible otherwise, not when it comes to any work about extreme situations, not when it is about war. Why listen to the HIJXS? Why write such uncomfortable, uneasy stories of that past after the 'return to democracy' in Peru? This has little to do with unveiling a truth. It is mostly an ethical choice from the present, to listen to such excluded stories that lived and continue living repression, be it by the state or society. Moreover, it is a choice based in the fact that, in the process, their stories became my own. So, more than unveiling a truth, the process has been about constructing our own truths as part of a collectivity that lived the internal war differently; a collectivity whose mere existence transgresses the narratives circulating about the conflict. A collective to which I belong as well, in a present we continue to struggle to construct for ourselves.

A last *postalita* from the edges of the HIJXS collective

Toñito
Lima, Peru, 2012

Yes, I'm Toñito. No, no. My name is not Toñito. I'm Izak. They called me Toñito, but they were the only ones who did so. I do remember being Toñito, I think it's the first name I remember actually. But I also remember ever so clearly the moment when Mom grabbed me by the arms saying, 'Listen to me, you are not Toñito, your name is Izak, don't ever forget that' in a very serious tone, agitated, *como desesperada*. I guess it was by the end of that period, when we lived in *la selva*.

The exact events were confusing, but the details of what happened in sharp still images are stuck in my head, still intact.

Then, all I remember is seeing my grandparents who went to pick me up, and the colours ... so intensely bright, all the imaginable shades of green of *la selva*, and the pop music by *Maná* playing everywhere. Even today those songs take me back to those times and those feelings, and those images. But I don't like dwelling on them, so I couldn't tell you how that makes me feel in the now because I really don't know. ... It's just that sometimes it's hard to breathe. ... No, it's not asthma ... it's just that I find it difficult to breathe. There's no explanation for it. I think it started when I used to go visit my dad in Castro Castro prison, on the other side of the city. Crossing Lima's downtown on those old buses, it always felt so grey and humid, *lúgubre* and sad. I don't like the city centre; I find it depressing and the smog just gets in the way of my breathing. I guess you can call it an allergy.

Going back to your question, only Abel calls me Toñito – so much can be contained in a name. I saw him in a large protest march in Lima, like 15 years later, but I immediately recognized him, from afar. So, I approached him and Abel was ... it was a thrilling moment ... all I said was 'Hi, I'm Toñito.'

13

Epilogue: *Testimonio* as Pedagogy

A conclusion presumes there is a way to end: that the writer (and later the reader) has come to some closure; that after such an intricate journey, complicated by/in/through the writing, there is an arrival point. And yet, what these pages have been about has no end. Experiences and stories of violence and loss outlive any war, well into the post-war period (and when does the post-war end?). Even after this book is finished, its stories continue unfolding, feeding different possible stories and interpretations.

Instead, I offer a possible way to engage pedagogically with this book and what we can learn from *testimonio*; that is to work through its lessons and renewed questions. My offer is inspired by the HIJXS' invitation to keep memory work open for a continuous rewriting. Rather than seeking to arrive at a new counter-narrative of the internal war, the group proposes to continue opening spaces for other silenced memories to enter the scene, for a chance to remake even our own most fixed memories, for the possibility of placing memories alongside one another in order to spark a conversation, and for cultivating the possible new stories that may emerge from that. Coming from a critical pedagogy tradition, we know power relations shape these exchanges and what is possible to emerge, but keeping ourselves open to be affected by memory work (such as *testimonio*) makes memory unfinished and subject to change, which is important to dismantle what we know until now.

This is what I mean by *testimonio* as pedagogy; both its process and content make available ways of knowing and learning that combine critical and creative traditions. I use here what Paulson (2023) calls an 'expansive understanding of pedagogy' based on diverse practices and philosophies of teaching and learning beyond the classroom. In our particular case, pedagogy refers to the ways in which teaching and learning about violence takes place over the course of our lives, in the present and the past. It is based on critical pedagogies and their understanding of power, together with creative pedagogies and their artful ways for imagining other knowledges.

In this book, we practised keeping close Anzaldúa's *borderlands* metaphor and Lather's *troubling* stance, which created a disposition for creative exploration, or what Freire termed an *epistemological curiosity*, and bell hooks inspired as *transgressive pedagogy*. This led us to challenge our binary thinking and established categories, which in turn pushed us towards an interconnected understanding of violence as part of us. We arrived at new stories that contest the victim–perpetrator dichotomy, the opposition of the fictional and the real, the simplistic narratives of 'terrorists' versus 'heroes', the separating of us and them, and the over-rehearsed stories that fail to convey how lives were lived in the war and, more importantly, how lives are lived with the violence of the present.

Testimonio-making process as pedagogy

Testimonio refers to the genre of testimonial narratives rooted in Latin American oral traditions; as a form of counter-history from lived experience it aims to raise awareness to transform past and present injustices. This book places *testimonio* within the field of education, drawing insights from Paulo Freire and Orlando Fals-Borda.

There is a rich history of using *testimonio* in the classroom beyond Latin America. The US feminist and migration studies use it to visibilize marginalized lives through their protagonists' voices, which has gained traction in education since the 1990s. Burciaga and Cruz Navarro recount its function: '*testimonio* as critical pedagogy encouraged a co-construction of knowledge and closer working relationship between two or more people, shaking/altering power relations' (2015: 39). The critical pedagogy impulse powered a widespread use of *testimonio* in educational spaces (from classrooms to museums and other learning spaces such as communities of practice) under an imperative of social transformation. The entry in the *Oxford Research Encyclopedia of Education* (Rodriguez-Campo, 2021) dedicated to '*Testimonio* in education' and the chapter titled '*Testimonio*' in the *SAGE Handbook of Qualitative Research* (Beverley, 2005) bear witness to its relevance in the field of education studies.

Testimonio, I propose, as pedagogical tool, a research method and methodology, altogether contributes to rethink the learning and knowledge-making process. In a classroom, for example, it develops connections with the varying experiences and knowledge that people's lives can offer and the experiences and knowledge that students/learners themselves bring into the classrooms (or any other learning spaces in less formal settings) and beyond. As a research method and methodology, *testimonio* compels researchers to re-envision their role in the process and their relationship with their participants (Rodriguez-Campo, 2021), who are to be considered as protagonists and knowledge-makers. In both cases, *testimonio* brings a distinctive pedagogical framework which recentres marginalized lived experiences, cultivates critical consciousness and promotes social justice transformations.

Memory and education studies, and within those, research with/about *testimonio* particularly, have opened questions of how do we as researchers deal with a series of tensions produced in the research process, and in consequence the difficulties of dealing with what knowledge is then possible while inhabiting (researching) such tensions. The book discussed several examples, such as the tense space between tellable and untellable stories in contexts of repression and violence (and its aftermath), or the tensions arising from the experiences where rather than transmitting memory, *testimonio* produces shifting memories and experiences, or the feeling that memory becomes an elusive object that is messy, unstable and constantly in the making.

This book contributes to the field by destabilizing a long-held tradition of *testimonio* and its sacrality; it moves beyond the traditional understanding to critically and creatively engage with its complexities. Inquiring into *testimonio* as a process of collective memory work over time and space resulted in learning to approach *testimonio* through the use of multiple epistemologies. *Testimonio* is thus a pedagogy in itself as it allows in its process not only to learn from people's lives about ourselves and our entangled lives, but also to learn to understand research from multiple ways of knowing to glimpse at memories of violence.

In our process of testimonial making with a group of (then) young adults in post-war Peru, we came up with three movements of inquiry to embrace multiple epistemologies. I named the three movements the realist, the politics and the poetics of memory. With these multiple epistemologies, we navigate the tensions arising from a collaborative activist inquiry in a highly repressive context. We could thus engage the contradiction between the demands of *testimonio* as denouncing political violence and *testimonio* as world-making, creating the possibility of imagining a life when violence resists remaining in the past.

The testimonial process offers a new lens to reflect on and theorize *testimonio* as pedagogy. Despite *testimonio*'s presence in educational settings and its recently gained attention in education and transitional justice studies, there is limited empirical research on the topic (Bellino et al, 2017). This study takes the invitation by Bellino and Williams (2017) to venture into 'pedagogies of imagining community', together with Segato's 'counter-pedagogies of cruelty' (2015), to expand the understanding of *testimonio* at the intersection of education and transitional justice. It does so by emphasizing the collaborative nature of co-constructing *testimonio* with the protagonists – a crucial process for producing knowledge differently, a knowledge that can be used for analytical and interpretive purposes in formal and informal educational spaces to examine questions of transitional justice – and also theoretically, by proposing the cycles of inquiry (the realist, the politics and the poetics) as an original approach for engaging with *testimonio* as pedagogy for social justice to anyone interested in engaging critically and creatively with human experiences and the legacies of violence.

By offering a novel theoretical lens for the production of *testimonio*, one that captures changes over time and space through the cycles of inquiry, it revamps *testimonio*'s importance for teaching and learning about the past, and as a research method to understand the present. A more critical engagement with *testimonio*, and other possibilities to produce testimonial narratives and to read/research them, provides new theoretical synergies between education and transitional justice scholarship, anchored in the importance of multiple epistemologies to produce (and consume) knowledge from conflict-ridden societies.

Three movements as cycles of inquiry for working with testimonio

Since knowledge production on political violence requires multiple epistemologies, working with memories of such violence through *testimonio* as critical and creative pedagogy is more productive where it embraces a cycles of inquiry approach.

The cyclical approach started with writing as inquiry while encountering and revisiting our *testimonio* and its process, a practice that came from the messiness of lives that experienced a particular involvement with violence, state repression and clandestine lives since early childhood. A writing that also took place from spaces of uncertainty and not-knowing while engaging with the HIJXS changing lives and desires in their changing but still highly repressive context. It was a writing that found a way to embrace the messiness, the fragmentary, the tentative, the unfinished (Biehl, 2013) and the wandering (Lather, 2007) that comes with the constant movement over fuzzy boundaries (Anzaldúa, 1987).

The first *realist* move is based on the testimonial encounters, which are recorded, and then edited as *testimonio*. The second move, the politics of memory, draws on the connections and negotiations with the context that produce the testimonial narratives, which in terms of practice results from revisiting in dialogue with the protagonists, the 'products' of the first move. The third move, the poetics of memory, deploys imagination and creativity to reflect on the process of *testimonio* making and its writing which trouble memory, voice and representation.

These parallel and seemingly contradictory modes of working and writing with memories (realist, politics, poetics) placed alongside are more productive than separated. It is not only that each contributes an additional layer or possibility for engagement with the testimonial, making other knowledges available, and adding to our understanding of memory work, but that together they also propose a more fragmented view of memories, exposing the impossible full-single-story and calling for attention to what lies in-between the three modalities of memory work, glimpsing at memory precisely in the frictions and gaps.

Troubling testimonio

Deciding from which stance I write and which pronouns to set to work has never been more problematic than in writing this epilogue. Are the final words mine or shared with the HIJXS? Where does my and their responsibility end? The borderlands between them and me, forged in the writing, have been ever present as an underlying thread.

Scholarly debates on memory and *testimonio* offer few insights about addressing the dilemmas of how to conduct memory work, and how to write *testimonio* in contexts where violence is not a matter of the past and it has both symbolic and material manifestations. *Testimonio*'s problematic methodological assumptions of my role as the 'absent' writer or objectively distanced researcher concerned me, as it did the 'heroic'/'redemptive' tone as a writing genre. Despite my (theoretical) misgivings, I accepted the HIJXS urgency to craft *testimonios* that they could put to use. I wanted to embark in that experience/experiment to see what we might produce with our conflicting views on *testimonio* and methodologies. Rather than clear-cut answers to these questions, our co-operative inquiry yielded stories from our situated practices (mine and the HIJXS). Something akin to Freire's situated praxis, the importance of a conscious and iterative cycling of action and reflection, a rooted learning through experience, that aims to be transformational.

There was in practice a struggle over meanings in our 'doing *testimonio*'. In my desire to engage with the HIJXS in a collaboration guided by a feminist ethics, I explored how to reappropriate the term *testimonio* to reflect our meanings and practices of what counts as activism or, more broadly, as political. This included our struggles over my role and theirs, our different views on violence and the war, and our changing positionings regarding the previous generation's politics. These dilemmas are shared with a broader field of reflections on memory work in post-war and post-authoritarian societies, and I resorted to troubling *testimonio*.

I think it was also an inherently subversive spirit (let's call it that) which led me to 'troubling' as a methodological stance and as a possibility. It was also probably our experiences of our parents' (semi-)clandestine lives that prompted me to explore creative writing and the imaginative. I found reassurance in Speedy's (2014) challenge to traditional scholarly writing that assumes a clear-cut distinction between the imagined (magical), the lived (agential) and the researched (critical) worlds, as if these three were completely separable experiences (or modes of experiencing the world). Rather, these are all entangled. Even in the imposed order of the cycles of inquiry designed to share these stories, there was always something that crept into the other sections. It was particularly challenging, for example, to justify a distinction between the politics and the poetics of *testimonio*. Ultimately, the second movement included reflections on writing that crossed into the third movement.

I faced another challenge in deciding which stories to map and how to account for their changes over time and space. Some HIJXS hardly recognize themselves in the 2007 *testimonio*; so much have they changed and so much has our relationship changed. My own journey has left me constantly tempted to rewrite them.[1] The HIJXS have reinterpreted and reshaped their stories, and some of those who did not make it in this project are now writing them. The focus on the process, on *testimonio* as practices rather than a fixed text, was an important one. It allowed us to reduce the anxiety that focusing on results brings, and to be more open to the twists and turns of the storytelling process from a more dialogical approach. It also provided the space for cultivating our relationship as a group and becoming an important reference to each other's lives. From all these, I learnt to be (slightly) more at ease with the fallibility of writing, and with the possibility that I got some of the stories wrong. At the same time, I learnt to trust that language and writing can be pushed and twisted to work for us if we keep a critical eye/hand on it, and if we let it surprise us when we further inquire into it.

A reflexive voice appears throughout the text, troubling it by posing questions, expressing doubts and telling stories of ongoing reflections. An undisciplined voice that comes in most cases from my several notebooks (a loosely kept research journal) with my own writings and quotes by others collected along the inquiry process; and in other cases reflections triggered by the writing itself, or instigated by revisiting the written text and finding something upsetting or troublesome; a thought or story that creeps in.

A fundamental purpose of my research, writing about and with the HIJXS group, has been to encourage readers to question the overly simplified stories of war and post-war. The writing then must perform a double act: it bears witness to our work of bearing witness to our lives during and after the violence in the country.

Three distinctive issues marked our collaborative experience. First, the constraints of Peruvian post-war politics meant that disclosing the

---

1   For most of my adult life I considered myself Nicaraguan, but after my fieldwork in 2012, which was my first time back to Peru after 20 years, I started using both countries to identify myself. And although I still felt more at home in Nicaragua than Peru, I could no longer kept my Peruvian side inside a keepsake box, but rather became open to embrace being from the in-between of Nicaragua and Peru. My politico-affective geographies have become more complicated than ever after this inquiry journey, which makes me wonder if I will ever settle in one place.

testimonios put us at risk. Second, after the first encounter with the group, I had the recorded *testimonios* and a rich collection of un-recorded material: my memories of talks and hanging out, some emails and online chats that have continued over the years, and several imagined conversations with them evoked by their stories. Third, individual *testimonios* failed to capture the energy of the collective, which led me to embrace collective conversations and practices for recreating each other's stories and other possible stories. Most importantly, our original purposes from 2007 changed by the time we revisited the *testimonios* in 2012/2013, and were definitely not the same by the end of the inquiry ten years later. With such instability of memories and of stories, how do we then do memory work?

I turned to creative writing and produced stories related to our work together called '*postalitas*' (little postcards) by distilling our conversations, providing a 'sense of them' through a snapshot of particular aspects of our stories. The *postalitas* were at the same time objects of inquiry for the group, and objects of communication, for sharing with other groups. We imagine *postalitas* can make the stories travel and interact with others; perhaps in a public exhibition in a real or virtual memory space.

Looking at *testimonio* as changing over time and space allowed me to experience the collective as it was growing, its energy and resources as a group to sustain each other. From there I learnt to think of *testimonio* as a collective endeavour, from wondering what to make of the shared use of particularly dark humour at unexpected moments that contrasted with the painful experiences? How to account for the way they supported each other just by being there, *acompañando* during difficult times related to either events in their past or the present in Peru? This forced me to reconnect with a critical and creative pedagogy where we do not learn as individuals but as part of a community and where imagination has its space. The *testimonio* process not only taught me to turn to the community aspect but also revealed itself as community-making when it sparked other memory process and contributed to building stronger bonds among the HIJXS and their surrounding communities.

Testimonio knowledge as pedagogical

Testimonio as pedagogy refers to learning from the process of constructing our lived experiences as testimonial narratives. And also to what is produced in such unfinished projects of embodied learning from reflecting on the experiential that connects the intimate and the public, the past and present, the politics and the poetics of narrating lives in the midst of violence. I refer here to the knowledge that *testimonio* brings and how we can learn from *testimonio*.

Individual–collective

What is the relationship between the individual and the collective in the production of *testimonio*, and what lessons can we draw from the inevitable fractures therein? The questions became relevant during the first fieldwork visit to Peru, where I had envisaged a collective writing exercise that would weave together the individual accounts we recorded in Cuba during encounters of the traditional *testimonio* kind (see Beverley, 2005). In those earlier accounts, the collective was always present as a mandate to produce *testimonio*, a shared desire to release their stories to the public.

I hoped the collective memory work would also address feminist critiques of the tendency in early *testimonio* to leave unproblematized the relationship between the individual and the collective (Moraga and Anzaldúa, 1983; Latina Feminist Group, 2001; Connolly, 2012). Newer methods for memory work, such as collective biography in its feminist poststructuralist version, make visible (and 'revisable') the discursive production of 'meanings and of selves'. It 'deconstructs the idea of the individual as one who can exist independent of various collectives, of discourse, of history, of time and of place' (Davies, 2000, cited in Davies and Gannon, 2006: 7).[2] Moreover, it proposes a collaborative writing method that ends up problematizing both the individual and the collective as always-in-the-making.

However well-armed with theoretical reflections, a collective idea of memory work and the importance of such collective effort, our process resulted in six *testimonios*, presented in the first movement. Additional hesitations to share and undertake public action also accumulated. I first read this as a failure to provide an account of the collective and honour the effort of building it.

Yet their bonds, love and solidarity became central both to our narratives (and my later, careful writing) and to our collective action. I wanted to honour such collective life and efforts, by turning my earlier narrative of failures – of the collective public action and of my collective writing methods – into a narrative of acts of resistance. The HIJXS resisted my researcher role, defining the collective, dissolving the group, the repression and stigma attached to their lives, the inherited old-left politics, and the main narratives of the internal war in Peru.

Seemingly intimate, the acts of narration performed in the testimonial work are at the same time political acts simply because they break down the traditional distinction between public and private (Butler, 2015). And more

---

[2] 'The truth that is accomplished in this process interests us not as a means to generate knowledge about the individual self of each storyteller, but as a means to provide knowledge about the ways in which individuals are made social, are discursively constituted in particular fleshy moments' (Davies and Gannon, 2006: 4).

complicatedly, in their refusal to subject themselves to the predetermined narrative of 'children of terrorists' the HIJXS openly defy the current politics of the Peruvian post-war by constructing other personal narratives of their present while at the same time reaffirming other ways of collective action. Important elements for the testimonial were the places where the narratives were constructed and played out, as well as the spaces available for them.

We can make sense of these issues by connecting them to the politics of memory work in a post-war society. The disappointments at the failure of public collective action, including writing a collective story, can be read differently: as a struggle to reimagine the political not solely as a public act to denounce and question hegemonic narratives, but also as daily acts of resistance that reclaim the individual within the collective and build affective bonds and solidarity. They are also political precisely because they challenge repressive politics and the breaking of the social fabric by violence in itself. It is no longer only the big heroic stories told in public spaces that matter and can produce change. The mere act of telling individual stories, with all the reverberations from the collectives and communities we are part of living inside those stories, and the risks taken in such an endeavour, represent a form of resistance against an official history that frames them through a victim–perpetrator binary in order to exclude them as their mere existence is considered a threat; a reminder of the terrorist threat that is used systematically to legitimize the mechanisms for state surveillance and violence.

In examining the question of how we address the collective in testimonial work, I first traced out the meaning of the collective for HIJXS, to then locate such meanings in the broader theoretical debates about the individual and the collective in testimonial production. Thus, I argue, the politics of memory within the HIJXS group reflects the 'political stakes in the ordinary' (Biehl, 2013), reclaiming the individual in the creation of *testimonios* as snapshots that give initial shape to their memories (temporarily fixing them) and can then be used for collective reflection.

Embodied listening

Nyssa Chow (2020) writes about embodied listening in oral history that applies to the particular listening demanded by the testimonial, a listening with

> the potential to record, elevate, and assert 'ways of being' and 'ways of knowing' our shared world that have been historically delegitimized and overlooked. Our embodied experiences are also our particular expertise on the world ... a particular education, one that shapes unique strategies of surviving and thriving; of sense-making; ways of seeing,

interpreting, and 'reading' the moments, politics, and interactions of daily life.

I came to fully understand embodied listening after my physical limitations forced me to take part differently. Listening to the HIJXS stories was so absorbing that it worked as an escape from bodily pain. This does not mean I listened better; sometimes I was worse at it. There were instances when increased pain made it hard to concentrate and impossible to stay in one position for long. During my stay in Cuba, I did nothing besides visiting doctors and hospitals for endless tests, physical therapy, needles and (at the time) strange alternative medicine treatments; I felt lost and outside of my environment. Living in Cuba, where the HIJXS could be more open about their histories, was an exceptional period in their lives as well as mine. Perhaps only such conditions of exceptionality make *testimonios* possible.

Testimonio demands a listening that also pays attention to the stories left out. It is important to remember that even in a long-held testimonial process, there will always be some stories left out. For example, as several lines of memory work in post-war or post-dictatorship Latin America can attest, the complexity of women's involvement during extremely violent times is one of the latest stories to come to light. In Peru, Theidon (2003; 2010) and Boutron (2012) problematize the lack of space to discuss women's participation during and after war. I, too, have been painfully aware that in writing women, I created a troubling re-presentation that still troubles me.

In these *testimonios*, the stories of the ways in which women participated in the war remain relatively absent, surrounded by silence and secrecy. Their complex involvement is reduced to safeguarding the family, caring for the imprisoned or undertaking *la denuncia* (the legal battle). While still wondering if I am (or this writing is) reproducing stereotypes of women, at the same time I did not find the possibility of doing otherwise since (ongoing) state repression, where what you say becomes a matter of life and death (or imprisonment), curtails the spaces women have for voice and action. Yet their situated resistances, in the decolonial feminist sense, may have been precisely the strategic use of widespread traditional female stereotypes to disguise their different and complicated modes of involvement. Viewed from this perspective, paradoxically stereotypes have provided a safe haven for their children, their political militancy, and the telling (or writing) of their HIJXS *testimonio*.

The HIJXS inherit the silences. Their interpretation of the histories of women are not subversive but compliant, not political but about (a de-politicized) family-care. The HIJXS do not challenge those silences as they have in other cases. They reproduce in their *testimonios* segregated stories of political participation, referring mainly to the men and in fewer cases to the women in the Tupac Amaru Revolutionary Movement. Only in very few cases, the intergenerational transmission of complicated memories led to silences being broken inside the safe space of the family. Thus the representations of women and their diverse modes of involvement remain hidden or misrepresented.

This book too reproduces that version of the story where women have marginal and depoliticized roles, roles anchored in care and safety rather than militant roles (who said caring work was not militant?). When it comes to war stories, it is difficult to harbour certainties. How can we be certain of what were women's roles? Perhaps more than any other, women's stories tell us that there is still so much we do not know. Recent developments in Peru supported our concern that a greater examination of women's and other silenced stories poses significant threats and ethical dilemmas.

Testimonio *as self-history-theory*

Testimonio is in close connection and lineage with oral history, and in particular critical oral history and indigenous storytelling methodologies as both give relevance to the process of constructing narratives of our lives. *Testimonio* is not data to be later analysed by expert knowledge, it is a narrative that already contains interpretations of their lived experiences. Even more *testimonio* is already a way of theory according to Anzaldúa's notion of autohistoria-teoria (self-history-theory).

Testimonio as a meaning-making activity over experiences that their protagonists struggle to make sense of, be this inside (and outside of) the telling space, which takes place because there are no fitting cultural frameworks available. The lived experiences are then considered embodied knowledge, and the testimonial space becomes the possibility to construct their own interpretation from their own frameworks. Such frameworks are not individual in the sense that they contain reverberations of discourses from the communities we live in, with or even against, and also in the sense that the knowledge it produces is always already relational.

Listening to some of the first testimonials, I felt the texture of a strong denouncing voice, proudly claiming a legacy, bringing the political in their parents' use of violence. It was a first attempt at naming and developing a language, which later changed after entering into contact with other stories of loss and violence. A process of reinterpretation follows once we place our stories alongside others.

Practices of naming what cannot be named, giving shape and language to a story are crucial to configuring a life. A similar understanding is expressed by an organization working from a marginalized urban space:

[A]ctions that are imperceptibly inserted into our daily lives: saying, qualifying, and distinguishing things are operations that both reflect and configure reality. If we want to put into motion other knowledges and other ways of generating knowledge, we have to play hard in the field of language and in the battle for words and concepts. (Carabancheleando, 2017: 37; my translation)

These tasks are possible if we pay attention to language as the first interpretation of the lived experience, and conversations with others to develop such language as its continuous reinterpretation. This supposes changing our view of those with such lived experiences. They are protagonists not only of what they lived but also of their meanings and (re-)interpretations. In that sense, they are knowledge bearers and the testimonial a knowledge-making process.

At the end, what I learnt from the written *testimonio* in the first movement and the reconstruction of the conditions surrounding their production is that they were situated and contingent, *the stories were told in the way that they could be told at their moment, just as they had been lived the way that they could be lived at their moment.*

> There are questions that remain … things we haven't even begun to ask ourselves and our parents because of the circumstances in which we had to live it all. We have to move from the melancholic state into being more active with what we inherited, with that dream of a different world as a possibility worth fighting for. We shouldn't keep it as a sad, sobbing history; we have to reclaim the laughter and the joy that are a big part of that entire story. The purpose is a political one, to highlight the workings of state repression against anything and anybody who attempts to change the system. (HIJXS participant, collective conversation, Havana, Cuba, 2007)

While writing, I posed my own reflections alongside those of the HIJXS regarding the individual–collective relationships, and how the collective was taking shape through the *testimonio experiencia*. It was after our first recordings (in Cuba) and during the revisiting stage (in Peru) that our present daily life gained relevance methodologically. It was through 'deep hanging out' that I realized the limited space for pre-designed methods. Instead, daily struggles that emerged incessantly (that is, job-seeking, family living arrangements, new conditions in prison, relatives' illness, and death) take over, affecting the possible conversations. Thus, affection, humour, drinking, solidarity and sense of belonging weaved a different narrative texture in the making of the HIJXS collective life.

> [W]e must attend to the ways that people's own struggles and visions of themselves and others create holes in dominant theories and

interventions and unleash a vital plurality: being in motion, ambiguous and contradictory, not reducible to a single narrative, projected into the future, transformed by recognition, and thus the very fabric of alternative world-making. (Biehl, 2013: 592)

Making space for the testimonial

The questions raised about my relationship with the HIJXS, the tensions between individual and collective lives, the role of places/spaces in the stories possible, and the presence of silences and secrets were important learnings. Equally important was the questioning of the relationship between real and fiction, how we relate to both when we engage in testimonial memory work, and ultimately what a realist mode of *testimonio* provided and what a creative writing move could bring upon.

Following Anzaldúa's borderlands metaphor led as to think of ourselves as being somewhere in-between the artificial categories of *victims and perpetrators* in Peru's internal war and the post-war context; of *real and fiction*, as memories are always already an intricate production between the remembered, the forgotten and the recreated; of *individual and collective*, as *testimonios* live somehow making such distinction problematic; and also of *practice and research*, because our collaborative work landed in the middle of those territories researching the/by doing, the process of producing *testimonio*.

These theoretical reflections were the ones I travelled with in my inquiry journey. They provided the grounding for approaching *testimonio* from a *troubling epistemology* (as an approach to knowledge(s) being produced in the doing), *methodology* (as a way into an inquiry with *testimonio* by 'poking holes' in it), and *method* by revisiting and using creative writing as a tool to spark new conversations and interrogating the narratives we were producing. And yet, during the course of this work and in constant dialogue with the HIJXS group, I encountered that in the process of *troubling* I produced even more troubles.

Beyond secluded spaces of recording and safe conversations, a violent repressive context pushes *testimonio* to become a mobile practice. With the HIJXS, we travelled, walked and wandered with our storied selves, resulting in a weaving of memories into places that transformed us and our stories in the process. In doing so, we occupied spaces differently, making room for our stories, all while allowing space to transform us with its 'almost magical' productive power.

Testimonio thus practised as an embodied 'doing and being-in-place' challenges the spaces/places of academic knowledge and their appropriation practices of knowledge-making. Even while occupying a precarious space in academia, our co-constructed embodied testimonial places/spaces became a platform for reconstructing underground memories of violence, resisting fixed narratives and fostering an entanglement of both realist accounts and creative imagination for the possibility of making new memories. Through movement and storytelling, we become co-producers of memory allowing ourselves to be affected by others (including spaces/places), enriching the landscape of our collective present. This highlights not only the embodied nature of *testimonio* but also its power to disrupt traditional knowledge spaces and its potential for creating new memory landscapes beyond the traditional spaces of education into pedagogies of community making.

Testimonio *and the politics of terrorism: a lens to read the present*

Theorizing the book's testimonial knowledge, as cycles of memory work, serves as a lens to read the present and its never-ending 'war of terror', where the label of 'terrorist' is increasingly and unscrupulously applied to a multiplicity of groups (and individuals) involved in diverse iterations of international and local conflicts and struggles. Anti-terrorist legislation based on the pre-emptive and ever-growing surveillance over citizens, with 'legal' exemptions that strip particular people of their basic human rights, has been created and applied with far-reaching consequences. In this world, the thread of the HIJXS memory work bears witness to and provides glimpses of how lives may unfold when your parents are labelled as terrorists. The repercussions are not only for the bodies living under such violent inscription, but for those around, and for our society as a whole as the 'threat' is used as pretext to silence dissent and to suppress individual and collective rights. As Manzoor-Khan (2022), speaking of the entanglements of terror and Islamophobia, suggests, we should be paying attention to what the terrorist discourse does, its immediate and broader effects, and how it works, including those who ultimately benefit from it.

The way Peruvian politics has unfolded since our testimonial work supports a long-held intuition; that exposing the silenced stories of those related to the armed groups poses significant threats and ethical dilemmas. The 2016 electoral campaign for the presidency in Peru, where the HIJXS were publicly involved, confirmed again that the violence of the conflict continues by other means. In that and the following campaigns, the media raised numerous accusations of 'terrorism' against the left as represented in whichever form or coalition.

In the post-electoral hangover, I wondered if we should change the familiar language we know and use to refer to our relatives or anyone involved in the insurgent groups, in particular those who were imprisoned. We may need to change our language if we want to be part of the conversation. Yet the terms of the conversation are already established, the available language – that of 'terrorism' (that so perfectly fits and feeds the global 'war on terror' after 9/11) – is imposed on all of us to refer to the violent struggles of the

1980s and 1990s. When the state demands that there be only one way to refer to the violence of the armed groups in the 1980s and 1990s, Raul Wiener (2015) argued it makes us 'captive' of their language.

Prisoners of their lexicon, we become also prisoners of a grammar that structures the scene; that both justifies state violence and strips those people it labels 'terrorists' of their human rights, making them disposable (Calveiro, 2008; Stern, 2015). We can see today that the state, the media, the military, and others, have successfully turned political struggles into 'terrorism' and those who oppose their model into 'terrorists' (or suspects of it, or in the new words I learnt in the electoral campaigns: 'pro-terrorists', 'philo-terrorists', 'terrorist-lover' or 'proto-terrorists'), leaving no space for political discussion, neither for critical conversations over the connections between violence and politics and the enduring effects of state violence, nor for learning and building other ways of doing politics. How do we engage with those we politically oppose outside a politics of fear and violence? How do we make conflict productive instead of destructive? How does it work for all of us instead of annihilating one or the other?

These were the questions confronting the HIJXS in their activism in 2016. In the present, the group continues more as a politically affective space to support each other and to hold conversations that cannot fit in other spaces. I also have renewed questions about research and its role as activism which informed my research and this book in its much revised form. I find it particularly enriching that we all wonder about our language, that we doubt the impulse to resort to taken-for-granted vocabularies and categories. As HIJXS, we are interested in entering into dialogue with others and other memories. After their/our own processes (individual and collective) of building safe spaces among themselves/ourselves, their/our families and their/our communities, the question now is how to talk to others outside those safe spaces we have built. *Testimonio*, as method and genre, which we adopted, wants an-other to engage with. Otherwise it threatens to become the over-rehearsed story that feminist collective biographers have warned us about (Davies and Gannon, 2006).

For making that dialogue possible, we need to be aware of and respect others' sensitivities, in particular their pain and loss in the internal war and after. For that we need to stop looking only at ourselves (and our communities) and instead occupy the small spaces we have now opened and entered, even if they are precarious and uncomfortable. This can allow us to enter the broader landscape of memories and contribute to a present that interrogates how the impunity of past violence keeps it alive in the present, and how violence is not of the past but continues in perhaps more subtle but not less lethal forms.

And maybe it is also true that we need to change our language in order to make that dialogue possible. But how to continue working within an imposed language; it is the violence of such imposition which makes it problematic. There must be another way; one that does not exclude some people and some lives to the point of elimination with the purpose of justifying state violence. The important struggle is not about spreading our language but opening the necessary space to create a new language. A language that can take in the diversity of lives and struggles including those who resort to violence in a political struggle against an already violent system. Perhaps, just perhaps, we can create a language, a new set of stories and future memories that give way to, and are nurtured by, living alongside one another. If this book contributes to creatively rethinking our language, it has gone some way to creating the possibility for other worlds of knowing and living.

References

Agüero, J.C. (2015) *Los rendidos: Sobre el don de perdonar*. Lima: Instituto de Estudios Peruanos.

Aguirre, C. (2012) 'Terruco de m … Insulto y estigma en la guerra sucia peruana', *Histórica*, 35(1), pp 103–139.

Alias Alejandro (2005) [Documentary film]. Cárdenas-Amelio, A. (Director). Sabotage Films GmbH. Germany.

Amnesty International (2003) 'The "anti-terrorism" legislation and its effects: an unfinished business in the transition to democracy'. London, May. AI Index: AMR 46/001/2003.

Anderson, J. (2004) 'Talking whilst walking: a geographical archaeology of knowledge', *Area*, 36(3), pp 254–261.

Andrews, M. (2007) *Shaping History: Narratives of Political Change*. 1st edn. Cambridge: Cambridge University Press.

Andrews, M. (2008) 'Never the last word: revisiting data', in M. Andrews, C. Squire and M. Tamboukou (eds) *Doing Narrative Research*. Los Angeles: SAGE, pp 86–101.

Anzaldúa, G. (1987) *Borderlands/La Frontera: The New Mestiza*. San Francisco: Aunt Lute.

Arfuch, L. (2013) 'La ciudad como autobiografía', *Bifurcaciones – Revista de Estudios Culturales Urbanos*, 12, pp 1–14.

Arias, A. (ed) (2001) *The Rigoberta Menchú Controversy*. Minneapolis: University of Minnesota Press.

Banks, A. and Banks, S.P. (eds) (1998) *Fiction and Social Research: By Ice or Fire*. Walnut Creek: AltaMira Press, SAGE.

Behar, R. (2003) *Translated Woman: Crossing the Border with Esperanza's Story*. 10th anniversary edition. Boston: Beacon Press.

Bellino, M.J. and Williams, J.H. (2017) *(Re)Constructing Memory: Education, Identity, and Conflict*. Rotterdam: Springer.

Bellino, M.J., Paulson, J. and Anderson Worden, E. (2017) 'Working through difficult pasts: toward thick democracy and transitional justice in education', *Comparative Education*, 53(3), pp 313–332.

Belsey, C. (2002) *Post-structuralism: A Very Short Introduction*. Oxford University Press.

Berg, R.H. (1994) 'Peasant responses to Shining Path in Andahuaylas', in D.S. Palmer (ed) *The Shining Path of Peru*. 2nd edn. New York: Palgrave Macmillan, pp 101–122.

Beverley, J. (2004) *Testimonio: On the Politics of Truth*. 1st edn. Minneapolis: University of Minnesota Press.

Beverley, J. (2005) 'Testimonio, subalternity and narrative authority', in N.K. Denzin and Y.S. Lincoln (eds) *The SAGE Handbook of Qualitative Research*. 3rd edn. Thousand Oaks: SAGE.

Biehl, J. (2013) 'Ethnography in the way of theory', *Cultural Anthropology*, 28(4), pp 573–597.

Blanchot, M. and Derrida, J. (2000) *The Instant of My Death / Demeure: Fiction and Testimony (Meridian, Stanford, California)*. 1st edn. Stanford: Stanford University Press.

Bondarevsky, L. (2003) *Che vo cachai*. vimeo.com/47696428. Argentina: Instituto Nacional de Cine y Artes Audiovisuales (INCAA).

Boutron, C. (2012) 'Reintegrating civilian life after combat: between invisibility and resistance. The experience of the Ronderas in Peru', in N. Duclos (ed) *War Veterans in Postwar Situations: Chenchnya, Serbia, Turkey, Peru, and Cote d'Ivorie*. New York: Palgrave Macmillan, pp 73–93.

Burciaga, R. and Cruz Navarro, N. (2015) 'Educational testimonio: critical pedagogy as mentorship', *New Directions for Higher Education*, 171, pp 33–41.

Burt, J.-M. (2006) '"Quien habla es terrorista": the political use of fear in Fujimori's Peru', *Latin American Research Review*, 41(3), pp 32–62.

Burt, J.-M. (2008) *Political Violence and the Authoritarian State in Peru: Silencing Civil Society*. Revised edn. New York: Palgrave Macmillan.

Burt, J.-M. (2009) 'Guilty as charged: the trial of former Peruvian president Alberto Fujimori for human rights violations', *International Journal of Transitional Justice*, 3(3), pp 384–405.

Burt, J.-M. and Cagley, C. (2013) 'Access to information, access to justice: the challenges to accountability in Peru', *SUR International Journal on Human Rights*, 10(18), pp 75–95.

Burt, J.-M. and Rodríguez, M. (2015) 'Justicia, verdad y memoria: el proceso penal para el caso de la masacre de Accomarca', in L. Huber and P. del Pino (eds) *Políticas en justicia transicional: miradas comparativas sobre el legado de la CVR*. Lima: IEP, pp 135–168.

Butler, J. (2015) *Notes Toward a Performative Theory of Assembly*. Cambridge: Harvard University Press.

Calveiro, P. (1998) *Poder y desaparición: los campos de concentración en Argentina*. Buenos Aires: Ediciones Colihue SRL.

Calveiro, P. (2006) 'Testimonio y memoria en el relato histórico', *Acta Poética*, 27(2), pp 65–86.

Calveiro, P. (2008) 'Acerca de la difícil relación entre violencia y resistencia', in M. López Maya, N. Iñigo Carrera and P. Calveiro (eds) *Luchas contrahegemónicas y cambios políticos recientes de América Latina.* Buenos Aires: Consejo Latinoamericano de Ciencias Sociales-CLACSO, pp 23–46.

Carabancheleando (ed) (2017) *Diccionario de las periferias: Métodos y saberes autónomos desde los barrios.* Madrid: Traficante de Sueños.

Carey-Webb, A. and Benz, S. (1996) *Teaching and Testimony: Rigoberta Menchu and the North American Classroom.* Albany: SUNY Press.

Carpenter, V. (ed) (2007) *A World Torn Apart: Representations of Violence in Latin American Narrative.* Oxford: Peter Lang.

Chow, N. (2020) *Listening for Embodied Knowledge: An Approach to the Oral History Interview.* 13 August. Columbia Oral History Master of Arts (OHMA). www.oralhistory.columbia.edu/calendar/People/ listening-for-embodied-knowledge-an-approach-to-the-oral-history-interview

Cixous, H. (1993) *Three Steps on the Ladder of Writing.* New York: Columbia University Press.

Clandinin, D.J. and Connelly, F.M. (2004) *Narrative Inquiry: Experience and Story in Qualitative Research.* 1st edn. San Francisco: Jossey Bass.

Clandinin, D.J., Lessard, S. and Caine, V. (2012) 'Reverberations of narrative inquiry: how resonant echoes of an inquiry with early school leavers shaped further inquiries', *Educacao, Sociedade & Culturas,* 7–24.

Clifford, J. (1997) *Routes: Travel and Translation in the Late Twentieth Century.* Cambridge: Harvard University Press.

Clifford, J. and Marcus, G.E. (1986) *Writing Culture: The Poetics and Politics of Ethnography.* Berkeley: University of California Press.

Clough, P. (2002) *Narratives and Fictions in Educational Research.* Buckingham: Open University Press.

Colombo, P. and Schindel, E. (2014) 'Introduction: the multi-layered memories of space', in E. Schindel and P. Colombo (eds) *Space and the Memories of Violence: Landscapes of Erasure, Disappearance and Exception.* Basingstoke: Palgrave Macmillan, pp 1–17.

Connolly, P. (2012) 'Testimonio and its travelers: feminist deployments of a genre at work', in L. Detwiler and J. Breckenridge (eds) *Pushing the Boundaries of Latin American Testimony: Meta-morphoses and Migrations.* New York: Palgrave Macmillan.

Counter Cartographies Collective, Dalton, C. and Mason-Deese, L. (2012) 'Counter (mapping) actions: mapping as militant research', *ACME: An International E-Journal for Critical Geographies,* 11(3), pp 439–466.

Coxshall, W. (2005) 'From the Peruvian Reconciliation Commission to ethnography', *PoLAR: Political and Legal Anthropology Review,* 28(2), pp 203–222.

Crandall, J. (ed) (2004) *Under Fire: The Organization and Representation of Violence.* Rotterdam: Witte de With, Center for Contemporary Art.

Cromotex Sindicato Textil Industrial (1980) *Compañeros, tomen nuestra sangre–: la lucha de los obreros de Cromotex*. Lima: Sindicato Textil Industrial Cromotex.

Crouch, D. (2010) 'Flirting with space: thinking landscape relationally', *Cultural Geographies*, 17(1), pp 5–18.

Cubilie, A. and Good, C. (2003) 'Introduction: the future of testimony', *Discourse*, 25(1), pp 4–18.

Cueto Rúa, S. (2010) 'Hijos de víctimas del terrorismo de Estado: Justicia, identidad y memoria en el movimiento de derechos humanos en Argentina, 1995–2008', *Historia Crítica*, 40, pp 122–145.

da Silva Catela, L. (2009) *No habrá flores en la tumba del pasado: La experiencia de reconstrucción del mundo de los familiares de desaparecidos*. 3rd edn. La Plata: Ediciones Al Margen.

Davies, B. and Gannon, S. (2006) *Doing Collective Biography: Investigating the Production of Subjectivity*. Maidenhead: Open University Press.

De Certeau, M. (1988) *The Practice of Everyday Life*. Translated by S. Rendall. Berkeley: University of California Press.

Degregori, C.I. (1994) 'Return to the past', in D.S. Palmer (ed) *The Shining Path of Peru*. 2nd edn. New York: Palgrave Macmillan, pp 51–62.

del Pino, P. and Agüero, J.C. (2014) *Cada Uno un Lugar de Memoria: Fundamentos Conceptuales del Lugar de la Memoria, la Tolerancia y la Inclusión Social*. LUM – Lugar de la Memoria, la Tolerancia y la Inclusión Social.

Denegri, F. (2003) 'Testimonio and its discontents', in S. Hart and R. Young (eds) *Contemporary Latin American Cultural Studies*. London: Arnold.

Denegri, F. and Hibbett, A. (eds) (2016) *Dando cuenta: estudios sobre el testimonio de la violencia política en el Perú (1980–2000)*. Lima: Fondo Editorial, PUCP.

Denzin, N.K. and Lincoln, Y.S. (2011) 'Introduction: the discipline and practice of qualitative research', in N.K. Denzin and Y.S. Lincoln (eds) *The SAGE Handbook of Qualitative Research*. 4th edn. Thousand Oaks: SAGE, pp 1–19.

Detwiler, L. and Breckenridge, J. (eds) (2012) *Pushing the Boundaries of Latin American Testimony: Meta-morphoses and Migrations*. New York: Palgrave Macmillan.

Drinot, P. (2009) 'For whom the eye cries: memory, monumentality, and the ontologies of violence in Peru', *Journal of Latin American Cultural Studies*, 18(1), pp 15–32.

Drinot, P. (2023) 'The internal enemy', *Fieldsights*, 30 March. https://culanth.org/fieldsights/the-internal-enemy

Durán, V., Messina, L. and Salvi, V. (2014) 'Espacios de Memoria: Controversias en torno a los usos y las estrategias de representación', *Clepsidra. Revista Interdisciplinaria de Estudios sobre Memoria*, 1(2), pp 6–11.

Durand, A. (2005) *Donde Habita el Olvido: los (H)usos de la Memoria y la Crisis del Movimiento Social en San Martín: Memoria, Política y Movimientos Sociales en la Región San Martín (1985–2000)*. Lima: Fondo Editorial de la Facultad de Ciencias Sociales, UNMSM.

Durand, A. (2015) '(Des) armar la palabra', *Revista Ideele – Revista del Instituto de Defensa Legal*, August. revistaideele.com/ideele/content/des-armar-la-palabra

Durand, A. (2023) *Estallido en los andes: movilización popular y crisis política en Perú*. Primera edición. Lima: La siniestra ensayos.

Emmel, N. and Clark, A. (2009) 'The methods used in connected lives: investigating networks, neighbourhoods and communities'. ESRC National Centre for Research Methods, NCRM Working Paper Series 06/09. eprints.ncrm.ac.uk/800

EPAF (2012) *De víctimas a ciudadanos: memorias de la violencia política en comunidades de la cuenca del río Pampas*. Lima: EPAF, Equipo peruano de antropología forense.

Esparza, M., Huttenbach, H.R. and Feierstein, D. (2009) *State Violence and Genocide in Latin America: The Cold War Years*. London: Routledge.

Etherington, K. (2007) 'Ethical research in reflexive relationships', *Qualitative Inquiry*, 13(5), pp 599–616.

Feitlowitz, M. (1999) *A Lexicon of Terror: Argentina and the Legacies of Torture*. New York: Oxford University Press.

Feldman, J.P. (2012) 'Exhibiting conflict: history and politics at the Museo de la Memoria de ANFASEP in Ayacucho, Peru', *Anthropological Quarterly*, 85(2), pp 487–518.

Forsey, M.G. (2010) 'Ethnography as participant listening', *Ethnography*, 11(4), pp 558–572.

Foucault, M. (1977) *Discipline and Punish: The Birth of the Prison*. New York: Pantheon Books.

Frank, A.W. (2005) 'What is dialogical research, and why should we do it?', *Qualitative Health Research*, 15(7), pp 964–974.

Freeman, M. (2007) 'Autobiographical understanding and narrative inquiry', in D.J. Clandinin (ed) *Handbook of Narrative Inquiry: Mapping a Methodology*. Thousand Oaks: SAGE, pp 120–145.

Freire, P. (1996) *Pedagogy of the Oppressed*. London and New York: Penguin Books.

Gandsman, A. (2006) 'Film reviews: The Blonds (Los Rubios), 2003. A film by Albertina Carri', *Journal of Latin American Anthropology*, 11(1), pp 253–255.

Gannon, S. (2006) 'The (im)possibilities of writing the self-writing: French poststructural theory and autoethnography', *Cultural Studies ↔ Critical Methodologies*, 6(4), pp 474–495.

Gatti, G. (2011) 'El lenguaje de las víctimas: silencios (ruidosos) y parodias (serias) para hablar (sin hacerlo) de la desaparición forzada de personas', *Universitas Humanística*, 72(72), pp 89–109.

Gatti, G. (2014) *Surviving Forced Disappearance in Argentina and Uruguay: Identity and Meaning*. New York: Palgrave Macmillan.

Gavilán, L. (2017) *Memorias de un soldado desconocido*. Segunda edición, revisada y aumentada. Lima: IEP, Instituto de Estudios Peruanos.

Gheerbrant, D. (2008) Interview by Ferrari, P., in *Capturing Reality: The Art of Documentary*. First Run Features, National Film Board of Canada. www.nfb.ca/film/capturing_reality

Geertz, C. (1973) *The Interpretation of Cultures: Selected Essays*. New York: Basic Books.

Geertz, C. (1988) 'Deep hanging out', *The New York Review of Books*, 22 October, pp 69–72.

Goffman, A. (2014) *On the Run: Fugitive Life in an American City*. Chicago: University of Chicago Press.

González, O. (2011) *Unveiling Secrets of War in the Peruvian Andes*. Chicago: University of Chicago Press.

Granados Moya, C. (2021) 'De la "guerra contraterrorista" al Congreso: El activismo político de los militares excombatientes en el Perú posconflicto', in R. Bedoya Forno, D. Delacroix, V. Robin Azevedo and T. Romero Barrios (eds) *La violencia que no cesa: huellas y persistencias del conflicto armado en el Perú contemporáneo*. Primera edición. Lima: Punto Cardinal.

Gready, P. (2008) 'The public life of narratives: ethics, politics, methods', in M. Andrews, C. Squire and M. Tamboukou (eds) *Doing Narrative Research*. Los Angeles: SAGE, pp 137–150.

Gugelberger, G.M. (1996) *The Real Thing: Testimonial Discourse and Latin America*. Durham, NC: Duke University Press.

Haig-Brown, C. (2003) 'Creating spaces: testimonio, impossible knowledge, and academe', *International Journal of Qualitative Studies in Education*, 16(3), pp 415–433.

Harvey, D. (2001) *Spaces of Capital: Towards a Critical Geography*. Hoboken: Taylor & Francis.

Heron, J. and Reason, P. (2001) 'The practice of co-operative inquiry: research with rather than on people', in P. Reason and H. Bradbury (eds) *Handbook of Action Research: Participative Inquiry and Practice*. London: SAGE, pp 179–188.

Hirsch, M. (2008) 'The generation of postmemory', *Poetics Today*, 29(1), pp 103–128.

Hite, K. (2007) '"The eye that cries": the politics of representing victims in contemporary Peru', *A Contracorriente*, 5(1), pp 108–134.

Holbraad, M. (2012) 'Truth beyond doubt: Ifá oracles in Havana', *HAU: Journal of Ethnographic Theory*, 2(1), pp 81–109.

Holdren, N. and Touza, S. (2005) 'Introduction to Colectivo Situaciones', *Ephemera: Theory and Politics in Organization*, 5(4), pp 595–601.

Infancia Clandestina [Clandestine Childhood] (2012) [Film]. Ávila, B. (Director). Argentina.

Isbell, B.J. (1994) 'Shining Path and peasant responses in rural Ayacucho', in D.S. Palmer (ed) *The Shining Path of Peru*. New York: Palgrave Macmillan, pp 77–99.

Isbell, B.J. (2005) 'Public secrets from Peru'. Billie Jean Isbell Andean Collection. https://hdl.handle.net/1813/2196

Isbell, B.J. (2009) *Finding Cholita*. 1st edn. Urbana: University of Illinois Press.

Jackson, A. and Mazzei, L.A. (2009) *Voice in Qualitative Inquiry: Challenging Conventional, Interpretive, and Critical Conceptions in Qualitative Research*. 1st edn. London: Routledge.

Jackson, A.Y. and Mazzei, L.A. (2011) *Thinking with Theory in Qualitative Research*. Abingdon and New York: Routledge.

Jacobo Timerman: Prisoner Without a Name, Cell Without a Number (1983) [Television Drama]. Yellen, L. (Director). Schiller Productions Inc. United States.

Jelin, E. (2003) *State Repression and the Labors of Memory*. Minneapolis: University of Minnesota Press.

Jelin, E. (2012) *Los Trabajos de la Memoria*. 2nd edn. Lima: Instituto de Estudios Peruanos.

Jelin, E. (2013) 'La situación de vejación de derechos no empezó con el conflicto armado interno ni terminó en el año 2000', Interviewed by Carmela Chávez. Seminario Internacional 'Miradas comparativas sobre el legado de la CVR', *Instituto de Democracia y Derechos Humanos – PUCP*. 28 August. https://idehpucp.pucp.edu.pe/boletin-eventos/elizabeth-jelin-la-situacion-de-vejacion-de-derechos-no-empezo-con-el-conflicto-armado-interno-ni-termino-en-el-ano-2000-3356/

Jelin, E. (2014) 'Las múltiples temporalidades del testimonio: el pasado vivido y sus legados presentes', *Clepsidra. Revista Interdisciplinaria de Estudios sobre Memoria*, 1(1), pp 140–163.

Jelin, E. and Langland, V. (eds) (2003) *Monumentos, memoriales y marcas territoriales*. Madrid: Siglo XXI de España Editores.

Jones, P., Bunce, G., Evans, J., Gibbs, H. and Hein, J.R. (2008) 'Exploring space and place with walking interviews', *Journal of Research Practice*, 4(2), pp 1–9.

Josselson, R. (1996) *Ethics and Process in the Narrative Study of Lives*. Thousand Oaks: SAGE.

Kaiser, S. (2005) *Postmemories of Terror: A New Generation Copes with the Legacy of the 'Dirty War'*. New York: Palgrave Macmillan.

Kletnicki, A. (2010) 'La ficción de la memoria: Un testimonio sobre la ausencia', *Aesthethika – Internacional sobre Subjetividad, Política y Arte*, 6(1), pp 20–29.

Kohan, M. (2014) 'New poetics of disappearance in Argentina', Conference Keynote in *New Poetics of Disappearance: Narrative, Violence and Memory. June 16–17, 2014*, Centre for the Study of Cultural Memory (University of London), Narratives of Terror and Disappearance (Universität Konstanz).

Kuhn, A. (2002) *Family Secrets: Acts of Memory and Imagination*. London: Verso.

La Serna, M. (2020) *With Masses and Arms: Peru's Tupac Amaru Revolutionary Movement*. Chapel Hill: University of North Carolina Press.

Lather, P. (1997) 'Drawing the line at angels: working the ruins of feminist ethnography', *International Journal of Qualitative Studies in Education*, 10(3), pp 285–304.

Lather, P. (2000a) 'Reading the image of Rigoberta Menchu: undecidability and language lessons', *International Journal of Qualitative Studies in Education*, 13(2), pp 153–162.

Lather, P. (2000b) 'Responsible practices of academic writing: troubling clarity II', in P.P. Trifonas (ed) *Revolutionary Pedagogies: Cultural Politics, Instituting Education, and the Discourse of Theory*. New York: Routledge, pp 289–311.

Lather, P. (2007) *Getting Lost: Feminist Efforts Toward a Double(d) Science*. SUNY Press.

Lather, P. (2009) 'Against empathy, voice and authenticity', in A. Jackson and L.A. Mazzei (eds) *Voice in Qualitative Inquiry: Challenging Conventional, Interpretive, and Critical Conceptions in Qualitative Research*. 1st edn. London: Routledge, pp 17–26.

Lather, P. and Smithies, C.S. (1997) *Troubling The Angels: Women Living With HIV/AIDS*. Boulder: Westview Press.

Latina Feminist Group (2001) *Telling to Live: Latina Feminist Testimonios*. Durham, NC: Duke University Press.

Lazzara, M.J. (2006) *Chile in Transition: The Poetics and Politics of Memory*. Gainesville: University Press of Florida.

Lefebvre, H. (1992) *The Production of Space*. Malden: Wiley-Blackwell.

Lessa, F. (2013) *Memory and Transitional Justice in Argentina and Uruguay: Against Impunity*. New York: Palgrave Macmillan.

Lewis-Kraus, G. (2016) 'The trials of Alice Goffman', *The New York Times*, 12 January. www.nytimes.com/2016/01/17/magazine/the-trials-of-alice-goffman.html

Lindbladh, J. (ed) (2008) *The Poetics of Memory in Post-Totalitarian Narration*. Lund: Centre for European Studies, Lund University.

Lorey, D.E. and Beezley, W.H. (2002) *Genocide, Collective Violence, and Popular Memory: The Politics of Remembrance in the Twentieth Century*. Wilmington: Scholarly Resources Inc.

Los Rubios [The Blonds] (2003) [Film]. Carri, A. (Director). Primer Plano Film Group (Argentina) Women Make Movies (USA – subtitled).

Luttrell, W. (2003) *Pregnant Bodies, Fertile Minds: Gender, Race and the Schooling of Pregnant Teens.* 1st edn. New York: Routledge.

Macher, S. (2007) *Recomendaciones vs realidades: avances y desafíos en el post-CVR Perú.* 1st edn. Lima: Instituto de Defensa Legal.

Macher, S. (2009) 'El Registro Único de Víctimas', *Revista Argumentos*, No. 4, Setiembre 2009. Instituto Estudios Peruanos. www.argumentos-historico.iep.org.pe/ articulos/el-registro-unico-de-victimas

Macher, S. (2014) *Hemos Avanzado? A 10 años de las recomendaciones de la Comisión de la Verdad y la Reconciliación.* Lima: Instituto de Estudios Peruanos.

Manrique, M.J. (2014) 'Generando la inocencia: creación, uso e implicaciones de la identidad de "inocente" en los periodos de conflicto y posconflicto en el Perú', *Bulletin de l'Institut français d'études andines*, 43(1), pp 53–73.

Manzoor-Khan, S. (2022) *Tangled in Terror: Uprooting Islamophobia.* London: Pluto Press.

Massey, D. (1992) 'Politics and space/time', *New Left Review*, 196, pp 65–84.

Massey, D. (2005) *For Space.* London: SAGE.

Mazzei, L.A. (2007) *Inhabited Silence in Qualitative Research: Putting Poststructural Theory to Work.* New York: Peter Lang.

McMurtrie, B. (2014) 'Secrets from Belfast: how Boston College's oral history of the Troubles fell victim to an international murder investigation?', *The Chronicle of Higher Education*, 26 January.

Méndez, C. (2021) 'The paths of terrorism in Peru: nineteenth to twenty-first centuries', in R. English (ed) *The Cambridge History of Terrorism.* Cambridge: Cambridge University Press, pp 420–452.

Meza, M. (2012) *El MRTA y las fuentes de la revolución en América Latina.* Doctoral Thesis on History. Colegio de Mexico, Mexico.

Milton, C.E. (2011) 'Defacing memory: (un)tying Peru's memory knots', *Memory Studies*, 4(2), pp 190–205.

Milton, C.E. (ed) (2014) *Art from a Fractured Past: Memory and Truth Telling in Post-Shining Path Peru.* Durham, NC: Duke University Press.

Moraga, C. and Anzaldúa, G. (1983) *This Bridge Called My Back: Writings by Radical Women of Colour.* 2nd edn. New York: Kitchen Table Press.

Nance, K. (2001) 'Disarming testimony: speakers' resistance to readers' defenses in Latin American testimonio', *Biography*, 24(3), pp 570–588.

Nance, K. (2006) *Can Literature Promote Justice? Trauma Narrative and Social Action in Latin American Testimonio.* Nashville: Vanderbilt University Press.

Nordstrom, C. and Robben, A.C.G.M. (1995) *Fieldwork Under Fire: Contemporary Studies of Violence and Survival.* Berkeley: University of California Press.

Nouzeilles, G. (2005) 'Postmemory cinema and the future of the past in Albertina Carri's Los Rubios', *Journal of Latin American Cultural Studies*, 14(3), pp 263–278.

Osgood, J. (2010) 'Narrative methods in the nursery: (re)-considering claims to give voice through processes of decision-making', *Reconceptualizing Educational Research Methodology*, 1(1), pp 14–28.

Paulson, J. (2023) 'Reparative pedagogies', in Y. Hutchinson, A.A. Cortez Ochoa, J. Paulson and L. Tikly (eds) *Decolonizing Education for Sustainable Futures*. Bristol: Bristol University Press, pp 220–240.

Perez, M.E. (2012) *Diario de una princesa montonera: 110% verdad*. Buenos Aires: Capital Intelectual.

Perez, M.E. (2013) 'Their lives after: theatre as testimony and the so-called "second generation" in post-dictatorship Argentina', *Journal of Romance Studies*, 13(3), pp 6–16.

Perez, M.E. (2014) 'The concentration camp and the "unhomely home": the disappearance of children in post-dictatorship Argentine theatre', in E. Schindel and P. Colombo (eds) *Space and the Memories of Violence: Landscapes of Erasure, Disappearance and Exception*. Basingstoke: Palgrave Macmillan, pp 119–131.

Peruvian Ombudsman Office (1999) [Defensoría del Pueblo] Informe sobre el establecimiento penitenciario de Yanamayo, Puno. Report No. 28, Lima, 31 de agosto de 1999.

Pollak, M. (2006) Translated by Da Silva Catela. 'Memoria, olvido, silencio: la producción social de identidades frente a situaciones límite'. La Plata: Al Margen.

Poole, D. and Rojas-Perez, I. (2011) 'Memories of reconciliation: photography and memory in postwar Peru', *e-misférica: After Truth*, 7(2). hemi.nyu.edu/hemi/en/e-misferica-72/poolerojas

Portelli, A. (1981) 'The peculiarities of oral history', *History Workshop Journal*, 12(1), pp 96–107.

Portugal, T. (2015) 'Batallas por el reconocimiento: lugares de memoria en el Perú', in C.I. Degregori, G. Salazar and R. Aroni (eds) *No hay mañana sin ayer: batallas por la memoria y consolidación democrática en el Perú*. Lima: Instituto de Estudios Peruanos, pp 71–236.

Precarias a la Deriva (2005) 'First stutterings of "Precarias a la Deriva"', *Caring Labor: An Archive*. caringlabor.wordpress.com/2010/12/14/precarias-a-la-deriva-first-stutterings-of-precarias-a-la-deriva/

Pushor, D. and Clandinin, D.J. (2009) 'The interconnections between narrative inquiry and action research', in S.E. Noffke and B. Somekh (eds) *The SAGE Handbook of Educational Action Research*. London: SAGE, pp 290–300.

Rajchenberg, E. and Héau-Lambert, C. (2004) 'Los silencios zapatistas', *Chiapas*, 16, pp 51–63.

Randall, M. (1985) *Testimonios: A Guide to Oral History*. Toronto: The Participatory Research Group.

Reason, P. and Bradbury, H. (2008) *The SAGE Handbook of Action Research: Participative Inquiry and Practice*. London: SAGE.

Reed, M. (2011) 'Somewhere between what is and what if: fictionalisation and ethnographic inquiry', *Changing English*, 18(1), pp 31–43.

Rénique, J.L. (2003) *La voluntad encarcelada: las 'luminosas trincheras de combate' de Sendero Luminoso del Perú*. Lima: Instituto de Estudios Peruanos.

Riaño-Alcalá, P. (2002) 'Remembering place: memory and violence in Medellin, Colombia', *Journal of Latin American Anthropology*, 7(1), pp 276–309.

Riaño-Alcalá, P. and Baines, E. (2011) 'The archive in the witness: documentation in settings of chronic insecurity', *International Journal of Transitional Justice*, 5(3), pp 412–433.

Richardson, L. (2002) 'Writing sociology', *Cultural Studies ↔ Critical Methodologies*, 2(3), pp 414–422.

Richardson, L. (2003) 'Poetic representation of interviews', in J.F. Gubrium and J.A. Holstein (eds) *Postmodern Interviewing*. London: SAGE, pp 187–202.

Richardson, L. and St. Pierre, E. (2005) 'Writing: a method of inquiry', in N.K. Denzin and Y.S. Lincoln (eds) *The SAGE Handbook of Qualitative Research*. 3rd edn. Thousand Oaks: SAGE.

Robertson, S.L. (2009) '"Spatializing" the sociology of education: stand points, entry points, vantage points', in M.W. Apple, S.J. Ball and L.A. Gandin (eds) *The Routledge International Handbook of the Sociology of Education*. London: Routledge, pp 15–26.

Robin Azevedo, V. (2021) *Los silencios de la guerra: memorias y conflicto armado en Ayacucho-Perú*. Lima: La Siniestra Ensayos.

Robin Azevedo, V. and Romero Barrios, T. (2023) 'Crisis sociopolítica, masacre y deshumanización', in G. Montoya Rivas and H. Quiroz (eds) *Estallido popular: protesta y masacre en Perú, 2022–2023*. Primera edición. Lima: Editorial Horizonte, pp 226–241.

Rodríguez, S. (1975) Playa Girón. *Días y Flores*. Havana: EGREM.

Rodriguez-Campo, M. (2021) 'Testimonio in education', in *Oxford Research Encyclopedia of Education*.

Rojas-Perez, I. (2013) 'Inhabiting unfinished pasts: law, transitional justice, and mourning in postwar Peru', *Humanity: An International Journal of Human Rights, Humanitarianism, and Development*, 4(1), pp 149–170.

Ros, A. (2012) *The Post-Dictatorship Generation in Argentina, Chile, and Uruguay: Collective Memory and Cultural Production*. New York: Palgrave Macmillan.

Ross, F.C. (2001) 'Speech and silence: women's testimony in the first five weeks of the South African Truth and Reconciliation Commission', in V. Das, A. Kleinman, M. Lock, M. Ramphele and P. Reynolds (eds) *Remaking a World: Violence, Social Suffering, and Recovery*. Berkeley: University of California Press, pp 250–278.

Ross, F.C. (2003) *Bearing Witness: Women and the Truth and Reconciliation Commission in South Africa*. London: Pluto Press.

Rothberg, M. (2014) 'Trauma theory, implicated subjects, and the question of Israel/Palestine', *Profession – Modern Language Association of America*, 2 May. http://profession.commons.mla.org/2014/05/02/trauma-theory-implicated-subjects-and-the-question-of-israelpalestine/

Salazar, C. (2013) 'A third world woman's text: between the politics of criticism and cultural politics', in S.B. Gluck and D. Patai (eds) *Women's Words: The Feminist Practice of Oral History*. New York: Routledge, pp 93–106.

Salgado Olivera, R. (2022) *De Silencios Y Otros Ruidos: Memorias de Un Hijo de La Guerra*. Lima: Punto Cardinal Editores.

Sánchez, M.M. (2007) 'Voces desplazadas: testimonios de mujeres víctimas de la violencia en Colombia', *Letras Femeninas*, 33(1), pp 119–152.

Saona, M. (2014) *Memory Matters in Transitional Peru*. Basingstoke: Palgrave Macmillan.

Schindel, E. and Colombo, P. (2014) *Space and the Memories of Violence: Landscapes of Erasure, Disappearance and Exception*. Basingstoke: Palgrave Macmillan.

Segato, R. (2015) *Contra-pedagogías de la crueldad*. Buenos Aires: Prometeo Libros.

Soja, E.W. (1996) *Thirdspace: Journeys to Los Angeles and Other Real-and-Imagined Places*. Wiley.

Solnit, R. (2001) *Wanderlust: A History of Walking*. New York: Penguin.

Sommer, D. (1991) 'No secrets: Rigoberta's guarded truth', *Women's Studies*, 20(1), pp 51–72.

Sommer, D. (1994) 'Resistant texts and incompetent readers', *Poetics Today*, 15(4), pp 523–551.

Sontag, S. (2004) *Regarding the Pain of Others*. New edn. London: Penguin.

Sosa, C. (2012) 'Queering kinship: the performance of blood and the attires of memory', *Journal of Latin American Cultural Studies*, 21(2), pp 221–233.

Sosa, C. and Serpente, A. (2012) 'Contemporary landscapes of Latin American cultural memory', *Journal of Latin American Cultural Studies*, 21(2), pp 159–163.

Sparkes, A. (2002) *Telling Tales in Sport and Physical Activity: A Qualitative Journey*. Champaign: Human Kinetics.

Speedy, J. (2008) *Narrative Inquiry and Psychotherapy*. Basingstoke: Palgrave Macmillan.

Speedy, J. (2014) 'Collaborative writing and ethical know-how: movement within the space around scholaship, the academy and the social research imaginary', in J. Speedy and J. Wyatt (eds) *Collaborative Writing as Inquiry*. Newcastle upon Tyne: Cambridge Scholars Publishing, pp 44–51.

Speedy, J. et al (2005) 'Failing to come to terms with things: a multi-storied conversation about poststructuralist ideas and narrative practices in response to some of life's failures', *Counselling and Psychotherapy Research: Linking Research with Practice*, 5(1), pp 65–74.

Stern, S.J. (2000) 'De la Memoria Suelta a la Memoria Emblematica: hacia el recordar y el olvidar como proceso historico (Chile, 1973–1998)', in M. Garcés and M. Olguín Tenorio (eds) *Memoria para un Nuevo Siglo: Chile, Miradas a la Segunda Mitad del Siglo XX*. Santiago: LOM Ediciones, pp 11–33.

Stern, S.J. (2015) 'Las verdades peligrosas: comisiones de la verdad y transiciones políticas latinoamericanas en perspectiva comparada', in L. Huber and P. del Pino (eds) *Políticas en justicia transicional: miradas comparativas sobre el legado de la CVR*. Lima: Instituto de Estudios Peruanos.

St. Pierre, E.A. (1997) 'Circling the text: nomadic writing practices', *Qualitative Inquiry*, 3(4), pp 403–417.

Strejilevich, N. (2006) 'Testimony: beyond the language of truth', *Human Rights Quarterly*, 28(3), pp 701–713.

Sullivan, A. (2010) 'The judgment against Fujimori for human rights violations', *American University International Law Review*, 25(4), pp 657–842.

Sykäri, V. (2012) 'Dialogic methodology and the dialogic space created after an interview', *Approaching Methodology – The Retrospective Methods Network*, 4, pp 80–88.

Tamboukou, M. (2008) 'A Foucauldian approach to narratives', in M. Andrews, C. Squire and M. Tamboukou (eds) *Doing Narrative Research*. Los Angeles: SAGE, pp 102–120.

Taussig, M. (1992) *The Nervous System*. New York: Routledge.

Taussig, M. (1999) *Defacement: Public Secrecy and the Labor of the Negative*. Stanford: Stanford University Press.

Taussig, M. (2005) *Law in a Lawless Land: Diary of a Limpieza in Colombia*. Chicago: University of Chicago Press.

Taylor, D. (2020) *¡Presente!: The Politics of Presence*. Durham, NC: Duke University Press.

Tello, M.E. (2012) *La Vida en Fuego: Un análisis antropológico sobre las memorias de la 'lucha armada' en los '70 en Argentina*. Tesis de Doctorado en Antropología Social. Universidad Autónoma de Madrid.

Theidon, K. (2003) 'Disarming the subject: remembering war and imagining citizenship in Peru', *Cultural Critique*, 54, pp 67–87.

Theidon, K. (2004) *Entre Projimos: el Conflicto Armado Interno y la Politica de la Reconciliacion en el Peru*. 1st edn. Lima: Instituto de Estudios Peruanos.

Theidon, K. (2010) 'Histories of innocence: postwar stories in Peru', in R. Shaw, L. Waldorf and P. Hazan (eds) *Localizing Transitional Justice: Interventions and Priorities After Mass Violence*. Stanford: Stanford University Press, pp 92–110.

Theidon, K. (2014) 'How was your trip? Self-care for researchers working and writing on violence'. Drugs, Security and Democracy Program, DSD Working Papers on Research Security No.2. Social Science Research Council.

Townsend, M. (2015) *'La Cautiva' Generates Polemic from the Peruvian State*. Panoramas – Center for Latin American Studies, University of Pittsburgh. www.panoramas.pitt.edu/art-and-culture/la-cautiva-generates-polemic-peruvian-state

Truth and Reconciliation Commission, TRC (2003a) Final Report. Vol VII. Chapter 2. Section 2.37 'Las ejecuciones extrajudiciales en el distrito de Los Molinos (1989)'. www.cverdad.org.pe/ifinal/

Truth and Reconciliation Commission, TRC (2003b) Final Report. Vol VIII. General Conclusions. www.cverdad.org.pe/ingles/ifinal/conclusiones.php

Truth and Reconciliation Commission, TRC (2003c) Final Report. Vol IX. Chapter 4. Recommendations. www.cverdad.org.pe/ifinal/

Truth and Reconciliation Commission, TRC (2003d) Final Report. Annex 1. Cronología 1978–2000. www.cverdad.org.pe/ifinal/

Tuck, E. and Yang, K.W. (2014) 'Unbecoming claims: pedagogies of refusal in qualitative research', *Qualitative Inquiry*, 20(6), pp 811–818.

Tuhiwai Smith, L. (2012) *Decolonizing Methodologies: Research and Indigenous Peoples*. 2nd edn. London: Zed Books.

Uccelli, F., Agüero, J.C. and Pease, M.A. (2013) *Secretos a voces. Memoria y educación en colegios públicos de Lima y Ayacucho*. Lima: Instituto de Estudios Peruanos.

Ugelvik, T. (2014) *Power and Resistance in Prison: Doing Time, Doing Freedom*. Basingstoke: Palgrave Macmillan.

Ulfe, M.E. (2009) 'Tantas Veces Lima: El museo de la memoria', *Coyuntura: Análisis Económico y Social de Actualidad. CISEPA-PUCP*, 5(26), pp 23–27.

Ulfe, M.E. and Milton, C.E. (2011) '¿Y, después de la verdad? El espacio público y las luchas por la memoria en la post CVR, Perú', *e-misférica: After Truth*, 7(2). hemi.nyu.edu/hemi/en/e-misferica-72/miltonulfe

Valenzuela, M. (2012) 'Sendero en la prisión: Apuntes etnográficos sobre los senderistas del penal Miguel Castro Castro', *Revista Argumentos – IEP*, 6(5), pp 1–7.

Van Maanen, J. (2011) *Tales of the Field: On Writing Ethnography*. 2nd revised edn. Chicago: University of Chicago Press.

Vargas Llosa, M. (1997) *Cartas a un joven novelista*. Barcelona: Ariel/Planeta.

Wiener, R. (2015) 'Los cautivos – Diario UNO', *Diario Uno*, 20 January. diariouno.pe/columna/los-cautivos/

Wilde, A. (1999) 'Irruptions of memory: expressive politics in Chile's transition to democracy', *Journal of Latin American Studies*, 31(2), pp 473–500.

Wilson, S. (2008) *Research is Ceremony: Indigenous Research Methods*. Black Point: Fernwood.

Winterson, J. (2011) *Why Be Happy When You Could Be Normal?* London: Random House.

Yúdice, G. (1996) 'Testimonio and postmodernism (1991)', in G.M. Gugelberger (ed) *The Real Thing: Testimonial Discourse and Latin America*. Durham, NC: Duke University Press, pp 42–57.

Index

References to endnotes show both the page number and the note number (231n3).